C-2394

THIS IS YOUR **PASSBOOK**® FOR ...

PRINCIPAL ADMINISTRATIVE ASSOCIATE

NATIONAL LEARNING CORPORATION®
passbooks.com

COPYRIGHT NOTICE

PASSBOOK® SERIES

THE *PASSBOOK® SERIES* has been created to prepare applicants and candidates for the ultimate academic battlefield – the examination room.

At some time in our lives, each and every one of us may be required to take an examination – for validation, matriculation, admission, qualification, registration, certification, or licensure.

Based on the assumption that every applicant or candidate has met the basic formal educational standards, has taken the required number of courses, and read the necessary texts, the *PASSBOOK® SERIES* furnishes the one special preparation which may assure passing with confidence, instead of failing with insecurity. Examination questions – together with answers – are furnished as the basic vehicle for study so that the mysteries of the examination and its compounding difficulties may be eliminated or diminished by a sure method.

This book is meant to help you pass your examination provided that you qualify and are serious in your objective.

The entire field is reviewed through the huge store of content information which is succinctly presented through a provocative and challenging approach – the question-and-answer method.

A climate of success is established by furnishing the correct answers at the end of each test.

You soon learn to recognize types of questions, forms of questions, and patterns of questioning. You may even begin to anticipate expected outcomes.

You perceive that many questions are repeated or adapted so that you can gain acute insights, which may enable you to score many sure points.

You learn how to confront new questions, or types of questions, and to attack them confidently and work out the correct answers.

You note objectives and emphases, and recognize pitfalls and dangers, so that you may make positive educational adjustments.

Moreover, you are kept fully informed in relation to new concepts, methods, practices, and directions in the field.

You discover that you arre actually taking the examination all the time: you are preparing for the examination by "taking" an examination, not by reading extraneous and/or supererogatory textbooks.

In short, this PASSBOOK®, used directedly, should be an important factor in helping you to pass your test.

PRINCIPAL ADMINISTRATIVE ASSOCIATE

DUTIES

Principal Administrative Associates, under general supervision, with some latitude for independent initiative and judgment, perform difficult and responsible office, supervisory or administrative functions utilizing manual and automated office systems. All Principal Administrative Associates perform related work.

Supervises a large office engaged in routine clerical activities or supervises a small office engaged in departmental, administrative or management activities; or performs difficult and responsible administrative or personnel management work. Supervises a group or section of subordinate personnel in the clerical and related activities performed in an income maintenance center. Performs difficult and responsible administrative work required for the conduct of hearings, control processing, and integrity of dispositions of parking violations; performs related work.

Under general supervision, with considerable latitude for the exercise of independent judgment, makes the necessary arrangements of services and activities in connection with public events, ceremonies, luncheons, and receptions.

Under direction, performs difficult and responsible administrative work in the capacity of Secretary to a very high level executive.

Under direction, with considerable latitude for independent action or decision, performs difficult and responsible supervisory or administrative work in any one or more of the following:

Administers all matters pertaining to the general municipal telephone system. Supervises a very large office engaged in routine clerical or personnel management work.

Under general direction and with wide latitude for the exercise of independent initiative and judgment performs the following:

Supervises an exceptionally large office engaged in routine clerical activities, or supervises a very large office engaged in departmental administrative or management activities. Performs exceptionally difficult and responsible independent, specialized administrative or management work related to accounts and budgeting, methods and organization, etc. Plans, directs and supervises a minimal personnel management program covering a large number of employees, or a well-developed personnel management program including several major personnel activities covering a moderate number of employees or performs appropriate professional duties in a personnel program headed by an employee of higher rank.

THE TEST

The multiple-choice test may include questions on the ability to understand written English words, sentences, paragraphs, etc.; the ability to write English words, sentences, paragraphs, etc., concisely and clearly so that others will understand; the ability to correctly perform numerical operations, such as adding, subtracting, dividing, multiplying and finding percentages; the ability to tell when something is wrong or is likely to go wrong; the ability to establish a course of action for yourself and/or subordinates to accomplish a specific goal; the ability to analyze a problem or situation and make appropriate judgments; principles and techniques of supervision; standards of proper employee conduct; and other related areas.

HOW TO TAKE A TEST

I. YOU MUST PASS AN EXAMINATION

A. WHAT EVERY CANDIDATE SHOULD KNOW

Examination applicants often ask us for help in preparing for the written test. What can I study in advance? What kinds of questions will be asked? How will the test be given? How will the papers be graded?

As an applicant for a civil service examination, you may be wondering about some of these things. Our purpose here is to suggest effective methods of advance study and to describe civil service examinations.

Your chances for success on this examination can be increased if you know how to prepare. Those "pre-examination jitters" can be reduced if you know what to expect. You can even experience an adventure in good citizenship if you know why civil service exams are given.

B. WHY ARE CIVIL SERVICE EXAMINATIONS GIVEN?

Civil service examinations are important to you in two ways. As a citizen, you want public jobs filled by employees who know how to do their work. As a job seeker, you want a fair chance to compete for that job on an equal footing with other candidates. The best-known means of accomplishing this two-fold goal is the competitive examination.

Exams are widely publicized throughout the nation. They may be administered for jobs in federal, state, city, municipal, town or village governments or agencies.

Any citizen may apply, with some limitations, such as the age or residence of applicants. Your experience and education may be reviewed to see whether you meet the requirements for the particular examination. When these requirements exist, they are reasonable and applied consistently to all applicants. Thus, a competitive examination may cause you some uneasiness now, but it is your privilege and safeguard.

C. HOW ARE CIVIL SERVICE EXAMS DEVELOPED?

Examinations are carefully written by trained technicians who are specialists in the field known as "psychological measurement," in consultation with recognized authorities in the field of work that the test will cover. These experts recommend the subject matter areas or skills to be tested; only those knowledges or skills important to your success on the job are included. The most reliable books and source materials available are used as references. Together, the experts and technicians judge the difficulty level of the questions.

Test technicians know how to phrase questions so that the problem is clearly stated. Their ethics do not permit "trick" or "catch" questions. Questions may have been tried out on sample groups, or subjected to statistical analysis, to determine their usefulness.

Written tests are often used in combination with performance tests, ratings of training and experience, and oral interviews. All of these measures combine to form the best-known means of finding the right person for the right job.

II. HOW TO PASS THE WRITTEN TEST

A. NATURE OF THE EXAMINATION

To prepare intelligently for civil service examinations, you should know how they differ from school examinations you have taken. In school you were assigned certain definite pages to read or subjects to cover. The examination questions were quite detailed and usually emphasized memory. Civil service exams, on the other hand, try to discover your present ability to perform the duties of a position, plus your potentiality to learn these duties. In other words, a civil service exam attempts to predict how successful you will be. Questions cover such a broad area that they cannot be as minute and detailed as school exam questions.

In the public service similar kinds of work, or positions, are grouped together in one "class." This process is known as *position-classification*. All the positions in a class are paid according to the salary range for that class. One class title covers all of these positions, and they are all tested by the same examination.

B. FOUR BASIC STEPS

1) Study the announcement

How, then, can you know what subjects to study? Our best answer is: "Learn as much as possible about the class of positions for which you've applied." The exam will test the knowledge, skills and abilities needed to do the work.

Your most valuable source of information about the position you want is the official exam announcement. This announcement lists the training and experience qualifications. Check these standards and apply only if you come reasonably close to meeting them.

The brief description of the position in the examination announcement offers some clues to the subjects which will be tested. Think about the job itself. Review the duties in your mind. Can you perform them, or are there some in which you are rusty? Fill in the blank spots in your preparation.

Many jurisdictions preview the written test in the exam announcement by including a section called "Knowledge and Abilities Required," "Scope of the Examination," or some similar heading. Here you will find out specifically what fields will be tested.

2) Review your own background

Once you learn in general what the position is all about, and what you need to know to do the work, ask yourself which subjects you already know fairly well and which need improvement. You may wonder whether to concentrate on improving your strong areas or on building some background in your fields of weakness. When the announcement has specified "some knowledge" or "considerable knowledge," or has used adjectives like "beginning principles of..." or "advanced ... methods," you can get a clue as to the number and difficulty of questions to be asked in any given field. More questions, and hence broader coverage, would be included for those subjects which are more important in the work. Now weigh your strengths and weaknesses against the job requirements and prepare accordingly.

3) Determine the level of the position

Another way to tell how intensively you should prepare is to understand the level of the job for which you are applying. Is it the entering level? In other words, is this the position in which beginners in a field of work are hired? Or is it an intermediate or advanced level? Sometimes this is indicated by such words as "Junior" or "Senior" in the class title. Other jurisdictions use Roman numerals to designate the level – Clerk I, Clerk II, for example. The word "Supervisor" sometimes appears in the title. If the level is not indicated by the title, check the description of duties. Will you be working under very close supervision, or will you have responsibility for independent decisions in this work?

4) Choose appropriate study materials

Now that you know the subjects to be examined and the relative amount of each subject to be covered, you can choose suitable study materials. For beginning level jobs, or even advanced ones, if you have a pronounced weakness in some aspect of your training, read a modern, standard textbook in that field. Be sure it is up to date and has general coverage. Such books are normally available at your library, and the librarian will be glad to help you locate one. For entry-level positions, questions of appropriate difficulty are chosen – neither highly advanced questions, nor those too simple. Such questions require careful thought but not advanced training.

If the position for which you are applying is technical or advanced, you will read more advanced, specialized material. If you are already familiar with the basic principles of your field, elementary textbooks would waste your time. Concentrate on advanced textbooks and technical periodicals. Think through the concepts and review difficult problems in your field.

These are all general sources. You can get more ideas on your own initiative, following these leads. For example, training manuals and publications of the government agency which employs workers in your field can be useful, particularly for technical and professional positions. A letter or visit to the government department involved may result in more specific study suggestions, and certainly will provide you with a more definite idea of the exact nature of the position you are seeking.

III. KINDS OF TESTS

Tests are used for purposes other than measuring knowledge and ability to perform specified duties. For some positions, it is equally important to test ability to make adjustments to new situations or to profit from training. In others, basic mental abilities not dependent on information are essential. Questions which test these things may not appear as pertinent to the duties of the position as those which test for knowledge and information. Yet they are often highly important parts of a fair examination. For very general questions, it is almost impossible to help you direct your study efforts. What we can do is to point out some of the more common of these general abilities needed in public service positions and describe some typical questions.

1) General information

Broad, general information has been found useful for predicting job success in some kinds of work. This is tested in a variety of ways, from vocabulary lists to questions about current events. Basic background in some field of work, such as sociology or economics, may be sampled in a group of questions. Often these are principles which have become familiar to most persons through exposure rather than through formal training. It is difficult to advise you how to study for these questions; being alert to the world around you is our best suggestion.

2) Verbal ability

An example of an ability needed in many positions is verbal or language ability. Verbal ability is, in brief, the ability to use and understand words. Vocabulary and grammar tests are typical measures of this ability. Reading comprehension or paragraph interpretation questions are common in many kinds of civil service tests. You are given a paragraph of written material and asked to find its central meaning.

3) Numerical ability

Number skills can be tested by the familiar arithmetic problem, by checking paired lists of numbers to see which are alike and which are different, or by interpreting charts and graphs. In the latter test, a graph may be printed in the test booklet which you are asked to use as the basis for answering questions.

4) Observation

A popular test for law-enforcement positions is the observation test. A picture is shown to you for several minutes, then taken away. Questions about the picture test your ability to observe both details and larger elements.

5) Following directions

In many positions in the public service, the employee must be able to carry out written instructions dependably and accurately. You may be given a chart with several columns, each column listing a variety of information. The questions require you to carry out directions involving the information given in the chart.

6) Skills and aptitudes

Performance tests effectively measure some manual skills and aptitudes. When the skill is one in which you are trained, such as typing or shorthand, you can practice. These tests are often very much like those given in business school or high school courses. For many of the other skills and aptitudes, however, no short-time preparation can be made. Skills and abilities natural to you or that you have developed throughout your lifetime are being tested.

Many of the general questions just described provide all the data needed to answer the questions and ask you to use your reasoning ability to find the answers. Your best preparation for these tests, as well as for tests of facts and ideas, is to be at your physical and mental best. You, no doubt, have your own methods of getting into an exam-taking mood and keeping "in shape." The next section lists some ideas on this subject.

IV. KINDS OF QUESTIONS

Only rarely is the "essay" question, which you answer in narrative form, used in civil service tests. Civil service tests are usually of the short-answer type. Full instructions for answering these questions will be given to you at the examination. But in case this is your first experience with short-answer questions and separate answer sheets, here is what you need to know:

1) Multiple-choice Questions

Most popular of the short-answer questions is the "multiple choice" or "best answer" question. It can be used, for example, to test for factual knowledge, ability to solve problems or judgment in meeting situations found at work.

A multiple-choice question is normally one of three types—
- It can begin with an incomplete statement followed by several possible endings. You are to find the one ending which *best* completes the statement, although some of the others may not be entirely wrong.
- It can also be a complete statement in the form of a question which is answered by choosing one of the statements listed.
- It can be in the form of a problem – again you select the best answer.

Here is an example of a multiple-choice question with a discussion which should give you some clues as to the method for choosing the right answer:

When an employee has a complaint about his assignment, the action which will *best* help him overcome his difficulty is to
- A. discuss his difficulty with his coworkers
- B. take the problem to the head of the organization
- C. take the problem to the person who gave him the assignment
- D. say nothing to anyone about his complaint

In answering this question, you should study each of the choices to find which is best. Consider choice "A" – Certainly an employee may discuss his complaint with fellow employees, but no change or improvement can result, and the complaint remains unresolved. Choice "B" is a poor choice since the head of the organization probably does not know what assignment you have been given, and taking your problem to him is known as "going over the head" of the supervisor. The supervisor, or person who made the assignment, is the person who can clarify it or correct any injustice. Choice "C" is, therefore, correct. To say nothing, as in choice "D," is unwise. Supervisors have and interest in knowing the problems employees are facing, and the employee is seeking a solution to his problem.

2) True/False Questions

The "true/false" or "right/wrong" form of question is sometimes used. Here a complete statement is given. Your job is to decide whether the statement is right or wrong.

SAMPLE: A roaming cell-phone call to a nearby city costs less than a non-roaming call to a distant city.

This statement is wrong, or false, since roaming calls are more expensive.
This is not a complete list of all possible question forms, although most of the others are variations of these common types. You will always get complete directions for

answering questions. Be sure you understand *how* to mark your answers – ask questions until you do.

V. RECORDING YOUR ANSWERS

Computer terminals are used more and more today for many different kinds of exams.

For an examination with very few applicants, you may be told to record your answers in the test booklet itself. Separate answer sheets are much more common. If this separate answer sheet is to be scored by machine – and this is often the case – it is highly important that you mark your answers correctly in order to get credit.

An electronic scoring machine is often used in civil service offices because of the speed with which papers can be scored. Machine-scored answer sheets must be marked with a pencil, which will be given to you. This pencil has a high graphite content which responds to the electronic scoring machine. As a matter of fact, stray dots may register as answers, so do not let your pencil rest on the answer sheet while you are pondering the correct answer. Also, if your pencil lead breaks or is otherwise defective, ask for another.

Since the answer sheet will be dropped in a slot in the scoring machine, be careful not to bend the corners or get the paper crumpled.

The answer sheet normally has five vertical columns of numbers, with 30 numbers to a column. These numbers correspond to the question numbers in your test booklet. After each number, going across the page are four or five pairs of dotted lines. These short dotted lines have small letters or numbers above them. The first two pairs may also have a "T" or "F" above the letters. This indicates that the first two pairs only are to be used if the questions are of the true-false type. If the questions are multiple choice, disregard the "T" and "F" and pay attention only to the small letters or numbers.

Answer your questions in the manner of the sample that follows:

32. The largest city in the United States is
  A. Washington, D.C.
  B. New York City
  C. Chicago
  D. Detroit
  E. San Francisco

1) Choose the answer you think is best. (New York City is the largest, so "B" is correct.)
2) Find the row of dotted lines numbered the same as the question you are answering. (Find row number 32)
3) Find the pair of dotted lines corresponding to the answer. (Find the pair of lines under the mark "B.")
4) Make a solid black mark between the dotted lines.

VI. BEFORE THE TEST

Common sense will help you find procedures to follow to get ready for an examination. Too many of us, however, overlook these sensible measures. Indeed, nervousness and fatigue have been found to be the most serious reasons why applicants fail to do their best on civil service tests. Here is a list of reminders:

- Begin your preparation early – Don't wait until the last minute to go scurrying around for books and materials or to find out what the position is all about.
- Prepare continuously – An hour a night for a week is better than an all-night cram session. This has been definitely established. What is more, a night a week for a month will return better dividends than crowding your study into a shorter period of time.
- Locate the place of the exam – You have been sent a notice telling you when and where to report for the examination. If the location is in a different town or otherwise unfamiliar to you, it would be well to inquire the best route and learn something about the building.
- Relax the night before the test – Allow your mind to rest. Do not study at all that night. Plan some mild recreation or diversion; then go to bed early and get a good night's sleep.
- Get up early enough to make a leisurely trip to the place for the test – This way unforeseen events, traffic snarls, unfamiliar buildings, etc. will not upset you.
- Dress comfortably – A written test is not a fashion show. You will be known by number and not by name, so wear something comfortable.
- Leave excess paraphernalia at home – Shopping bags and odd bundles will get in your way. You need bring only the items mentioned in the official notice you received; usually everything you need is provided. Do not bring reference books to the exam. They will only confuse those last minutes and be taken away from you when in the test room.
- Arrive somewhat ahead of time – If because of transportation schedules you must get there very early, bring a newspaper or magazine to take your mind off yourself while waiting.
- Locate the examination room – When you have found the proper room, you will be directed to the seat or part of the room where you will sit. Sometimes you are given a sheet of instructions to read while you are waiting. Do not fill out any forms until you are told to do so; just read them and be prepared.
- Relax and prepare to listen to the instructions
- If you have any physical problem that may keep you from doing your best, be sure to tell the test administrator. If you are sick or in poor health, you really cannot do your best on the exam. You can come back and take the test some other time.

VII. AT THE TEST

The day of the test is here and you have the test booklet in your hand. The temptation to get going is very strong. Caution! There is more to success than knowing the right answers. You must know how to identify your papers and understand variations in the type of short-answer question used in this particular examination. Follow these suggestions for maximum results from your efforts:

1) Cooperate with the monitor

The test administrator has a duty to create a situation in which you can be as much at ease as possible. He will give instructions, tell you when to begin, check to see that you are marking your answer sheet correctly, and so on. He is not there to guard you, although he will see that your competitors do not take unfair advantage. He wants to help you do your best.

2) Listen to all instructions

Don't jump the gun! Wait until you understand all directions. In most civil service tests you get more time than you need to answer the questions. So don't be in a hurry. Read each word of instructions until you clearly understand the meaning. Study the examples, listen to all announcements and follow directions. Ask questions if you do not understand what to do.

3) Identify your papers

Civil service exams are usually identified by number only. You will be assigned a number; you must not put your name on your test papers. Be sure to copy your number correctly. Since more than one exam may be given, copy your exact examination title.

4) Plan your time

Unless you are told that a test is a "speed" or "rate of work" test, speed itself is usually not important. Time enough to answer all the questions will be provided, but this does not mean that you have all day. An overall time limit has been set. Divide the total time (in minutes) by the number of questions to determine the approximate time you have for each question.

5) Do not linger over difficult questions

If you come across a difficult question, mark it with a paper clip (useful to have along) and come back to it when you have been through the booklet. One caution if you do this – be sure to skip a number on your answer sheet as well. Check often to be sure that you have not lost your place and that you are marking in the row numbered the same as the question you are answering.

6) Read the questions

Be sure you know what the question asks! Many capable people are unsuccessful because they failed to *read* the questions correctly.

7) Answer all questions

Unless you have been instructed that a penalty will be deducted for incorrect answers, it is better to guess than to omit a question.

8) Speed tests

It is often better NOT to guess on speed tests. It has been found that on timed tests people are tempted to spend the last few seconds before time is called in marking answers at random – without even reading them – in the hope of picking up a few extra points. To discourage this practice, the instructions may warn you that your score will be "corrected" for guessing. That is, a penalty will be applied. The incorrect answers will be deducted from the correct ones, or some other penalty formula will be used.

9) Review your answers

If you finish before time is called, go back to the questions you guessed or omitted to give them further thought. Review other answers if you have time.

10) Return your test materials

If you are ready to leave before others have finished or time is called, take ALL your materials to the monitor and leave quietly. Never take any test material with you. The monitor can discover whose papers are not complete, and taking a test booklet may be grounds for disqualification.

VIII. EXAMINATION TECHNIQUES

1) Read the general instructions carefully. These are usually printed on the first page of the exam booklet. As a rule, these instructions refer to the timing of the examination; the fact that you should not start work until the signal and must stop work at a signal, etc. If there are any *special* instructions, such as a choice of questions to be answered, make sure that you note this instruction carefully.

2) When you are ready to start work on the examination, that is as soon as the signal has been given, read the instructions to each question booklet, underline any key words or phrases, such as *least, best, outline, describe* and the like. In this way you will tend to answer as requested rather than discover on reviewing your paper that you *listed without describing*, that you selected the *worst* choice rather than the *best* choice, etc.

3) If the examination is of the objective or multiple-choice type – that is, each question will also give a series of possible answers: A, B, C or D, and you are called upon to select the best answer and write the letter next to that answer on your answer paper – it is advisable to start answering each question in turn. There may be anywhere from 50 to 100 such questions in the three or four hours allotted and you can see how much time would be taken if you read through all the questions before beginning to answer any. Furthermore, if you come across a question or group of questions which you know would be difficult to answer, it would undoubtedly affect your handling of all the other questions.

4) If the examination is of the essay type and contains but a few questions, it is a moot point as to whether you should read all the questions before starting to answer any one. Of course, if you are given a choice – say five out of seven and the like – then it is essential to read all the questions so you can eliminate the two that are most difficult. If, however, you are asked to answer all the questions, there may be danger in trying to answer the easiest one first because you may find that you will spend too much time on it. The best technique is to answer the first question, then proceed to the second, etc.

5) Time your answers. Before the exam begins, write down the time it started, then add the time allowed for the examination and write down the time it must be completed, then divide the time available somewhat as follows:

- If 3-1/2 hours are allowed, that would be 210 minutes. If you have 80 objective-type questions, that would be an average of 2-1/2 minutes per question. Allow yourself no more than 2 minutes per question, or a total of 160 minutes, which will permit about 50 minutes to review.
- If for the time allotment of 210 minutes there are 7 essay questions to answer, that would average about 30 minutes a question. Give yourself only 25 minutes per question so that you have about 35 minutes to review.

6) The most important instruction is to *read each question* and make sure you know what is wanted. The second most important instruction is to *time yourself properly* so that you answer every question. The third most important instruction is to *answer every question.* Guess if you have to but include something for each question. Remember that you will receive no credit for a blank and will probably receive some credit if you write something in answer to an essay question. If you guess a letter – say "B" for a multiple-choice question – you may have guessed right. If you leave a blank as an answer to a multiple-choice question, the examiners may respect your feelings but it will not add a point to your score. Some exams may penalize you for wrong answers, so in such cases *only*, you may not want to guess unless you have some basis for your answer.

7) Suggestions
    a. Objective-type questions
        1. Examine the question booklet for proper sequence of pages and questions
        2. Read all instructions carefully
        3. Skip any question which seems too difficult; return to it after all other questions have been answered
        4. Apportion your time properly; do not spend too much time on any single question or group of questions
        5. Note and underline key words – *all, most, fewest, least, best, worst, same, opposite,* etc.
        6. Pay particular attention to negatives
        7. Note unusual option, e.g., unduly long, short, complex, different or similar in content to the body of the question
        8. Observe the use of "hedging" words – *probably, may, most likely,* etc.
        9. Make sure that your answer is put next to the same number as the question
        10. Do not second-guess unless you have good reason to believe the second answer is definitely more correct
        11. Cross out original answer if you decide another answer is more accurate; do not erase until you are ready to hand your paper in
        12. Answer all questions; guess unless instructed otherwise
        13. Leave time for review

    b. Essay questions
        1. Read each question carefully
        2. Determine exactly what is wanted. Underline key words or phrases.
        3. Decide on outline or paragraph answer

4. Include many different points and elements unless asked to develop any one or two points or elements
5. Show impartiality by giving pros and cons unless directed to select one side only
6. Make and write down any assumptions you find necessary to answer the questions
7. Watch your English, grammar, punctuation and choice of words
8. Time your answers; don't crowd material

8) Answering the essay question

Most essay questions can be answered by framing the specific response around several key words or ideas. Here are a few such key words or ideas:

M's: manpower, materials, methods, money, management
P's: purpose, program, policy, plan, procedure, practice, problems, pitfalls, personnel, public relations
  a. Six basic steps in handling problems:
    1. Preliminary plan and background development
    2. Collect information, data and facts
    3. Analyze and interpret information, data and facts
    4. Analyze and develop solutions as well as make recommendations
    5. Prepare report and sell recommendations
    6. Install recommendations and follow up effectiveness

  b. Pitfalls to avoid
    1. *Taking things for granted* – A statement of the situation does not necessarily imply that each of the elements is necessarily true; for example, a complaint may be invalid and biased so that all that can be taken for granted is that a complaint has been registered
    2. *Considering only one side of a situation* – Wherever possible, indicate several alternatives and then point out the reasons you selected the best one
    3. *Failing to indicate follow up* – Whenever your answer indicates action on your part, make certain that you will take proper follow-up action to see how successful your recommendations, procedures or actions turn out to be
    4. *Taking too long in answering any single question* – Remember to time your answers properly

IX. AFTER THE TEST

Scoring procedures differ in detail among civil service jurisdictions although the general principles are the same. Whether the papers are hand-scored or graded by machine we have described, they are nearly always graded by number. That is, the person who marks the paper knows only the number – never the name – of the applicant. Not until all the papers have been graded will they be matched with names. If other tests, such as training and experience or oral interview ratings have been given, scores will be combined. Different parts of the examination usually have different weights. For example, the written test might count 60 percent of the final grade, and a rating of training and experience 40 percent. In many jurisdictions, veterans will have a certain number of points added to their grades.

After the final grade has been determined, the names are placed in grade order and an eligible list is established. There are various methods for resolving ties between those who get the same final grade – probably the most common is to place first the name of the person whose application was received first. Job offers are made from the eligible list in the order the names appear on it. You will be notified of your grade and your rank as soon as all these computations have been made. This will be done as rapidly as possible.

People who are found to meet the requirements in the announcement are called "eligibles." Their names are put on a list of eligible candidates. An eligible's chances of getting a job depend on how high he stands on this list and how fast agencies are filling jobs from the list.

When a job is to be filled from a list of eligibles, the agency asks for the names of people on the list of eligibles for that job. When the civil service commission receives this request, it sends to the agency the names of the three people highest on this list. Or, if the job to be filled has specialized requirements, the office sends the agency the names of the top three persons who meet these requirements from the general list.

The appointing officer makes a choice from among the three people whose names were sent to him. If the selected person accepts the appointment, the names of the others are put back on the list to be considered for future openings.

That is the rule in hiring from all kinds of eligible lists, whether they are for typist, carpenter, chemist, or something else. For every vacancy, the appointing officer has his choice of any one of the top three eligibles on the list. This explains why the person whose name is on top of the list sometimes does not get an appointment when some of the persons lower on the list do. If the appointing officer chooses the second or third eligible, the No. 1 eligible does not get a job at once, but stays on the list until he is appointed or the list is terminated.

X. HOW TO PASS THE INTERVIEW TEST

The examination for which you applied requires an oral interview test. You have already taken the written test and you are now being called for the interview test – the final part of the formal examination.

You may think that it is not possible to prepare for an interview test and that there are no procedures to follow during an interview. Our purpose is to point out some things you can do in advance that will help you and some good rules to follow and pitfalls to avoid while you are being interviewed.

What is an interview supposed to test?

The written examination is designed to test the technical knowledge and competence of the candidate; the oral is designed to evaluate intangible qualities, not readily measured otherwise, and to establish a list showing the relative fitness of each candidate – as measured against his competitors – for the position sought. Scoring is not on the basis of "right" and "wrong," but on a sliding scale of values ranging from "not passable" to "outstanding." As a matter of fact, it is possible to achieve a relatively low score without a single "incorrect" answer because of evident weakness in the qualities being measured.

Occasionally, an examination may consist entirely of an oral test – either an individual or a group oral. In such cases, information is sought concerning the technical knowledges and abilities of the candidate, since there has been no written examination for this purpose. More commonly, however, an oral test is used to supplement a written examination.

Who conducts interviews?

The composition of oral boards varies among different jurisdictions. In nearly all, a representative of the personnel department serves as chairman. One of the members of the board may be a representative of the department in which the candidate would work. In some cases, "outside experts" are used, and, frequently, a businessman or some other representative of the general public is asked to serve. Labor and management or other special groups may be represented. The aim is to secure the services of experts in the appropriate field.

However the board is composed, it is a good idea (and not at all improper or unethical) to ascertain in advance of the interview who the members are and what groups they represent. When you are introduced to them, you will have some idea of their backgrounds and interests, and at least you will not stutter and stammer over their names.

What should be done before the interview?

While knowledge about the board members is useful and takes some of the surprise element out of the interview, there is other preparation which is more substantive. It *is* possible to prepare for an oral interview – in several ways:

1) Keep a copy of your application and review it carefully before the interview

This may be the only document before the oral board, and the starting point of the interview. Know what education and experience you have listed there, and the sequence and dates of all of it. Sometimes the board will ask you to review the highlights of your experience for them; you should not have to hem and haw doing it.

2) Study the class specification and the examination announcement

Usually, the oral board has one or both of these to guide them. The qualities, characteristics or knowledges required by the position sought are stated in these documents. They offer valuable clues as to the nature of the oral interview. For example, if the job involves supervisory responsibilities, the announcement will usually indicate that knowledge of modern supervisory methods and the qualifications of the candidate as a supervisor will be tested. If so, you can expect such questions, frequently in the form of a hypothetical situation which you are expected to solve. NEVER go into an oral without knowledge of the duties and responsibilities of the job you seek.

3) Think through each qualification required

Try to visualize the kind of questions you would ask if you were a board member. How well could you answer them? Try especially to appraise your own knowledge and background in each area, *measured against the job sought*, and identify any areas in which you are weak. Be critical and realistic – do not flatter yourself.

4) Do some general reading in areas in which you feel you may be weak

For example, if the job involves supervision and your past experience has NOT, some general reading in supervisory methods and practices, particularly in the field of human relations, might be useful. Do NOT study agency procedures or detailed manuals. The oral board will be testing your understanding and capacity, not your memory.

5) Get a good night's sleep and watch your general health and mental attitude

You will want a clear head at the interview. Take care of a cold or any other minor ailment, and of course, no hangovers.

What should be done on the day of the interview?

Now comes the day of the interview itself. Give yourself plenty of time to get there. Plan to arrive somewhat ahead of the scheduled time, particularly if your appointment is in the fore part of the day. If a previous candidate fails to appear, the board might be ready for you a bit early. By early afternoon an oral board is almost invariably behind schedule if there are many candidates, and you may have to wait. Take along a book or magazine to read, or your application to review, but leave any extraneous material in the waiting room when you go in for your interview. In any event, relax and compose yourself.

The matter of dress is important. The board is forming impressions about you – from your experience, your manners, your attitude, and your appearance. Give your personal appearance careful attention. Dress your best, but not your flashiest. Choose conservative, appropriate clothing, and be sure it is immaculate. This is a business interview, and your appearance should indicate that you regard it as such. Besides, being well groomed and properly dressed will help boost your confidence.

Sooner or later, someone will call your name and escort you into the interview room. *This is it.* From here on you are on your own. It is too late for any more preparation. But remember, you asked for this opportunity to prove your fitness, and you are here because your request was granted.

What happens when you go in?

The usual sequence of events will be as follows: The clerk (who is often the board stenographer) will introduce you to the chairman of the oral board, who will introduce you to the other members of the board. Acknowledge the introductions before you sit down. Do not be surprised if you find a microphone facing you or a stenotypist sitting by. Oral interviews are usually recorded in the event of an appeal or other review.

Usually the chairman of the board will open the interview by reviewing the highlights of your education and work experience from your application – primarily for the benefit of the other members of the board, as well as to get the material into the record. Do not interrupt or comment unless there is an error or significant misinterpretation; if that is the case, do not hesitate. But do not quibble about insignificant matters. Also, he will usually ask you some question about your education, experience or your present job – partly to get you to start talking and to establish the interviewing "rapport." He may start the actual questioning, or turn it over to one of the other members. Frequently, each member undertakes the questioning on a particular area, one in which he is perhaps most competent, so you can expect each member to participate in the examination. Because time is limited, you may also expect some rather abrupt switches in the direction the questioning takes, so do not be upset by it. Normally, a board member will not pursue a single line of questioning unless he discovers a particular strength or weakness.

After each member has participated, the chairman will usually ask whether any member has any further questions, then will ask you if you have anything you wish to add. Unless you are expecting this question, it may floor you. Worse, it may start you off on an extended, extemporaneous speech. The board is not usually seeking more information. The question is principally to offer you a last opportunity to present further qualifications or to indicate that you have nothing to add. So, if you feel that a significant qualification or characteristic has been overlooked, it is proper to point it out in a sentence or so. Do not compliment the board on the thoroughness of their examination – they have been sketchy, and you know it. If you wish, merely say, "No thank you, I have nothing further to add." This is a point where you can "talk yourself out" of a good impression or fail to present an important bit of information. Remember, *you close the interview yourself.*

The chairman will then say, "That is all, Mr. _____, thank you." Do not be startled; the interview is over, and quicker than you think. Thank him, gather your belongings and take your leave. Save your sigh of relief for the other side of the door.

How to put your best foot forward

Throughout this entire process, you may feel that the board individually and collectively is trying to pierce your defenses, seek out your hidden weaknesses and embarrass and confuse you. Actually, this is not true. They are obliged to make an appraisal of your qualifications for the job you are seeking, and they want to see you in your best light. Remember, they must interview all candidates and a non-cooperative candidate may become a failure in spite of their best efforts to bring out his qualifications. Here are 15 suggestions that will help you:

1) Be natural – Keep your attitude confident, not cocky

If you are not confident that you can do the job, do not expect the board to be. Do not apologize for your weaknesses, try to bring out your strong points. The board is interested in a positive, not negative, presentation. Cockiness will antagonize any board member and make him wonder if you are covering up a weakness by a false show of strength.

2) Get comfortable, but don't lounge or sprawl

Sit erectly but not stiffly. A careless posture may lead the board to conclude that you are careless in other things, or at least that you are not impressed by the importance of the occasion. Either conclusion is natural, even if incorrect. Do not fuss with your clothing, a pencil or an ashtray. Your hands may occasionally be useful to emphasize a point; do not let them become a point of distraction.

3) Do not wisecrack or make small talk

This is a serious situation, and your attitude should show that you consider it as such. Further, the time of the board is limited – they do not want to waste it, and neither should you.

4) Do not exaggerate your experience or abilities

In the first place, from information in the application or other interviews and sources, the board may know more about you than you think. Secondly, you probably will not get away with it. An experienced board is rather adept at spotting such a situation, so do not take the chance.

5) If you know a board member, do not make a point of it, yet do not hide it

Certainly you are not fooling him, and probably not the other members of the board. Do not try to take advantage of your acquaintanceship – it will probably do you little good.

6) Do not dominate the interview

Let the board do that. They will give you the clues – do not assume that you have to do all the talking. Realize that the board has a number of questions to ask you, and do not try to take up all the interview time by showing off your extensive knowledge of the answer to the first one.

7) Be attentive

You only have 20 minutes or so, and you should keep your attention at its sharpest throughout. When a member is addressing a problem or question to you, give him your undivided attention. Address your reply principally to him, but do not exclude the other board members.

8) Do not interrupt

A board member may be stating a problem for you to analyze. He will ask you a question when the time comes. Let him state the problem, and wait for the question.

9) Make sure you understand the question

Do not try to answer until you are sure what the question is. If it is not clear, restate it in your own words or ask the board member to clarify it for you. However, do not haggle about minor elements.

10) Reply promptly but not hastily

A common entry on oral board rating sheets is "candidate responded readily," or "candidate hesitated in replies." Respond as promptly and quickly as you can, but do not jump to a hasty, ill-considered answer.

11) Do not be peremptory in your answers

A brief answer is proper – but do not fire your answer back. That is a losing game from your point of view. The board member can probably ask questions much faster than you can answer them.

12) Do not try to create the answer you think the board member wants

He is interested in what kind of mind you have and how it works – not in playing games. Furthermore, he can usually spot this practice and will actually grade you down on it.

13) Do not switch sides in your reply merely to agree with a board member

Frequently, a member will take a contrary position merely to draw you out and to see if you are willing and able to defend your point of view. Do not start a debate, yet do not surrender a good position. If a position is worth taking, it is worth defending.

14) Do not be afraid to admit an error in judgment if you are shown to be wrong

The board knows that you are forced to reply without any opportunity for careful consideration. Your answer may be demonstrably wrong. If so, admit it and get on with the interview.

15) Do not dwell at length on your present job

The opening question may relate to your present assignment. Answer the question but do not go into an extended discussion. You are being examined for a *new* job, not your present one. As a matter of fact, try to phrase ALL your answers in terms of the job for which you are being examined.

Basis of Rating

Probably you will forget most of these "do's" and "don'ts" when you walk into the oral interview room. Even remembering them all will not ensure you a passing grade. Perhaps you did not have the qualifications in the first place. But remembering them will help you to put your best foot forward, without treading on the toes of the board members.

Rumor and popular opinion to the contrary notwithstanding, an oral board wants you to make the best appearance possible. They know you are under pressure – but they also want to see how you respond to it as a guide to what your reaction would be under the pressures of the job you seek. They will be influenced by the degree of poise you display, the personal traits you show and the manner in which you respond.

ABOUT THIS BOOK

This book contains tests divided into Examination Sections. Go through each test, answering every question in the margin. At the end of each test look at the answer key and check your answers. On the ones you got wrong, look at the right answer choice and learn. Do not fill in the answers first. Do not memorize the questions and answers, but understand the answer and principles involved. On your test, the questions will likely be different from the samples. Questions are changed and new ones added. If you understand these past questions you should have success with any changes that arise. Tests may consist of several types of questions. We have additional books on each subject should more study be advisable or necessary for you. Finally, the more you study, the better prepared you will be. This book is intended to be the last thing you study before you walk into the examination room. Prior study of relevant texts is also recommended. NLC publishes some of these in our Fundamental Series. Knowledge and good sense are important factors in passing your exam. Good luck also helps. So now study this Passbook, absorb the material contained within and take that knowledge into the examination. Then do your best to pass that exam.

———

EXAMINATION SECTION

EXAMINATION SECTION
TEST 1

DIRECTIONS: Each question or incomplete statement is followed by several suggested answers or completions. Select the one that BEST answers the question or completes the statement. *PRINT THE LETTER OF THE CORRECT ANSWER IN THE SPACE AT THE RIGHT.*

Questions 1–5.

DIRECTIONS: Questions 1 through 5 consist of sentences each of which contains one under-lined word whose meaning you are to identify by marking your answer either A, B, C, or D.

EXAMPLE

Public employees should avoid <u>unethical</u> conduct.
The word unethical, as used in the sentence, means, most nearly,
  A. fine   B. dishonest   C. polite   D. sleepy
The correct answer is dishonest (B). Therefore, you should mark your answer B.

1. Employees who can produce a <u>considerable</u> amount of good work are very valuable.   1.____
     The word *considerable,* as used in the sentence, means, most nearly,

     A. large   B. potential   C. necessary   D. frequent

2. No person should <u>assume</u> that he knows more than anyone else.   2.____
     The word *assume,* as used in the sentence, means, most nearly,

     A. verify   B. hope   C. suppose   D. argue

3. The parties decided to <u>negotiate</u> through the night.   3.____
     The word *negotiate,* as used in the sentence, means, most nearly,

     A. suffer   B. play   C. think   D. bargain

4. Employees who have <u>severe</u> emotional problems may create problems at work.   4.____
     The word *severe,* as used in the sentence, means, most nearly,

     A. serious   B. surprising   C. several   D. common

5. Supervisors should try to be as <u>objective</u> as possible when dealing with subordinates.   5.____
     The word *objective,* as used in the sentence, means, most nearly,

     A. pleasant   B. courteous   C. fair   D. strict

Questions 6–10.

DIRECTIONS: In each of Questions 6 through 10, *one* word is wrongly used because it is *NOT* in keeping with the intended meaning of the statement. First, decide which word is wrongly used; then select as your answer the right word which really belongs in its place.

EXAMPLE

The employee told ill and requested permission to leave early.
  A. felt   B. considered   C. cried   D. spoke
The word *"told"* is clearly wrong and not in keeping with the intended meaning of the quota-tion.

1

The word *"felt"* (A), however, would clearly convey the intended meaning of the sentence. Option A is correct. Your answer space, therefore, would be marked A.

6. Only unwise supervisors would deliberately overload their subordinates in order to create themselves look good.   6._____

    A. delegate   B. make   C. reduce   D. produce

7. In a democratic organization each employee is seen as a special individual kind of fair treatment,   7._____

    A. granted   B. denial   C. perhaps   D. deserving

8. In order to function the work flow in an office you should begin by identifying each important procedure being performed in that office.   8._____

    A. uniformity   B. study   C. standards   D. reward

9. A wise supervisor tries to save employees' time by simplifying forms or adding forms where possible.   9._____

    A. taxing   B. supervising   C. eliminating   D. protecting

10. A public agency, whenever it changes its program, should give requirements to the need for retraining its employees.   10._____

    A. legislation   B. consideration   C. permission   D. advice

Questions 11-15.

DIRECTIONS: Answer each of Questions 11 through 15 ONLY on the basis of the reading passage preceding each question.

11. Things may not always be what they seem to be. Thus, the wise supervisor should analyze his problems and determine whether there is something there that does not meet the eye. For example, what may seem on the surface to be a personality clash between two subordinates may really be a problem of faulty organization, bad communication, or bad scheduling.   11._____
Which one of the following statements BEST supports this passage?

    A. The wise supervisor should avoid personality clashes.
    B. The smart supervisor should figure out what really is going on.
    C. Bad scheduling is the result of faulty organization.
    D. The best supervisor is the one who communicates effectively.

12. Some supervisors, under the pressure of meeting deadlines, become harsh and dictatorial to their subordinates. However, the supervisor most likely to be effective in meeting deadlines is one who absorbs or cushions pressures from above.
According to the passage, if a supervisor wishes to meet deadlines, it is MOST important that he

    A. be informative to his superiors
    B. encourage personal initiative among his subordinates
    C. become harsh and dictatorial to his subordinates
    D. protects his subordinates from pressures from above

12.____

13. When giving instructions, a supervisor must always make clear his meaning, leaving no room for misunderstanding. For example, a supervisor who tells a subordinate to do a task "*as soon as possible*" might legitimately be understood to mean either "*it's top priority*" or "*do it when you can.*"
Which of the following statements is BEST supported by the passage?

    A. Subordinates will attempt to avoid work by deliberately distorting instructions.
    B. Instructions should be short, since brief instructions are the clearest.
    C. Less educated subordinates are more likely to honestly misunderstand instructions.
    D. A supervisor should give precise instructions that cannot be misinterpreted.

13.____

14. Practical formulas are often suggested to simplify what a supervisor should know and how he should behave, such as the four F's (be firm, fair, friendly, and factual). But such simple formulas are really broad principles, not necessarily specific guides in a real situation.
According to the passage, simple formulas for supervisory behavior

    A. are superior to complicated theories and principles
    B. not always of practical use in actual situations
    C. useful only if they are fair and factual
    D. would be better understood if written in clear language

14.____

15. Many management decisions are made far removed from the actual place of operations. Therefore, there is a great need for reliable reports and records and, the larger the organization, the greater is the need for such reports and records.
According to the passage, management decisions made far from the place of operations are

    A. dependent to a great extent on reliable reports and records
    B. sometimes in error because of the great distances involved
    C. generally unreliable because of poor communications
    D. generally more accurate than on–the–scene decisions

15.____

16. Assume that you have just been advanced to a supervisory administrative position and have been assigned as supervisor to a new office with subordinates you do not know, The BEST way for you to establish good relations with these new subordinates would be to

    A. announce that all actions of the previous supervisor are now cancelled
    B. hold a meeting and warn them that you will not tolerate loafing on the job
    C. reassign all your subordinates to new tasks on the theory that a thorough shake–up is good for morale
    D. act fairly and show helpful interest in their work

16.____

17. One of your subordinates asks you to let her arrive at work 15 minutes later than usual but leave for the day 15 minutes later than she usually does. This is temporarily necessary, your subordinate states, because of early morning medication she must give her sick child.
Which of the following would be the *MOST* appropriate action for you to take?

    A. *Suggest* to your subordinate that she choose another family doctor
    B. *Warn* your subordinate that untruthful excuses are not acceptable
    C. *Tell* your subordinate that you will consider the request and let her know very shortly
    D. *Deny* the request since late arrival at work interferes with work performance

17.____

18. A young newly–hired employee asked his supervisor several times for advice on private financial matters. The supervisor commented, in a friendly manner, that he considered it undesirable to give such advice.
The supervisor's response was

    A. *unwise;* the supervisor missed an opportunity to advise the employee on an important matter
    B. *wise;* if the financial advice was wrong, it could damage the supervisor's relationship with the subordinate
    C. *unwise;* the subordinate will take up the matter with his fellow workers and probably get poor advice
    D. *wise;* the supervisor should never advise subordinates on any matter

18.____

19. Which of the following is the MOST justified reason for a supervisor to pay any serious attention to a subordinate's off–the–job behavior? The

    A. subordinate's life style is different from the supervisor's way of life
    B. subordinate has become well–known as a serious painter of fine art
    C. subordinate's work has become very poor as a result of his or her personal problems
    D. subordinate is a reserved person who, at work, seldom speaks of personal matters

19.____

4

20. One of your subordinates complains to you that you assign him to the least pleasant jobs more often than anyone else. You are disturbed by this complaint since you believe you have always rotated such assignments on a fair basis.
    Of the following, it would be BEST for you to tell the complaining subordinate that

    A. you will review your past assignment records and discuss the matter with him further
    B. complaints to supervisors are not the wise way to get ahead on the job
    C. disciplinary action will follow if the complaint is not justified
    D. he may be correct, but you do not have sufficient time to verify the complaint

20.____

21. Assume that you have called one of your subordinates into your office to talk about the increasing number of careless errors in her work. Until recently, this subordinate had been doing good work, but this is no longer so. Your subordinate does not seem to respond to your questions about the reason for her poor work.
    In these circumstances, your *next* step should be to tell her

    A. that her continued silence will result in severe disciplinary action
    B. to request an immediate transfer from your unit
    C. to return when she is ready to respond
    D. to be more open with you so that her work problem can be identified

21.____

22. Assume that you are given a complicated assignment with a tight deadline set by your superior. Shortly after you begin work you realize that, if you are to do a top quality job, you cannot possibly meet the deadline.
    In these circumstances, what should be your FIRST course of action?

    A. *Continue* working as rapidly as possible, hoping that you will meet the deadline after all
    B. *Request* the assignment be given to an employee whom you believe works faster
    C. *Advise* your superior of the problem and see whether the deadline can be extended
    D. *Advise* your superior that the deadline cannot be met and, therefore, you will not start the job

22.____

23. Assume that a member of the public comes to you to complain about a long–standing practice of your agency. The complaint seems to be justified.
    Which one of the following is the BEST way for you to handle this situation?

    A. *Inform* the complainant that you will have the agency practice looked into and that he will be advised of any action taken
    B. *Listen* politely, express sympathy, and state that you see no fault in the practice
    C. *Express* agreement with the practice on the ground that it has been in effect for many years
    D. *Advise* the complainant that things will work out well in good time

23.____

24. One of your subordinates tells you that he sees no good reason for having departmental   24._____
safety rules.
Which one of the following replies would be BEST for you to make?

    A. Rules are meant to be obeyed without question.
    B. All types of rules are equally important.
    C. Safety rules are meant to protect people from injury.
    D. If a person is careful enough, he doesn't have to observe safety rules.

25. Assume that a supervisor, when he issues instructions to his subordinates, usually   25._____
names his superior as the source of these instructions.
This practice is, generally,

    A. *wise,* since if things go wrong, the subordinates will know whom to blame
    B. *unwise,* since it may give the subordinates the impression that the supervisor
doesn't really support the instructions
    C. *wise,* since it clearly invites the subordinates to go to higher authority if they don't
like the instructions
    D. *unwise,* since the subordinates may thereby be given too much information

---

KEY (CORRECT ANSWERS)

1.	A		11.	B
2.	C		12.	D
3.	D		13.	D
4.	A		14.	B
5.	C		15.	A
6.	B		16.	D
7.	D		17.	C
8.	B		18.	B
9.	C		19.	C
10.	B		20.	A

21.	D
22.	C
23.	A
24.	C
25.	B

TEST 2

DIRECTIONS: Each question or incomplete statement is followed by several suggested answers or completions. Select the one that *BEST* answers the question or completes the statement. *PRINT THE LETTER OF THE CORRECT ANSWER IN THE SPACE AT THE RIGHT*

1. An office aide is assigned as a receptionist in a busy office. The office aide often has stretches of idle time between visitors.
   In this situation, the supervisor should

   1.____

   A. *give* the receptionist non–urgent clerical jobs which can quickly be done at the reception desk
   B. *offer* all office aides an opportunity to volunteer for this assignment
   C. *eliminate* the receptionist assignment
   D. *continue* the arrangement unchanged, because receptionist duties are so important nothing should interfere with them

2. A supervisor can MOST correctly assume that an employee is not performing up to his usual standard when the employee does not handle a task as skillfully as

   2.____

   A. do other employees who have received less training
   B. do similar employees having comparable work experience
   C. he has handled it in several recent instances
   D. the supervisor himself could handle it

3. Assume that you receive a suggestion that you direct all the typists in a typing pool to complete the identical quantity of work each day.
   For you to adopt this suggestion would be

   3.____

   A. *advisable;* it will demonstrate the absence of supervisory favoritism
   B. *advisable;* all employees in a given title should be treated identically
   C. *inadvisable;* a supervisor should decide on work standards without interference from others
   D. *inadvisable;* it ignores variations in specific assignments and individual skills

4. A certain supervisor encouraged her subordinates to tell her if they become aware of possible job problems.
   This practice is *good* MAINLY because

   4.____

   A. early awareness of job problems allows more time for seeking solutions
   B. such expected job problems may not develop
   C. the supervisor will be able to solve the job problem without consulting other people
   D. the supervisor will be able to place responsibility for poor work

5. Some supervisors will discuss with a subordinate how he is doing on the job only when indicating his mistakes or faults.
   Which of the following is the MOST likely result of such a practice?

   5.____

   A. The subordinate will become discouraged and frustrated.
   B. Management will set work standards too low.
   C. The subordinate will be favorably impressed by the supervisor's frankness.
   D. Supervisors will avoid creating any impression of favoritism.

6. A supervisor calls in a subordinate he supervises to discuss the subordinate's annual   6._____
   work performance, indicating his work deficiencies and also praising his job strengths.
   The subordinate nods his head as if in agreement with his supervisor's comments on
   both his strengths and weaknesses, but actually says nothing, even after the supervisor
   has completed his comments. At this point, the supervisor should

   A. end the session and assume that the subordinate agrees completely with the eval-
      uation
   B. end the session, since all the subordinate's good and bad points have been identi-
      fied
   C. ask the subordinate whether the criticism is justified, and, if so, what he, the super-
      visor, can do to help
   D. thank the subordinate for being so fair–minded in accepting the criticism in a posi-
      tive manner

7. The successful supervisor is often one who gives serious attention to his subordinates'   7._____
   needs for job satisfaction. A supervisor who believes this statement is MOST likely to

   A. treat all subordinates in an identical manner, irrespective of individual differences
   B. permit each subordinate to perform his work as he wishes, within reasonable limits
   C. give all subordinates both criticism and praise in equal measure
   D. provide each subordinate with as much direct supervision as possible

8. Assume that you are supervising seven subordinates and have been asked by your   8._____
   superior to prepare an especially complex report due today. Its completion will take the
   rest of the day. You break down the assignment into simple parts and give a different part
   to each subordinate.
   If you were to explain the work of each subordinate to more than one subordinate, your
   decision would be

   A. *wise;* this would prevent boredom
   B. *unwise;* valuable time would be lost
   C. *wise;* your subordinates would become well–rounded
   D. *unwise;* your subordinates would lose their competitive spirit

9. Suppose that an office associate whom you supervise has given you a well–researched   9._____
   report on a problem in an area in which he is expert. However, the report lacks solutions
   or recommendations. You know this office associate to be fearful of stating his opinions.
   In these circumstances, you should tell him that

   A. you will seek recommendations on the problem from other, even if less expert,
      office associates
   B. his work is unsatisfactory, in hope of arousing him to greater assertiveness
   C. you need his advise and expertise, to help you reach a decision on the problem
   D. his uncooperative behavior leaves you no choice but to speak to your superior

10. If a supervisor wishes to have the work of his unit completed on schedule, it is usually MOST important to   10.____

    A. avoid listening to employees' complaints, thereby discouraging dissatisfaction
    B. perform much of the work himself, since he is generally more capable
    C. observe employees continuously, so they do not slacken their efforts
    D. set up the work carefully, then stay informed as to how it is moving

11. Of the following agencies, the one MOST likely to work out a proposed budget close to its real needs is   11.____

    A. a newly–created agency staffed by inexperienced administrators
    B. funded with a considerable amount of money
    C. an existing agency which intends to install new, experimental systems for doing its work
    D. an existing agency which can base its estimate on its experience during the past few years

12. Assume that you are asked to prepare a report on the expected costs and benefits of a proposed:new program to be installed in your office. However, you are aware that certain factors are not really measurable in dollars and cents.
As a result, you should   12.____

    A. *identify* the non–measurable factors and state why they are important
    B. *assign* a fixed money value to all factors that are not really measurable
    C. *recommend* that programs containing non–measurable factors should be dropped
    D. *assume* that the non–measurable factors are really unimportant

13. Assume that you are asked for your opinion as to the necessity for hiring more employees to perform certain revenue–producing work in your office.
The information that you will MOST likely need in giving an informed opinion is   13.____

    A. whether public opinion would favor hiring additional employees
    B. an estimate of the probable additional revenue compared with the additional personnel costs
    C. the total cots of all city operations in contrast to all city revenues
    D. the method by which present employees would be selected for promotion in an expanded operation

14. The *most* reasonable number of subordinates for a supervisor to have is BEST determined by the   14.____

    A. average number of subordinates other supervisors have
    B. particular responsibilities given to the supervisor
    C. supervisor's educational background
    D. personalities of the subordinates assigned to the supervisor

15. Most subordinates would need less supervision if they knew what they were supposed to do.
An ESSENTIAL first step in fixing in subordinates' minds exactly what is required of them is to

    A. *require* that supervisors be firm in their supervision of subordinates
    B. *encourage* subordinates to determine their own work standards
    C. *encourage* subordinates to submit suggestions to improve procedures
    D. *standardize* and simplify procedures and logically schedule activities

15.____

16. Assume that you have been asked to recommend an appropriate office layout to correspond with a just completed office reorganization.
Which of the following is it MOST advisable to recommend?

    A. *Allocate* most of the space for traffic flow
    B. *Use* the center area only for traffic flow
    C. *situate* close to each other those units whose work is closely related
    D. *Group* in an out–of–the–way corner the supply and file cabinets

16.____

17. Although an organization chart will illustrate the formal structure of an agency, it will seldom show a true picture of its actual workings.
Which of the following BEST explains this statement? Organization charts

    A. are often prepared by employees who may exaggerate their own importance
    B. usually show titles and sometimes names rather than the actual contacts and movements between employees
    C. are likely to discourage the use of official titles, and in so doing promote greater freedom in human relations
    D. usually show the informal arrangements and dealings between employees

17.____

18. Assume that a supervisor of a large unit has a variety of tasks to perform, and that he gives each of his subordinates just one set of tasks to do. He never rotates subordinates from one set of tasks to another.
Which one of the following is the MOST likely *advantage* to be gained by this practice?

    A. Each subordinate will get to know all the tasks of the unit.
    B. The subordinate will be encouraged to learn all they can about all the unit's tasks.
    C. Each subordinate will become an expert in his particular set of tasks.
    D. The subordinates will improve their opportunities for promotion.

18.____

19. Listed below are four steps commonly used in trying to solve administrative problems. These four steps are not listed in the order in which they normally would be taken. If they were listed in the proper order, which step should be taken *FIRST*?
    I. Choosing the most practical solution to the problem
    II. Analyzing the essential facts about the problem
    III. Correctly identifying the problem
    IV. Following up to see if the solution chosen really works
The CORRECT answer is:

    A. III   B. I   C. II   D. IV

19.____

20. Assume that another agency informally tells you that most of your agency's reports are coming to them with careless errors made by many of your office aides.
Which one of the following is MOST likely to solve this problem?

    A. *Require* careful review of all outgoing reports by the supervisors of the office aides
    B. *Request* the other agency to make necessary corrections whenever such errors come to their attention
    C. *Ask* the other agency to submit a written report on this situation
    D. *Establish* a small unit to review all reports received from other agencies

20.____

21. Assume that you supervise an office which gets two kinds of work. One kind is high–priority and must be done within two days. The other kind of work must be done within two weeks.
Which one of the following instructions would be MOST reasonable for you to give to your subordinates in this office?

    A. If a backlog builds up during the day, clean the backlog up first, regardless of priority
    B. Spend half the day doing priority work and the other half doing non–priority work
    C. Generally do the priority work first as soon as it is received
    D. Usually do the work in the order in which it comes in, priority or non–priority

21.____

22. An experienced supervisor should do advance planning of his subordinates' work assignments and schedules.
Which one of the following is the BEST reason for such advance planning? It

    A. enables the supervisor to do less supervision
    B. will assure the assignment of varied duties
    C. will make certain a high degree of discipline among subordinates
    D. helps make certain that essential operations are adequately covered

22.____

23. Agencies are required to evaluate the performance of their employees.
Which one of the following would generally be POOR evaluation practice by an agency rater? The rater

    A. regularly observes the performance of the employee being rated
    B. in evaluating the employee, acquaints himself with the employee's job
    C. uses objective standards in evaluating the employee being rated
    D. uses different standards in evaluating men and women

23.____

24. A good supervisor should have a clear idea of the quantity and quality of his subordinates' work.
Which one of the following sources would normally provide a supervisor with the LEAST reliable information about a subordinate's work performance?

    A. Discussion with a friend of the subordinate
    B. Comments by other supervisors who have worked recently with the subordinate
    C. Opinions of fellow workers who work closely with the subordinate on a daily basis
    D. Comparison with work records of others doing similar work during the same period of time

24.____

25. In order to handle the ordinary work of an office, a, supervisor sets up standard work pro-   25.____
    cedures.
    The MOST likely benefit of this is to reduce the need to

    A. motivate employees to do superior work
    B. rethink what has to be done every time a routine matter comes up
    C. keep records and write reports
    D. change work procedures as new situations come up

    _____

KEY (CORRECT ANSWERS

1.	A		11.	D
2.	C		12.	A
3.	D		13.	B
4.	A		14.	B
5.	A		15.	D
6.	C		16.	C
7.	B		17.	B
8.	B		18.	C
9.	C		19.	A
10.	D		20.	A

21.	C
22.	D
23.	D
24.	A
25.	B

_____

EXAMINATION SECTION
TEST 1

DIRECTIONS: Each question or incomplete statement is followed by several suggested answers or completions. Select the one that BEST answers the question or completes the statement. *PRINT THE LETTER OF THE CORRECT ANSWER IN THE SPACE AT THE RIGHT.*

1. In almost every organization, there is a nucleus of highly important functions commonly designated as *management.* Which of the following statements BEST characterizes *management?*   1.____

    A. Getting things done through others
    B. The highest level of intelligence in any organization
    C. The process whereby democratic and participative activities are maximized
    D. The *first among equals*

2. Strategies in problem-solving are important to anyone aspiring to advancement in the field of administration. Which of the following is BEST classified as the first step in the process of problem-solving?   2.____

    A. Collection and organization of data
    B. The formulation of a plan
    C. The definition of the problem
    D. The development of a method and methodology

3. One of the objectives of preparing a budget is to   3.____

    A. create optimistic goals which each department can attempt to meet
    B. create an overall company goal by combining the budgets of the various departments
    C. be able to compare planned expenditures against actual expenditures
    D. be able to identify accounting errors

4. The rise in demand for *systems* personnel in industrial and governmental organizations over the past five years has been extraordinary.
In which of the following areas would a *systems* specialist assigned to an agency be LEAST likely to be of assistance?   4.____

    A. Developing, recommending, and establishing an effective cost and inventory system
    B. Development and maintenance of training manuals
    C. Reviewing existing work procedures and recommending improvements
    D. Development of aptitude tests for new employees

5. Management experts have come to the conclusion that the traditional forms of motivation used in industry and government, which emphasize authority over and economic rewards for the employee, are no longer appropriate.
To which of the following factors do such experts attribute the GREATEST importance in producing this change?   5.____

    A. The desire of employees to satisfy material needs has become greater and more complex.

B. The desire for social satisfaction has become the most important aspect of the job for the average worker.

C. With greater standardization of work processes, there has been an increase in the willingness of workers to accept discipline.

D. In general, employee organizations have made it more difficult for management to fire an employee.

6. In preparing a budget, it is usually considered advisable to start the initial phases of preparation at the operational level of management.
Of the following, the justification that management experts usually advance as MOST reasonable for this practice is that operating managers, as a consequence of their involvement, will

6.____

A. develop a background in finance or accounting
B. have an understanding of the organizational structure
C. tend to feel responsible for carrying out budget objectives
D. have the ability to see the overall financial picture

7. An administrative officer has been asked by his superior to write a concise, factual report with objective conclusions and recommendations based on facts assembled by other researchers.
Of the following factors, the administrative officer should give LEAST consideration to

7.____

A. the educational level of the person or persons for whom the report is being prepared
B. the use to be made of the report
C. the complexity of the problem
D. his own feelings about the importance of the problem

8. In an agency, upon which of the following is a supervisor's effectiveness MOST likely to depend?
The

8.____

A. degree to which a supervisor allows subordinates to participate in the decision-making process and the setting of objectives
B. degree to which a supervisor's style meets management's objectives and subordinates' needs
C. strength and forcefulness of the supervisor in pursuing his objectives
D. expertise and knowledge the supervisor has about the specific work to be done

9. For authority to be effective, which of the following is the MOST basic requirement?
Authority must be

9.____

A. absolute   B. formalized   C. accepted   D. delegated

10. Management no longer abhors the idea of employees taking daily work breaks, but prefers to schedule such breaks rather than to allot to each employee a standard amount of free time to be taken off during the day as he wishes. Which of the following BEST expresses the reason management theorists give for the practice of scheduling such breaks?

10.____

A. Many jobs fall into natural work units which are scheduled, and the natural time to take a break is at the end of the unit.

B. Taking a scheduled break permits socialization and a feeling of accomplishment.

C. Managers have concluded that scheduling rest periods seems to reduce the incidence of unscheduled ones.

D. Many office workers who really need such breaks are hesitant about taking them unless they are scheduled.

11. The computer represents one of the major developments of modern technology. It is widely used in both scientific and managerial activities because of its many advantages. Which of the following is NOT an advantage gained by management in the use of the computer?
A computer

    11.____

A. provides the manager with a greatly enlarged memory so that he can easily be provided with data for decision making

B. relieves the manager of basic decision-making responsibility, thereby giving him more time for directing and controlling

C. performs routine, repetitive calculations with greater precision and reliability than employees

D. provides a capacity for rapid simulations of alternative solutions to problem solving

12. A supervisor of a unit in a division is usually responsible for all of the following EXCEPT

    12.____

A. the conduct of subordinates in the achievement of division objectives

B. maintaining quality standards in the unit

C. the protection and care of materials and equipment in the unit

D. performing the most detailed tasks in the unit himself

13. You have been assigned to teach a new employee the functions and procedures of your office.
In your introductory talk, which of the following approaches is PREFERABLE?

    13.____

A. Advise the new employee of the employee benefits and services available to him, over and above his salary.

B. Discuss honestly the negative aspects of departmental procedures and indicate methods available to overcome them.

C. Give the new employee an understanding of the general purpose of office procedures and functions and of their relevance to departmental objectives.

D. Give a basic and detailed explanation of the operations of your office, covering all functions and procedures.

14. It is your responsibility to assign work to several clerks under your supervision. One of the clerks indignantly refuses to accept an assignment and asks to be given something else. He has not yet indicated why he does not want the assignment, but is sitting there glaring at you, awaiting your reaction.
Of the following, which is the FIRST action you should take?

    14.____

A. Ask the employee into your office in order to reprimand him and tell him emphatically that he must accept the assignment.

B. Talk to the employee privately in an effort to find the reason for his indignation and refusal, and then base your action upon your findings.

C. Let the matter drop for a day or two to allow the employee to cool off before you insist that he accept the assignment.
D. Inform the employee quietly and calmly that as his supervisor you have selected him for this assignment and that you fully expect him to accept it.

15. Administrative officers are expected to be able to handle duties delegated to them by their supervisors and to be able, as they advance in status, to delegate tasks to assistants.
When considering whether to delegate tasks to a subordinate, which of the following questions should be LEAST important to an administrative officer?
In the delegated tasks,

   A. how significant are the decisions to be made, and how much consultation will be involved?
   B. to what extent is uniformity and close coordination of activity required?
   C. to what extent must speedy-on-the-spot decisions be made?
   D. to what extent will delegation relieve the administrative officer of his burden of responsibility?

15._____

16. A functional forms file is a collection of forms which are grouped by

   A. purpose   B. department   C. title   D. subject

16._____

17. All of the following are reasons to consult a records retention schedule except one.
Which one is that?
To determine

   A. whether something should be filed
   B. how long something should stay in file
   C. who should be assigned to filing
   D. when something on file should be destroyed

17._____

18. Listed below are four of the steps in the process of preparing correspondence for filing.
If they were to be put in logical sequence, the SECOND step would be

   A. preparing cross-reference sheets or cards
   B. coding the correspondence using a classification system
   C. sorting the correspondence in the order to be filed
   D. checking for follow-up action required and preparing a follow-up slip

18._____

19. New material added to a file folder should USUALLY be inserted

   A. in the order of importance (the most important in front)
   B. in the order of importance (the most important in back)
   C. chronologically (most recent in front)
   D. chronologically (most recent in back)

19._____

20. An individual is looking for a name in the white pages of a telephone directory.
Which of the following BEST describes the system of filing found there?
A(n)_____ file

   A. alphabetic   B. sequential
   C. locator   D. index

20._____

21. The MAIN purpose of a tickler file is to 21._____
    A. help prevent overlooking matters that require future attention
    B. check on adequacy of past performance
    C. pinpoint responsibility for recurring daily tasks
    D. reduce the volume of material kept in general files

22. Which of the following BEST describes the process of reconciling a bank statement? 22._____
    A. Analyzing the nature of the expenditures made by the office during the preceding month
    B. Comparing the statement of the bank with the banking records maintained in the office
    C. Determining the liquidity position by reading the bank statement carefully
    D. Checking the service charges noted on the bank statement

23. From the viewpoint of preserving agency or institutional funds, which of the following is the LEAST acceptable method for making a payment? 23._____
    A check made out to
    A. cash   B. a company
    C. an individual   D. a partnership

24. In general, the CHIEF economy of using multicopy forms is in 24._____
    A. the paper on which the form is printed   B. printing the form
    C. employee time   D. carbon paper

25. Suppose your supervisor has asked you to develop a form to record certain information needed. 25._____
    The FIRST thing you should do is to

    A. determine the type of data that will be recorded repeatedly so that it can be pre-printed
    B. study the relationship of the form to the job to be accomplished so that the form can be planned
    C. determine the information that will be recorded in the same place on each copy of the form so that it can be used as a check
    D. find out who will be responsible for supplying the information so that space can be provided for their signatures

26. An administrative officer in charge of a small fund for buying office supplies has just writ-ten a check to Charles Laird, a supplier, and has sent the check by messenger to him. A half-hour later, the messenger telephones the administrative officer. He has lost the check. 26._____
    Which of the following is the MOST important action for the administrative officer to take under these circumstances?

    A. Ask the messenger to return and write a report describing the loss of the check.
    B. Make a note on the performance record of the messenger who lost the check.
    C. Take the necessary steps to have payment stopped on the check.
    D. Refrain from doing anyting since the check may be found shortly.

27. A petty cash fund is set up PRIMARILY to   27.____

    A. take care of small investments that must be made from time to time
    B. take care of small expenses that arise from time to time
    C. provide a fund to be used as the office wants to use it with little need to maintain records
    D. take care of expenses that develop during emergencies, such as machine breakdowns and fires

28. Of the following, which is usually the MOST important guideline in writing business letters?   28.____
A letter should be

    A. neat
    B. written in a formalized style
    C. written in clear language intelligible to the reader
    D. written in the past tense

29. Suppose you are asked to edit a policy statement. You note that personal pronouns like *you, we,* and *I* are used freely.   29.____
Which of the following statements BEST applies to this use of personal pronouns?
It

    A. is proper usage because written business language should not be different from carefully spoken business language
    B. requires correction because it is ungrammatical
    C. is proper because it is clearer and has a warmer tone
    D. requires correction because policies should be expressed in an impersonal manner

30. Good business letters are coherent.   30.____
To be coherent means to

    A. keep only one unifying idea in the message
    B. present the total message
    C. use simple, direct words for the message
    D. tie together the various ideas in the message

31. Proper division of a letter into paragraphs requires that the writer of business letters should, as much as possible, be sure that   31.____

    A. each paragraph is short
    B. each paragraph develops discussion of just one topic
    C. each paragraph repeats the theme of the total message
    D. there are at least two paragraphs for every message

32. An editor is given a letter with this initial paragraph: 32.____
We have received your letter, which we read with interest, and we are happy to respond to your question. In fact, we talked with several people in our office to get ideas to send to you.
Which of the following is it MOST reasonable for the editor to conclude?
The paragraph is

A. concise
B. communicating something of value
C. unnecessary
D. coherent

33. As soon as you pick up the phone, a very angry caller begins immediately to complain about city agencies and *red tape*. He says that he has been shifted to two or three different offices. It turns out that he is seeking information which is not immediately available to you. You believe you know, however, where it can be found. Which of the following actions is the BEST one for you to take?

    33._____

    A. To eliminate all confusion, suggest that the caller write the mayor stating explicitly what he wants.
    B. Apologize by telling the caller how busy city agencies now are, but also tell him directly that you do not have the information he needs.
    C. Ask for the caller's telephone number and assure him you will call back after you have checked further.
    D. Give the caller the name and telephone number of the person who might be able to help, but explain that you are not positive he will get results.

34. Suppose that one of your duties is to dictate responses to routine requests from the public for information. A letter writer asks for information which, as expressed in a one-sentence, explicit agency rule, cannot be given out to the public.
Of the following ways of answering the letter, which is the MOST efficient?

    34._____

    A. Quote verbatim that section of the agency rules which prohibits giving this information to the public.
    B. Without quoting the rule, explain why you cannot accede to the request and suggest alternative sources.
    C. Describe how carefully the request was considered before classifying it as subject to the rule forbidding the issuance of such information.
    D. Acknowledge receipt of the letter and advise that the requested information is not released to the public.

35. Suppose you assist in supervising a staff which has rather high morale, and your own supervisor asks you to poll the staff to find out who will be able to work overtime this particular evening to help complete emergency work.
Which of the following approaches would be MOST likely to win their cooperation while maintaining their morale?

    35._____

    A. Tell them that the better assignments will be given only to those who work overtime.
    B. Tell them that occasional overtime is a job requirement .
    C. Assure them they'll be doing you a personal favor.
    D. Let them know clearly why the overtime is needed.

36. Suppose that you have been asked to write and to prepare for reproduction new departmental vacation leave regulations.
After you have written the new regulations, all of which fit on one page, which one of the following would be the BEST method of reproducing 1000 copies?

    36._____

    A. An outside private printer, because you can best maintain confidentiality using this technique
    B. Xeroxing, because the copies will have the best possible appearance

C.   Typing copies, because you will be certain that there are the fewest possible errors

D.   Including it in the next company newsletter

37.   Administration is the center, but not necessarily the source, of all ideas for procedural improvement.
The MOST significant implication that this principle bears for the administrative officer is that

    A.   before procedural improvements are introduced, they should be approved by a majority of the staff

    B.   it is the unique function of the administrative officer to derive and introduce procedural improvements

    C.   the administrative officer should derive ideas and suggestions for procedural improvement from all possible sources, introducing any that promise to be effective

    D.   the administrative officer should view employee grievances as the chief source of procedural improvements

37.____

38.   Your bureau is assigned an important task.
Of the following, the function that you, as an administrative officer, can LEAST reasonably be expected to perform under these circumstances is

    A.   division of the large job into individual tasks

    B.   establishment of *production lines* within the bureau

    C.   performance personally of a substantial share of all the work

    D.   check-up to see that the work has been well done

38.____

39.   Suppose that you have broken a complex job into its smaller components before making assignments to the employees under your jurisdiction.
Of the following, the LEAST advisable procedure to follow from that point is to

    A.   give each employee a picture of the importance of his work for the success of the total job

    B.   establish a definite line of work flow and responsibility

    C.   post a written memorandum of the best method for performing each job

    D.   teach a number of alternative methods for doing each job

39.____

40.   As an administrative officer, you are requested to draw up an organization chart of the whole department.
Of the following, the MOST important characteristic of such a chart is that it will

    A.   include all peculiarities and details of the organization which distinguish it from any other

    B.   be a schematic representation of purely administrative functions within the department

    C.   present a modification of the actual departmental organization in the light of principles of scientific management

    D.   present an accurate picture of the lines of authority and responsibility

40.____

KEY (CORRECT ANSWERS)

1.	A	11.	B	21.	A	31.	B
2.	C	12.	D	22.	B	32.	C
3.	C	13.	C	23.	A	33.	C
4.	D	14.	B	24.	C	34.	A
5.	D	15.	D	25.	B	35.	D
6.	C	16.	A	26.	C	36.	B
7.	D	17.	C	27.	B	37.	C
8.	B	18.	A	28.	C	38.	C
9.	C	19.	C	29.	D	39.	D
10.	C	20.	A	30.	D	40.	D

TEST 2

DIRECTIONS: Each question or incomplete statement is followed by several suggested answers or completions. Select the one that BEST answers the question or completes the statement. *PRINT THE LETTER OF THE CORRECT ANSWER IN THE SPACE AT THE RIGHT.*

Questions 1-10.

DIRECTIONS: In each of Questions 1 through 10, a pair of related words written in capital letters is followed by four other pairs of words. For each question, select the pair of words which MOST closely expresses a relationship similar to that of the pair in capital letters.

SAMPLE QUESTION:

BOAT - DOCK
    A. airplane - hangar   B. rain - snow
    C. cloth - cotton   D. hunger - food

Choice A is the answer to this sample question since, of the choices given, the relationship between airplane and hangar is most similar to the relationship between boat and dock.

1. AUTOMOBILE - FACTORY   1.____

    A. tea - lemon   B. wheel - engine
    C. pot - flower   D. paper - mill

2. GIRDER - BRIDGE   2.____

    A. petal - flower   B. street - sidewalk
    C. meat - vegetable   D. sun - storm

3. RADIUS - CIRCLE   3.____

    A. brick - building   B. tie - tracks
    C. spoke - wheel   D. axle - tire

4. DISEASE - RESEARCH   4.____

    A. death - poverty   B. speech - audience
    C. problem - conference   D. invalid - justice

5. CONCLUSION - INTRODUCTION   5.____

    A. commencement - beginning   B. housing - motor
    C. caboose - engine   D. train - cabin

6. SOCIETY - LAW   6.____

    A. baseball - rules   B. jury - law
    C. cell - prisoner   D. sentence - jury

7. PLAN - ACCOMPLISHMENT   7.____

    A. deed - fact   B. method - success
    C. graph - chart   D. rules - manual

8. ORDER - GOVERNMENT   8.____

    A. chaos - administration   B. confusion - pandemonium
    C. rule - stability   D. despair - hope

9. TYRANNY - FREEDOM   9.____

    A. despot - mob   B. wealth - poverty
    C. nobility - commoners   D. dictatorship - democracy

10. FAX - LETTER   10.____

    A. hare - tortoise   B. lie - truth
    C. number - word   D. report - research

Questions 11-16.

DIRECTIONS: Answer Questions 11 through 16 SOLELY on the basis of the information
                       given in the passage below.

       Inherent in all organized endeavors is the need to resolve the individual differences involved in conflict. Conflict may be either a positive or negative factor, since it may lead to creativity, innovation, and progress, on the one hand, or it may result, on the other hand, in a deterioration or even destruction of the organization. Thus, some forms of conflict are desirable, whereas others are undesirable and ethically wrong.
       There are three management strategies which deal with interpersonal conflict. In the "divide-and-rule strategy", management attempts to maintain control by limiting the conflict to those directly involved and preventing their disagreement from spreading to the larger group. The "suppression-of-differences strategy" entails ignoring conflicts or pretending they are irrelevant. In the "working-through-differences strategy", management actively attempts to solve or resolve intergroup or interpersonal conflicts. Of the three strategies, only the last directly attacks and has the potential for eliminating the causes of conflict. An essential part of this strategy, however, is its employment by a committed and relatively mature management team.

11. According to the above passage, the *divide-and-rule strategy* for dealing with conflict is   11.____
     the attempt to

    A. involve other people in the conflict
    B. restrict the conflict to those participating in it
    C. divide the conflict into positive and negative factors
    D. divide the conflict into a number of smaller ones

12. The word *conflict* is used in relation to both positive and negative factors in this passage. 12.____
     Which one of the following words is MOST likely to describe the activity which the word
     conflict, in the sense of the passage, implies?

    A. Competition   B. Cooperation
    C. Confusion   D. Aggression

13. According to the above passage, which one of the following characteristics is shared by 13.____
     both the *suppression-of-differences strategy* and the *divide-and-rule strategy?*

    A. Pretending that conflicts are irrelevant
    B. Preventing conflicts from spreading to the group situation

23

    C.   Failure to directly attack the causes of conflict
    D.   Actively attempting to resolve interpersonal conflict

14. According to the above passage, the successful resolution of interpersonal conflict   14.____
requires

    A.   allowing the group to mediate conflicts between two individuals
    B.   division of the conflict into positive and negative factors
    C.   involvement of a committed, mature management team
    D.   ignoring minor conflicts until they threaten the organization

15. Which can be MOST reasonably inferred from the above passage?   15.____
A conflict between two individuals is LEAST likely to continue when management uses

    A.   the *working-through-differences strategy*
    B.   the *suppression-of-differences strategy*
    C.   the *divide-and-rule strategy*
    D.   a combination of all three strategies

16. According to the above passage, a desirable result of conflict in an organization is when   16.____
conflict

    A.   exposes production problems in the organization
    B.   can be easily ignored by management
    C.   results in advancement of more efficient managers
    D.   leads to development of new methods

Questions 17-23.

DIRECTIONS: Answer Questions 17 through 23 SOLELY on the basis of the information
given in the passage below.

Modern management places great emphasis on the concept of communication. The communication process consists of the steps through which an idea or concept passes from its inception by one person, the sender, until it is acted upon by another person, the receiver. Through an understanding of these steps and some of the possible barriers that may occur, more effective communication may be achieved. The first step in the communication process is ideation by the sender. This is the formation of the intended content of the message he wants to transmit. In the next step, encoding, the sender organizes his ideas into a series of symbols designed to communicate his message to his intended receiver. He selects suitable words or phrases that can be understood by the receiver, and he also selects the appropriate media to be used-for example, memorandum, conference, etc. The third step is transmission of the encoded message through selected channels in the organizational structure. In the fourth step, the receiver enters the process by tuning in to receive the message. If the receiver does not function, however, the message is lost. For example, if the message is oral, the receiver must be a good listener. The fifth step is decoding of the message by the receiver, as for example, by changing words into ideas. At this step, the decoded message may not be the same idea that the sender originally encoded because the sender and receiver have different perceptions regarding the meaning of certain words.

Finally, the receiver acts or responds. He may file the information, ask for more information, or take other action. There can be no assurance, however, that communication has taken place unless there is some type of feedback to the sender in the form of an acknowledgement that the message was received.

17. According to the above passage, *ideation* is the process by which the 17.____

    A. sender develops the intended content of the message
    B. sender organizes his ideas into a series of symbols
    C. receiver tunes in to receive the message
    D. receiver decodes the message

18. In the last sentence of the passage, the word *feedback* refers to the process by which the 18.____
sender is assured that the

    A. receiver filed the information
    B. receiver's perception is the same as his own
    C. message was received
    D. message was properly interpreted

19. Which one of the following BEST shows the order of the steps in the communication pro- 19.____
cess as described in the passage?

    A. 1- ideation   2- encoding
        3- decoding   4- transmission
        5- receiving   6- action
        7- feedback to the sender

    B. 1- ideation   2- encoding
        3- transmission   4- decoding
        5- receiving   6- action
        7- feedback to the sender

    C. 1- ideation   2- decoding
        3- transmission   4- receiving
        5- encoding   6- action
        7- feedback to the sender

    D. 1- ideation   2- encoding
        3- transmission   4- receiving
        5- decoding   6- action
        7- feedback to the sender

20. Which one of the following BEST expresses the main theme of the passage? 20.____

    A. Different individuals have the same perceptions regarding the meaning of words.
    B. An understanding of the steps in the communication process may achieve better
        communication.
    C. Receivers play a passive role in the communication process.
    D. Senders should not communicate with receivers who transmit feedback.

21. The above passage implies that a receiver does NOT function properly when he 21.____

    A. transmits feedback   B. files the information
    C. is a poor listener   D. asks for more information

22. Which of the following, according to the above passage, is included in the SECOND step of the communication process?   22.____

    A. Selecting the appropriate media to be used in transmission
    B. Formulation of the intended content of the message
    C. Using appropriate media to respond to the receiver's feedback
    D. Transmitting the message through selected channels in the organization

23. The above passage implies that the *decoding process* is MOST NEARLY the reverse of the _____ process.   23.____

    A. transmission   B. receiving
    C. feedback   D. encoding

Questions 24-27.

DIRECTIONS: Answer Questions 24 through 27 SOLELY on the basis of the information given in the paragraph below.

    A personnel researcher has at his disposal various approaches for obtaining information, analyzing it, and arriving at conclusions that have value in predicting and affecting the behavior of people at work. The type of method to be used depends on such factors as the nature of the research problem, the available data, and the attitudes of those people being studied to the various kinds of approaches. While the experimental approach, with its use of control groups, is the most refined type of study, there are others that are often found useful in personnel research. Surveys, in which the researcher obtains facts on a problem from a variety of sources, are employed in research on wages, fringe benefits, and labor relations. Historical studies are used to trace the development of problems in order to understand them better and to isolate possible causative factors. Case studies are generally developed to explore all the details of a particular problem that is representative of other similar problems. A researcher chooses the most appropriate form of study for the problem he is investigating. He should recognize, however, that the experimental method, commonly referred to as the scientific method, if used validly and reliably, gives the most conclusive results.

24. The above statement discusses several approaches used to obtain information on particular problems.   24.____
Which of the following may be MOST reasonably concluded from the paragraph?
A(n)

    A. historical study cannot determine causative factors
    B. survey is often used in research on fringe benefits
    C. case study is usually used to explore a problem that is unique and unrelated to other problems
    D. experimental study is used when the scientific approach to a problem fails

25. According to the above paragraph, all of the following are factors that may determine the type of approach a researcher uses EXCEPT   25.____

    A. the attitudes of people toward being used in control groups
    B. the number of available sources
    C. his desire to isolate possible causative factors
    D. the degree of accuracy he requires

26. The words *scientific method,* used in the last sentence of the paragraph, refer to a type of   26.____
study which, according to the paragraph,

    A. uses a variety of sources
    B. traces the development of problems
    C. uses control groups
    D. analyzes the details of a representative problem

27. Which of the following can be MOST reasonably concluded from the above paragraph?   27.____
In obtaining and analyzing information on a particular problem, a researcher employs
the method which is the

    A. most accurate   B. most suitable
    C. least expensive   D. least time-consuming

Questions 28-31.

DIRECTIONS: The graph below indicates at 5-year intervals the number of citations issued
for various offenses from the year 1990 to the year 2010. Answer Questions 28
through 31 according to the information given in this graph.

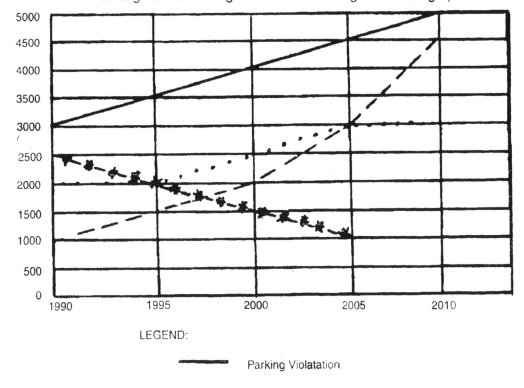

LEGEND:

—————— Parking Violatation

— — — Drug Use

• • • • Dangerous Weapons

🐟🐟🐟🐟 Improper Dress

28. Over the 20-year period, which offense shows an AVERAGE rate of increase of more   28.____
than 150 citations per year?

    A. Parking Violations   B. Dangerous Weapons
    C. Drug Use   D. None of the above

29. Over the 20-year period, which offense shows a CONSTANT rate of increase or decrease?   29.____

    A. Parking Violations   B. Drug Use
    C. Dangerous Weapons   D. Improper Dress

30. Which offense shows a TOTAL INCREASE OR DECREASE of 50% for the full 20-year period?   30.____

    A. Parking Violations   B. Drug Use
    C. Dangerous Weapons   D. Improper Dress

31. The percentage increase in total citations issued from 1995 to 2000 is MOST NEARLY   31.____

    A. 7%   B. 11%   C. 21%   D. 41%

Questions 32-35.

DIRECTIONS: The chart below shows the annual average number of administrative actions completed for the four divisions of a bureau. Assume that the figures remain stable from year to year.

                 Answer Questions 32 through 35 SOLELY on the basis of information given in the chart.

Administrative Actions	DIVISIONS				
	W	X	Y	Z	Totals
Telephone Inquiries Answered	8,000	6,800	7,500	4,800	27,100
Interviews Conducted	500	630	550	500	2,180
Applications Processed	15,000	18,000	14,500	9,500	57,000
Letters Typed	2,500	4,400	4,350	3,250	14,500
Reports Completed	200	250	100	50	600
Totals	26,200	30,080	27,000	18,100	101,380

32. In which division is the number of Applications Processed the GREATEST percentage of the total Administrative Actions for that division?   32.____

    A. W   B. X   C. Y   D. Z

33. The bureau chief is considering a plan that would consolidate the typing of letters in a separate unit. This unit would be responsible for the typing of letters for all divisions in which the number of letters typed exceeds 15% of the total number of Administrative Actions. Under this plan, which of the following divisions would CONTINUE to type its own letters?   33.____

    A. W and X   B. W, X, and Y
    C. X and Y   D. X and Z

34. The setting up of a central information service that would be capable of answering 25% of the whole bureau's telephone inquiries is under consideration. Under such a plan, the divisions would gain for other activities that time previously spent on telephone inquiries. Approximately how much total time would such a service gain for all four divisions if it requires 5 minutes to answer the average telephone inquiry? _____ hours.

    A. 500   B. 515   C. 565   D. 585

34._____

35. Assume that the rate of production shown in the table can be projected as accurate for the coming year and that monthly output is constant for each type of administrative action within a division. Division Y is scheduled to work exclusively on a 4-month long special project during that year. During the period of the project, Division Y's regular workload will be divided evenly among the remaining divisions.
    Using the figures in the table, what would be MOST NEARLY the percentage increase in the total Administrative Actions completed by Division Z for the year?

    A. 8%   B. 16%   C. 25%   D. 50%

35._____

36. You have conducted a traffic survey at 10 two-lane bridges and find the traffic between 4:30 and 5:30 P.M. averages 665 cars per bridge that hour. You can't find the tabulation sheet for Bridge #7, but you know that 6066 cars were counted at the other 9 bridges. Determine from this how many must have been counted at Bridge #7.

    A. 584   B. 674   C. 665   D. 607

36._____

37. You pay temporary help $11.20 per hour and regular employees $12.00 per hour. Your workload is temporarily heavy, so you need 20 hours of extra regular employees' time to catch up. If you do this on overtime, you must pay time-and-a-half. If you use temporary help, it takes 25% more time to do the job.
    What is the difference in cost between the two alternatives?

    A. $20 more for temporary   B. $40 more for temporary
    C. $80 more for regular   D. $136 more for regular

37._____

38. An experienced clerk can process the mailing of annual forms in 9 days. A new clerk takes 14 days to process them.
    If they work together, how many days MOST NEARLY will it take to do the processing?

    A. $4\frac{1}{2}$ B. $5\frac{1}{2}$ C. $6\frac{1}{2}$ D. 7

38._____

39. A certain administrative aide is usually able to successfully handle 27% of all telephone inquiries without assistance. In a particular month, he receives 1200 inquiries and handles 340 of them successfully on his own. How many more inquiries has he handled successfully in that month than would have been expected of him based on his usual rate?

    A. 10   B. 16   C. 24   D. 44

39._____

40. Suppose that on a scaled drawing of an office building floor, 1/2 inch represents three feet of actual floor dimensions.
    A floor which is, in fact, 75 feet wide and 132 feet long has which of the following dimensions on this scaled drawing? _____ inches wide and _____ inches long.

    A. 9.5; 20.5   B. 12.5; 22
    C. 17; 32   D. 25; 44

40._____

41. In a division of clerks and stenographers, 15 people are currently employed, 20% of whom are stenographers.
   If management plans are to maintain the current number of stenographers, but to increase the clerical staff to the point where 12% of the total staff are stenographers, what is the MAXIMUM number of additional clerks that should be hired to meet these plans?

   A. 3   B. 8   C. 10   D. 12

    41.____

42. Suppose that a certain agency had a 2005 budget of $1,100,500. The 2006 budget was 7% higher than that of 2005, and the 2007 budget was 8% higher than that of 2006. Of the following, which one is MOST NEARLY that agency's budget for 2007?

   A. $1,117,624
   C. $1,265,575
   B. $1,261,737
   D. $1,271,738

    42.____

Question's 43-50.

DIRECTIONS: Your office keeps a file card record of the work assignments for all the employees in a certain bureau. On each card is the employee's name, a work assignment code number, and the date of this assignment. In this filing system, the employee's name is filed alphabetically, the work assignment code is filed numerically, and the date of the assignment is filed chronologically (earliest date first).

Each of Questions 43 through 50 represents five cards to be filed, numbered (1) through (5) shown in Column I. Each card is made up of the employee's name, a work assignment code number shown in parentheses, and the date of this assignment. The cards are to be filed according to the following rules:

First: File in alphabetical order;
Second: When two or more cards have the same employee's name, file according to the work assignment number, beginning with the lowest number.
Third: When two or more cards have the same employee's name and same assignment number, file according to the assignment date beginning with earliest date.

Column II shows the cards arranged in four different orders. Pick the answer (A, B, C, or D) in Column II which shows the cards arranged correctly according to the above filing rules.

SAMPLE QUESTION:

Column I				Column II					
(1) Cluney	(486503)	6/17/07	A.	2,	3,	4,	1,	5
(2) Roster	(246611)	5/10/06	B.	2,	5,	1,	3,	4
(3) Altool	(711433)	10/15/07	C.	3,	2,	1,	4,	5
(4) Cluney	(527610)	12/18/06	D.	3,	5,	1,	4,	2
(5) Cluney	(486500)	4/8/07						

The correct way to file the cards is:

(3) Altool	(711433)	10/15/07
(5) Cluney	(486500)	4/8/07
(1) Cluney	(486503)	6/17/07
(4) Cluney	(527610)	12/18/06
(2) Roster	(246611)	5/10/06

The correct filing order is shown by the numbers in front of each name (3, 5, 1, 4, 2). The answer to the sample question is the letter in Column II in front of the numbers 3, 5, 1, 4, 2. This answer is D.

43.   43._____

		Column I				Column II			
(1)	Prichard	(013469)	4/6/06	A.	5,	4,	3,	2,	1
(2)	Parks	(678941)	2/7/06	B.	1,	2,	5,	3,	4
(3)	Williams	(551467)	3/6/05	C.	2,	1,	5,	3,	4
(4)	Wilson	(551466)	8/9/02	D.	1,	5,	4,	3,	2
(5)	Stanhope	(300014)	8/9/02						

44.   44._____

(1)	Ridgeway	(623809)	8/11/06	A.	5,	1,	3,	4,	2
(2)	Travers	(305439)	4/5/02	B.	5,	1,	3,	2,	4
(3)	Tayler	(818134)	7/5/03	C.	1,	5,	3,	2,	4
(4)	Travers	(305349)	5/6/05	D.	1,	5,	4,	2,	3
(5)	Ridgeway	(623089)	10/9/06						

45.   45._____

(1)	Jaffe	(384737)	2/19/06	A.	3,	5,	2,	4,	1
(2)	Inez	(859176)	8/8/07	B.	3,	5,	2,	1,	4
(3)	Ingrahm	(946460)	8/6/04	C.	2,	3,	5,	1,	4
(4)	Karp	(256146)	5/5/05	D.	2,	3,	5,	4,	1
(5)	Ingrahm	(946460)	6/4/05						

46.   46._____

(1)	Marrano	(369421)	7/24/04	A.	1,	5,	3,	4,	2
(2)	Marks	(652910)	2/23/06	B.	3,	5,	4,	2,	1
(3)	Netto	(556772)	3/10/07	C.	2,	4,	1,	5,	3
(4)	Marks	(652901)	2/17/07	D.	4,	2,	1,	5,	3
(5)	Netto	(556772)	6/17/05						

47.   47._____

(1)	Abernathy	(712467)	6/23/05	A.	5,	3,	1,	2,	4
(2)	Acevedo	(680262)	6/23/03	B.	5,	4,	2,	3,	1
(3)	Aaron	(967647)	1/17/04	C.	1,	3,	5,	2,	4
(4)	Acevedo	(680622)	5/14/02	D.	2,	4,	1,	5,	3
(5)	Aaron	(967647)	4/1/00						

48.   48._____

(1)	Simon	(645219)	8/19/05	A.	4,	1,	2,	5,	3
(2)	Simon	(645219)	9/2/03	B.	4,	5,	2,	1,	3
(3)	Simons	(645218)	7/7/05	C.	3,	5,	2,	1,	4
(4)	Simms	(646439)	10/12/06	D.	5,	1,	2,	3,	4
(5)	Simon	(645219)	10/16/02						

49.   49._____

(1)	Rappaport	(312230)	6/11/06	A.	4,	3,	1,	2,	5
(2)	Rascio	(777510)	2/9/05	B.	4,	3,	1,	5,	2
(3)	Rappaport	(312230)	7/3/02	C.	3,	4,	1,	5,	2
(4)	Rapaport	(312330)	9/6/05	D.	5,	2,	4,	3,	1
(5)	Rascio	(777501)	7/7/05						

50.

(1)	Johnson	(843250)	6/8/02	A.	1,	3,	2,	4,	5
(2)	Johnson	(843205)	4/3/05	B.	1,	3,	2,	5,	4
(3)	Johnson	(843205)	8/6/02	C.	3,	2,	1,	4,	5
(4)	Johnson	(843602)	3/8/06	D.	3,	2,	1,	5,	4
(5)	Johnson	(843602)	8/3/05						

50.____

———

KEY (CORRECT ANSWERS)

1.	D	11.	B	21.	C	31.	B	41.	C
2.	A	12.	A	22.	A	32.	B	42.	D
3.	C	13.	C	23.	D	33.	A	43.	C
4.	C	14.	C	24.	B	34.	C	44.	A
5.	C	15.	A	25.	D	35.	B	45.	C
6.	A	16.	D	26.	C	36.	A	46.	D
7.	B	17.	A	27.	B	37.	C	47.	A
8.	C	18.	C	28.	C	38.	B	48.	B
9.	D	19.	D	29.	A	39.	B	49.	B
10.	A	20.	B	30.	C	40.	B	50.	D

———

EXAMINATION SECTION
TEST 1

DIRECTIONS: Each question or incomplete statements is followed by several suggested answers or completions. Select the one that BEST answers the question or completes the statement. *PRINT THE LETTER OF THE CORRECT ANSWER IN THE SPACE AT THE RIGHT.*

1. The one of the following which BEST characterizes an agency in which delegation of authority is practiced on an organization-wide level is that the agency is

    A. autocratic
    B. authoritarian
    C. centralized
    D. decentralized

1.____

2. The concept of the *chain of command* is MOST similar to which one of the following concepts?

    A. Span of control
    B. Matrix or task-force organization
    C. Scalar principle
    D. Functional departmentation

2.____

3. The one of the following techniques which is NOT conducive to the establishment of an effective working relationship between employees and supervisors is

    A. periodic discussion of job performance with employees
    B. listening to employees when they discuss their job difficulties
    C. observation of employees on the job, in both individual and group situations, in order to help them with job performance
    D. treating all employees the same with respect to job performance and individual behavior

3.____

4. Which of the following is a valid, commonly-raised objection to the establishment of work standards for office clerical workers?

    A. Routine clerical work is not subject to accurate measurement.
    B. Clerical work standards can only lower employee morale by creating undue pressure to produce work rapidly.
    C. Work standards are not effective tools for planning, scheduling, and routing clerical work.
    D. Some phases of many clerical jobs, such as telephone answering or information gathering, cannot be readily or accurately measured.

4.____

5. Of the following, the feature which is LEAST characteristic of almost all successful staff relationships with line managers is that the staff employee

    A. is primarily a representative of his supervisor
    B. receives a salary at least equal to the average salary of his supervisor's direct line subordinates
    C. relies largely on persuasion to get his ideas put into effect
    D. is prepared to submerge his own personality and his own desire for recognition and see others often receive more recognition than he receives

5.____

6. The one of the following systems which has, as its principal objective, the storage of items in files so that they may be readily found when needed is called
   A. information retrieval
   B. simulation
   C. critical path
   D. PERT

6._____

7. A detailed description of the steps to be taken in order to accomplish a job is MOST appropriately called a

   A. policy
   B. rule
   C. procedure
   D. principle

7._____

8. In choosing the best place in the executive hierarchy to which to assign the task of making a certain type of decision, which one of the following questions should normally be LEAST important?

   A. Who knows the facts on which the decision will be based, or who can obtain them most readily?
   B. Who has the most adequate supply of current forms on which the decision is normally recorded?
   C. Who has the capacity to make sound decisions?
   D. How significant is the decision?

8._____

9. Of the following, the action which is LEAST likely to be either expressed or implied every time a manager delegates work to a subordinate is that the manager

   A. creates a need for a new class of positions
   B. indicates what work the subordinate is to do
   C. grants the subordinate some authority
   D. creates an obligation for the subordinate who accepts the work to try to complete it

9._____

10. Of the following, the LEAST appropriate use of organizational charts is to

    A. depict standard operating procedures
    B. indicate lines of responsibility
    C. indicate the relative level of key positions
    D. portray organizations graphically

10._____

11. The one of the following considerations which is generally LEAST important in deciding whether to automate a management operation by using a computer is whether the computer

    A. possesses a suitable array of programmed actions that might be taken
    B. can draw upon available data for information as to which alternative is best
    C. is already familiar to the staff of the organization
    D. can issue findings in a way that will facilitate the decision-making process

11._____

12. In evaluating a proposal to establish a library in your agency, it is generally considered LEAST necessary to determine

    A. the average time staff members spend on preparatory research when assigned to projects
    B. how often junior professional and technical staff members are sent out to *look something up* in a local library

12._____

C. how much time and money agency executives devote to telephoning around the country seeking information before making decisions
D. the quality of the research done by executives and scientists in the agency

13. In determining the number and type of tasks that should be combined into a single job, the one of the following which is normally the LEAST useful factor to consider is the   13.____

    A. benefit of functional specialization
    B. benefit of tall pyramid organization structures in increasing decentralization
    C. need for coordination of tasks with each other
    D. effect of the tasks assigned on the morale of the employee

14. Of the following, the one which is LEAST likely to be an objective of systems and procedures analysis is to   14.____

    A. eliminate as many unessential forms and records as feasible
    B. simplify forms in content and method of preparation
    C. mechanize repetitive, routine tasks
    D. expand as many of the forms as possible

15. A specific managerial function encompasses all of the following: the establishment of an intentional structure of roles through determination and enumeration of the activities required to achieve the goals of an enterprise and each part of it, the grouping of these activities, the assignment of such groups of activities to a manager, the delegation of authority to carry them out, and provision for coordination of authority and informational relationships horizontally and vertically in the organization structure.
Of the following, the MOST appropriate term for this entire managerial function is   15.____

    A. organizing   B. directing
    C. controlling   D. staffing

16. The optimum number of subordinates that a supervisor can supervise effectively generally tends to vary INVERSELY with the   16.____

    A. percentage of the supervisor's time devoted to supervision rather than operations
    B. repetition of activities
    C. degree of centralization of decision-making within the supervisor's unit
    D. ability of subordinates

17. Under certain circumstances, a top manager may desire to strengthen the position of his staff people by granting them concurring authority, so that no action may be taken in a functional area by subordinate line officials until a designated staff employee agrees to the action. For example, office managers may have to get the approval of the agency personnel officer before hiring a new employee. This approach is likely to be MOST valid under which one of the following conditions?   17.____

    A. The top manager refrains from indicating the grounds on which the staff employee may grant or withhold his approval of line proposals.
    B. The point of view represented by the staff employee is particularly important, and the possible delay in action will not be serious.
    C. It is more important to fix specific accountability for failure to take appropriate action than for wrong actions taken.
    D. The top manager gives speed priority over prudence.

18. The inclusion of the *reason why* by a superior in his written orders to his subordinates normally is MOST likely to   18._____

    A. encourage belief by the subordinates in the meaning and intent of the order
    B. be a waste of valuable time for both superior and subordinates
    C. be useful principally where the superior has no power to enforce the order
    D. discourage effective two-way communication between superior and subordinates

19. The one of the following which is generally the BEST justification for an administrator's search for alternative methods of attaining a given objective of the unit he heads is that such-search   19._____

    A. always turns up a better method of attaining objectives than that currently in use
    B. helps to make certain that the best method has a chance to be found and evaluated
    C. helps to insure that his peers realize that the existing method of attaining the objective is not the best
    D. is a good way to train the unit's staff in the organization's operational procedures

20. *Managing-by-Objectives* tends to place PRINCIPAL emphasis upon which of the following?   20._____

    A. Use of primarily qualitative goals at all management levels
    B. Use of trait-appraisal systems based upon personality factors
    C. Use of primarily qualitative goals at lower management levels as contrasted with primarily quantitative goals at higher management levels
    D. Goals which are clear and verifiable

21. Which one of the following BEST identifies the two most important considerations which generally should determine the degree of management decentralization desirable in a given situation?   21._____
The
    A. age of the subordinate executives to whom decisions may be delegated and the number of courses in management that they have completed
    B. number of skills and the competence possessed by subordinate executives and the distribution of the necessary information to the points of decision
    C. ratio of the salary of the superior executives to the salary of the subordinate executives and the number of titles on the executive staff
    D. number of titles in the executive staff and the distribution of information to those various titles

22. Which one of the following is generally LEAST likely to occur at mid-level management as a result of installing an electronic data processing system?   22._____
    A. The time that managers will be required to spend on the controlling function will increase.
    B. The number of contacts that managers will have with subordinates will increase.
    C. Additional time will be needed to train people for managerial positions.
    D. There will be an increase in the volume of information presented to managers for analysis.

23. The concept that the major source of managerial authority is derived from the subordinate's acceptance of the manager's power is MOST closely identified with

    A. Luther Gulick   B. John D. Mooney
    C. Frederick W. Taylor   D. Chester I. Barnard

23._____

24. The one of the following which is generally the principal objection to a pure *functional organization,* as compared with a pure *line organization,* is that

    A. there is a tendency to overload intermediate and supervisory management at each succeeding level of organization with wide and varied duties
    B. authority flows in an unbroken line from top management to the worker
    C. workers must often report to two or more supervisors
    D. there is a lack of specialization at the supervisory level

24._____

25. The appraisal of subordinates and their performance is an integral part of the supervisor's job. There is wide agreement that several basic principles must be taken into account by supervisors involved in the appraisal process in order to perform this function correctly. The one of the statements below which LEAST represents a basic principle of the appraisal process is:
Appraisal(s)

    A. should be based more on performance of definite tasks than on personality considerations
    B. of long-range potential should rely most heavily on subjective judgment of that potential
    C. involves the use of value judgments by the supervisor and does, therefore, require reference to pre-established standards
    D. should aim at emphasizing subordinates' strengths rather than weaknesses

25._____

26. Of the following, the INITIAL step in the decision-making procedure normally is

    A. evaluation of alternatives
    B. implementing the chosen course of action
    C. listing potential solutions
    D. diagnosis and problem definition

26._____

27. Management textbooks are LEAST likely to define coordination as

    A. a concern for harmonious and unified action directed toward a common objective
    B. the essence of management, since the basic purpose of management is the achievement of harmony of individual effort toward the accomplishment of group goals
    C. the orderly arrangement of group effort to provide unity of action in pursuit of common purpose
    D. the transmittal of messages from senders to receivers, involving acts of persuasion of regulation, or simply the rendering of information

27._____

28. A number of important assumptions underlie the modern human relations approach to management and administration. The one of the following which is NOT an assumption integral to the human relations school of thought is that

28.____

    A. employee participation is essential to higher productivity
    B. employees are motivated solely by monetary factors
    C. teamwork is indispensable for organization growth and survival
    D. free-flow communications must be established and maintained for organizational effectiveness

29. Of the following, the MAIN purpose of systematic manpower planning is to

29.____

    A. analyze the levels of skill needed by each worker
    B. analyze causes of current vacancies, such as resignations, discharges, retirements, transfers, or promotions
    C. save money by eliminating useless jobs
    D. provide for the continuous and proper staffing of the workforce

30. A Planning-Programming-Budget System (PPBS) is PRIMARILY intended to do which of the following?

30.____

    A. Improve control through a budgeting-by-line-item system
    B. Plan and program budgets by objective rather than by function
    C. Raise money for social welfare programs
    D. Reduce budgets by planning and programming unspent funds

———

KEY (CORRECT ANSWERS)

1.	D	11.	C	21.	B
2.	C	12.	D	22.	A
3.	D	13.	B	23.	D
4.	D	14.	D	24.	C
5.	B	15.	A	25.	B
6.	A	16.	C	26.	D
7.	C	17.	B	27.	D
8.	B	18.	A	28.	B
9.	A	19.	B	29.	D
10.	A	20.	D	30.	B

———

TEST 2

DIRECTIONS: Each question or incomplete statements is followed by several suggested answers or completions. Select the one that BEST answers the question or completes the statement. *PRINT THE LETTER OF THE CORRECT ANSWER IN THE SPACE AT THE RIGHT.*

1. The one of the following which is a basic advantage of microform record system (e.g., microfilm, microfiche) over a conventional filing system is that a microform system

    A. provides a compact method of grouping and systematizing records
    B. provides records which are immediately available without special equipment
    C. eliminates the need for specially trained personnel
    D. eliminates entirely the inadvertent loss of records

1.____

2. In the planning of office space for the various bureaus and divisions of an agency, the one of the following arrangements which is generally considered to be MOST desirable in a conventional layout is to

    A. locate offices where employees do close and tedious work, such as accounting, and also offices of high-level executives away from windows so that distractions will be minimal
    B. locate *housekeeping* offices such as data processing and the mailroom very close to the high executive offices to increase convenience for the executives
    C. locate departments so that the work flow proceeds in an uninterrupted manner
    D. centralize the executive suite for maximum availability and public exposure

2.____

3. Generally, the one of the following that is LEAST likely to be an essential step in a records retention plan is

    A. storing inactive records
    B. checking for accuracy of all records to be retained
    C. classification of all records
    D. making an inventory of all agency records

3.____

4. The PRINCIPAL asset of an office layout diagram, as contrasted with the more abstract organization charts and flowcharts, is that an office layout diagram is

    A. more readily adaptable to strictly conceptual studies
    B. pictorial and therefore easier to understand
    C. suitable for showing both manual and machine processing operations, whereas organization charts and flowcharts may only be used for manual processing operations
    D. better suited for summarizing the number of work units produced at each step

4.____

5. One of the assistants whom you supervise displays apparent familiarity toward a businessman who deals with your agency. This assistant spends more time with this person than the nature of his business would warrant, and you have observed that they are occasionally seen leaving the office together for lunch. In several instances, when this businessman comes into the office and this assistant is not at his desk, the businessman will not deal with any other staff member but will, instead, leave the office and return later when that particular employee is available.
Of the following courses of action, the FIRST one you should take is to

5.____

A. audit the agency's books and records pertaining to this businessman
B. rebuke the assistant for unprofessional conduct at the next staff meeting and warn him of disciplinary action if the practice is not discontinued forthwith
C. advise your agency head of the action by the businessman and the assistant that has been described in the above paragraph
D. reassign the assistant to duties that will not bring him into contact with any businessman

6. The one of the following factors which generally is the BEST justification for keeping higher inventories of supplies and equipment is an expected   6._____

    A. decline in demand
    B. price increase
    C. decline in prices
    D. increase in interest charges and storage costs

7. Statistical sampling is often used in administrative operations PRIMARILY because it enables   7._____

    A. administrators to determine the characteristics of appointed or elected officials
    B. decisions to be made based on mathematical and scientific fact
    C. courses of action to be determined by scientifically-based computer programs
    D. useful predictions to be made from relatively small samples

8. According to United States Department of Labor figures, the PRINCIPAL source of disabling injuries to office workers is   8._____

    A. flying objects and falling objects
    B. striking against equipment
    C. falls and slips
    D. handling materials

9. To expedite the processing of applications issued by your agency, you ask your assistant to design a form that will be used by your typists. After several discussions, he presents you with a draft that requires the typist to use 23 tabular-stop positions.
Such a form would PROBABLY be considered   9._____

    A. *undesirable;* typists would now have to soft-roll the platen to make the typing fall on the lines
    B. *desirable;* the fill-in operation by typists would be speeded up
    C. *undesirable;* proper vertical alignment of data would be made difficult by the number of tabular-stop positions required
    D. *desirable;* it would force the typists to utilize the tabular-stop device

Question 10.

DIRECTIONS: Following are five general instructions to file clerks which might appear in the proposed filing manual for an agency:

    1. *Follow instructions generally; if you have a suggestion for improvement in the filing methods, install it after notifying the file supervisor who will duly authorize a change in the manual.*

2. *You may discuss the contents of files with fellow employees or outsiders, but do NOT give papers from the file to any person whose duties have no relation to the material requested.*

3. *All special instructions must be given by the file supervisor. Any problems that arise outside the regular routine of filing must be decided by the file supervisor, not by a fellow clerk.*

4. *You will not be held responsible for your own errors; thus, refrain from asking other workers for instructions. No one is more interested in helping you in your training than your file supervisor.*

5. *Speed is the first essential in filing; make it your primary consideration - quick finding of filed material is the real test of your efficiency.*

10. Which of the choices listed below BEST identifies those of the above statements that should or should not be followed by agencies in the functioning of their filing sections? Instruction(s) _____ should be followed; instructions _____ should not be followed.

    A. 1, 2, 3; 4, 5   B. 3; 1, 2, 4, 5
    C. 2, 4; 1, 3, 5   D. 1, 3; 2, 4, 5

10.____

11. Listed below are five steps in the process of staffing:
    I.   Authorization for staffing
    II.   Manpower planning
    III. Development of applicant sources
    IV. Evaluation of applicants
    V.   Employment decisions and offers

The one of the following sequences which is generally the MOST logical arrangement of the above steps is:

    A. I, II, III, IV, V   B. II, I, III, IV, V
    C. III, I, II, IV, V   D. II, III, I, IV, V

11.____

12. Job enrichment is LEAST likely to lead to

    A. fewer employee grievances
    B. increased employee productivity
    C. people acting as adjuncts of increased automation
    D. increased employee morale

12.____

13. Of the following, programmed instruction would usually be MOST effective in teaching

    A. principles of decision-making
    B. technical skills and knowledge
    C. good judgment
    D. executive management ability

13.____

14. Assume that a group has been working effectively with a contributing nonconformist in its midst.
The BEST of the following reasons for the group to retain the nonconformist *generally* is that

    A. nonconformists stimulate groups to think
    B. he may be their boss some day
    C. nonconformists usually are fun to work with
    D. another nonconformist will usurp his role

14.____

15. The *grievance-arbitration* process involves systematic union-management deliberation   15.____
regarding a complaint that is work-or contract-related. An
outcome that does NOT result from this process is

    A. a communications channel from the rank-and-file workers to higher management is
developed or improved
    B. the contract is immediately changed to provide justice for both parties
    C. both labor and management identify those parts of the contract that need to be
clarified and modified in subsequent negotiations
    D. the language of the agreement is informally translated into understandable terms for
the parties bound by it

16. In government, job evaluation is the process of determining the relative worth of the vari-   16.____
ous jobs in an organization so that differential wages can be paid. Job evaluation is
based on several basic assumptions.
Of the assumptions listed below, the MOST questionable is that

    A. the cash payments in government should be substantially higher than those in
local private industry
    B. it is logical to pay the most for jobs that contribute most to the organization
    C. people feel more fairly treated if wages are based on the relative worth of their jobs
    D. the best way to achieve the goals of the enterprise is to maintain a wage structure
based on job worth

17. Of the following, the training method that normally provides the instructor with the LEAST   17.____
feedback from the trainees is

    A. the lecture method
    B. the conference method
    C. simulation or gaming techniques
    D. seminar instruction

18. Insufficient and inappropriate delegation of work assignments is MOST often the fault of   18. ___

    A. subordinates who are unwilling to accept responsibility for their own mistakes
    B. a paternal attitude on the part of management
    C. the immediate supervisor
    D. subordinates who are too willing to take on extra responsibility

19. As contrasted with expense budgets, capital budgets are MORE likely to   19. ___

    A. be used for construction of physical facilities
    B. be designed for a shorter time period
    C. include personal service expenditures
    D. include fringe benefits

20. During the first quarter of a year, a division's production rate was 1.26 man-hours per   20. ___
work unit produced. For the second quarter of that year, all other factors (e.g., size of staff,
character of work unit, etc.) remained constant, except that the manner of reporting
production rate was changed to work units per man-hour instead of man-hours per work
unit. During that second quarter, the unit's production rate was .89 work units per man-
hour.

On the basis of the above information, it would be MOST NEARLY CORRECT to conclude that the division's production rate during the second quarter was *approximately* _____ than during the first quarter.

A. 30% lower   B. 10% lower
C. 10% higher   D. 30% higher

Questions 21-22.

DIRECTIONS: Answer Questions 21 and 22 on the basis of the following information.

The five bureaus within a department sent the following budget requests to the department head:

> Bureau A - $10 million
> Bureau B - $12 million
> Bureau C - $18 million
> Bureau D - $6 million
> Bureau E - $4 million

After reviewing all of these requests, the department head decided to reduce these requests so that they would total only $40 million. He considered the following two options to accomplish this:

Option I- *Reduce the requests of Bureaus A, B, and D by an equal dollar amount. Reduce the dollar amount request of Bureau C by 2 ½ times the dollar amount that he reduces the request of Bureau B. Reduce the dollar amount request of Bureau E by 1/2 of the dollar amount that he reduces the request of Bureau B.*

Option II- *First, reduce the dollar amount request of all five bureaus by 15%. Then, the remaining reduction required by the entire department would be achieved by further reducing the resulting budget requests of Bureaus B and C by an equal dollar amount each.*

21. Under Option I, the dollar amount request for Bureau E, after reduction by the department head, would be MOST NEARLY _____ millions.   21._____

    A. $1 2/3   B. $2 1/3   C. $3 1/6   D. $3 1/2

22. Under Option II, the dollar amount of the request of Bureau B, after both reductions were made by the department head, would be MOST NEARLY _____ millions.   22._____

    A. $8   B. $9   C. $10   D. $11

23. The Summary of finding of a long management report intended for typical manager Should generally appear   23._____
    A. at the very beginning of the report
    B. at the end of the report
    C. throughout the report
    D. in the middle of the report

24. Of the following, the BIGGEST disadvantage in allowing a free flow of communications in an agency is that such a free flow   24._____

    A. decreases creativity
    B. increases the use of the *grapevine*
    C. lengthens the chain of command
    D. reduces the executive's power to direct the flow of information

25. A downward flow of authority in an organization is one example of _____ communica-   25.____
    tions.

    A. horizontal   B. informal
    C. circular   D. vertical

26. Workers who belong to a cohesive group are generally thought to   26.____

    A. have more job-related anxieties than those who do not
    B. be less well-adjusted than those who do not
    C. derive little satisfaction from the group
    D. conform to group norms more closely than those in noncohesive groups

27. The one of the following which BEST exemplifies negative motivation is   27.____

    A. a feeling on the part of the worker that the work is significant
    B. monetary rewards offered the worker for high levels of output
    C. reducing or withholding the worker's incentive rewards when performance is medi-
        ocre
    D. nonmonetary rewards given the worker, such as publicizing a good suggestion

28. Of the following, the one that would be MOST likely to block effective communication is   28.____

    A. concentration only on the issues at hand
    B. lack of interest or commitment
    C. use of written reports
    D. use of charts and graphs

29. Many functions formerly centralized in a department of personnel have been decentral-   29.____
    ized, in whole or in part, to operating agencies.
    The one of the following personnel functions which has been LEAST decentralized is

    A. position evaluation
    B. investigation of non-competitive employees
    C. investigation of competitive employees
    D. jurisdictional classification

30. In making a position analysis for a duties classification, the one of the following factors   30.____
    which MUST be considered is the _____the incumbent.

    A. capabilities of
    B. qualifications of
    C. efficiency attained by
    D. responsibility assigned to

_____

KEY (CORRECT ANSWERS)

1.	A	11.	B	21.	C
2.	C	12.	C	22.	B
3.	B	13.	B	23.	A
4.	B	14.	A	24.	D
5.	C	15.	B	25.	D
6.	B	16.	A	26.	D
7.	D	17.	A	27.	C
8.	C	18.	C	28.	B
9.	C	19.	A	29.	D
10.	B	20.	C	30.	D

EXAMINATION SECTION

Questions 1-5.

1. Whatever the method, the necessity to keep up with the dynamics of an organization is   1.____
   the point on which many classification plans go awry. The budgetary approach to "positions," for example, often leads to using for recruitment and pay purposes a position
   authorized many years earlier for quite a different purpose than currently contemplated –
   making perhaps the title, the class, and the qualifications required inappropriate to the
   current need. This happens because executives overlook the stability that takes place in
   job duties and fail to reread an initial description of the job before saying, as they scan a
   list of titles, "We should fill this position right away." Once a classification plan is adopted,
   it is pointless to do anything less than provide for continuous, painstaking maintenance
   on a current basis, else once different positions that have actually become similar to
   each other remain in different classes, and some former cognates that have become
   quite different continue in the same class. Such a program often seems expensive. But to
   stint too much on this out-of-pocket cost may create still higher hidden costs growing out
   of lowered morale, poor production, delayed operating programs, excessive pay for simple work, and low pay for responsible work (resulting in poorly qualified executives and
   professional men) – all normal concomitants of inadequate, hasty, or out-of-date classification.

   A. evolution   B. personnel
   C. disapproved   D. forward

2. At first sight, it may seem that there is little or no difference between the usableness of a   2.____
   manual and the degree of its use. But there is a difference. A manual may have all the
   qualities which make up the usable manual and still not be used. Take this instance as an
   example: Suppose you have a satisfactory manual but issue instructions from day to day
   through the avenue of bulletins, memorandums, and other informational releases. Which
   will the employee use, the manual or the bulletin which passes over his desk? He will, of
   course, use the latter, for some obsolete material will not be contained in this manual.
   Here we have a theoretically usable manual which is unused because of the other ave-
   nues by which procedural information may be issued.

   A. countermand   B. discard
   C. intentional   D. worthwhile

3. By reconcentrating control over its operations in a central headquarters, a firm is able to extend the influence of automation to many, if not all, of its functions – from inventory and payroll to production, sales, and personnel. In so doing, businesses freeze all the elements of the corporate function in their relationship to one another and to the overall objectives of the firm. From this total systems concept, companies learn that computers can accomplish much more than clerical and accounting jobs. Their capabilities can be tapped to perform the traditional applications (payroll processing, inventory control, accounts payable, and accounts receivable) as well as newer applications such as spotting deviations from planned programs (exception reporting), adjusting planning schedules, forecasting business trends, simulating market conditions, and solving production problems. Since the office manager is a manager of information and each of these applications revolves around the processing of data, he must take an active role in studying and improving the system under his care.

3.____

    A. maintaining   B. inclusion
    C. limited   D. visualize

4. In addition to the formal and acceptance theories of the source of authority, although perhaps more closely related to the latter, is the belief that authority is generated by personal qualifies of technical competence. Under this heading is the individual who has made, in effect, subordinates of others through sheer force of personality, and the engineer or economist who exerts influence by furnishing answers or sound advice. These may have no actual organizational authority, yet their advice may be so eagerly sought and so unerringly followed that it appears to carry the weight of an order.
But, above all, one cannot discount the importance of formal authority with its institutional foundations. Buttressed by the qualities of leadership implicit in the acceptance theory, formal authority is basic to the managerial job. Once abrogated, it may be delegated or withheld, used or misused, and be effective in capable hands or be ineffective in inept hands.

4.____

    A. selected   B. delegation
    C. limited   D. possessed

5. Since managerial operations in organizing, staffing, directing, and controlling are designed to support the accomplishment of enterprise objectives, planning logically precedes the execution of all other managerial functions. Although all the functions intermesh in practice, planning is unique in that it establishes the objectives necessary for all group effort. Besides, plans must be made to accomplish these objectives before the manager knows what kind of organization relationships and personal qualifications are needed, along which course subordinates are to be directed, and what kind of control is to be applied. And, of course, each of the other managerial functions must be planned if they are to be effective.
Planning and control are inseparable – the Siamese twins of management. Unplanned action cannot be controlled, for control involves keeping activities on course by correcting deviations from plans. Any attempt to control without plans would be meaningless, since there is no way anyone can tell whether he is going where he wants to go – the task of control – unless first he knows where he wants to go – the task of planning. Plans thus preclude the standards of control.

5.____

    A. coordinating   B. individual
    C. furnish   D. follow

Questions 6-7.

DIRECTIONS: Answer Questions 6 and 7 SOLELY on the basis of information given in the fol-
                 lowing paragraph.
  *In-basket tests are often used to assess managerial potential. The exercise consists of a
set of papers that would be likely to be found in the in-basket of an administrator or manager
at any given time, and requires the individuals participating in the examination to indicate how
they would dispose of each item found in the in-basket. In order to handle the in-basket effectively, they must successfully manage their time, refer and assign some work to subordinates,
juggle potentially conflicting appointments and meetings, and arrange for follow-up of problems generated by the items in the in-basket. In other words, the in-basket test is attempting
to evaluate the participants' abilities to organize their work, set priorities, delegate, control,
and make decisions.*

6.   According to the above paragraph, to succeed in an in-basket test, an administrator must   6.____

     A.   be able to read very quickly
     B.   have a great deal of technical knowledge
     C.   know when to delegate work
     D.   arrange a lot of appointments and meetings

7.   According to the above paragraph, all of the following abilities are indications of manage-   7.____
     rial potential EXCEPT the ability to

     A.   organize and control   B.   manage time
     C.   write effective reports   D.   make appropriate decisions

Questions 8-9.

DIRECTIONS: Answer Questions 8 and 9 SOLELY on the basis of information given in the fol-
                 lowing paragraph.
  *One of the biggest mistakes of government executives with substantial supervisory
responsibility is failing to make careful appraisals of performance during employee probationary periods. Many a later headache could have been avoided by prompt and full appraisal
during the early months of an employee's assignment. There is not much more to say about
this except to emphasize the common prevalence of this oversight, and to underscore that for
its consequences, which are many and sad, the offending managers have no one to blame
but themselves.*

8.   According to the above passage, probationary periods are   8.____

     A.   a mistake, and should not be used by supervisors with large responsibilities
     B.   not used properly by government executives
     C.   used only for those with supervisory responsibility
     D.   the consequence of management mistakes

9. The one of the following conclusions that can MOST appropriately be drawn from the   9.____
    above passage is that

    A. management's failure to appraise employees during their probationary period is a
        common occurrence
    B. there is not much to say about probationary periods, because they are unimportant
    C. managers should blame employees for failing to use their probationary periods
        properly
    D. probationary periods are a headache to most managers

Questions 10-12.

DIRECTIONS: Answer Questions 10 through 12 SOLELY on the basis of information given in
              the following paragraph.

*The common sense character of the merit system seems so natural to most Americans
that many people wonder why it should ever have been inoperative. After all, the American
economic system, the most phenomenal the world has ever known, is also founded on a rug-
ged selective process which emphasizes the personal qualities of capacity, industriousness,
and productivity. The criteria may not have always been appropriate and competition has not
always been fair, but competition there was, and the responsibilities and the rewards – with
exceptions, of course – have gone to those who could measure up in terms of intelligence,
knowledge, or perseverance. This has been true not only in the economic area, in the money-
making process, but also in achievement in the professions and other walks of life.*

10. According to the above paragraph, economic rewards in the United States have   10.____

     A. always been based on appropriate, fair criteria
     B. only recently been based on a competitive system
     C. not gone to people who compete too ruggedly
     D. usually gone to those people with intelligence, knowledge, and perseverance

11. According to the above passage, a merit system is   11.____

     A. an unfair criterion on which to base rewards
     B. unnatural to anyone who is not American
     C. based only on common sense
     D. based on the same principles as the American economic system

12. According to the above passage, it is MOST accurate to say that   12.____

     A. the United States has always had a civil service merit system
     B. civil service employees are very rugged
     C. the American economic system has always been based on a merit objective
     D. competition is unique to the American way of life

Questions 13-15.

DIRECTIONS: The management study of employee absence due to sickness is an effective tool in planning. Answer Questions 13 through 15 SOLELY on the data given below.

Number of days absent per worker (sickness)	1	2	3	4	5	6	7	8 or Over
Number of workers	76	23	6	3	1	0	1	0

Total Number of Workers: 400
Period Covered: January 1 - December 31

13. The total number of man days lost due to illness was 13.____

    A. 110   B. 137   C. 144   D. 164

14. What percent of the workers had 4 or more days absence due to sickness? 14.____

    A. .25%   B. 2.5%   C. 1.25%   D. 12.5%

15. Of the 400 workers studied, the number who lost no days due to sickness was 15.____

    A. 190   B. 236   C. 290   D. 346

Questions 16-18.

DIRECTIONS: In the graph below, the lines labeled "A" and "B" represent the cumulative progress in the work of two file clerks, each of whom was given 500 consecutively numbered applications to file in the proper cabinets over a five-day work week. Answer Questions 16 through 18 SOLELY upon the data provided in the graph.

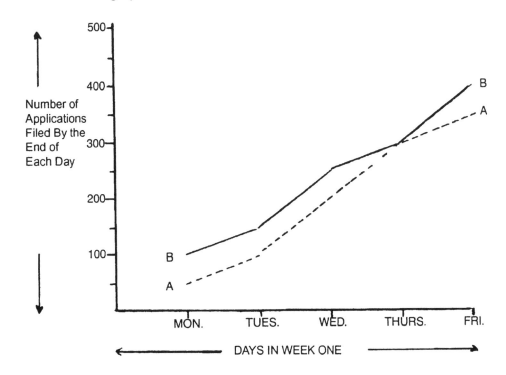

16. The day during which the LARGEST number of applications was filed by both clerks was   16.____

    A. Monday   B. Tuesday   C. Wednesday   D. Friday

17. At the end of the second day, the percentage of applications STILL to be filed was   17.____

    A. 25%   B. 50%   C. 66%   D. 75%

18. Assuming that the production pattern is the same the following week as the week shown in the chart, the day on which the file clerks will FINISH this assignment will be   18.____

    A. Monday   B. Tuesday   C. Wednesday   D. Friday

Questions 19-21.

DIRECTIONS: The following chart shows the differences between the rates of production of employees in Department D in 1996 and 2006. Answer Questions 19 through 21 SOLELY on the basis of the information given in the chart.

Number of Employees Producing Work-Units Within Range in 1996	Number of Work-Units Produced	Number of Employees Producing Work-Units Within Range in 2006
7	500 - 1000	4
14	1001 - 1500	11
26	1501 - 2000	28
22	2001 - 2500	36
17	2501 - 3000	39
10	3001 - 3500	23
4	3501 - 4000	9

19. Assuming that within each range of work-units produced the average production was at the mid-point at that range (e.g., category 500 - 1000 = 750), then the AVERAGE number of work-units produced per employee in 1996 fell into the range   19.____

    A. 1001 - 1500   B. 1501 - 2000
    C. 2001 - 2500   D. 2501 - 3000

20. The ratio of the number of employees producing more than 2000 work-units in 1996 to the number of employees producing more than 2000 work-units in 2006 is *most nearly*   20.____

    A. 1:2   B. 2:3   C. 3:4   D. 4:5

21. In Department D, which of the following were GREATER in 2006 than in 1996?   21.____
    I. Total number of employees
    II. Total number of work-units produced
    III. Number of employees producing 2000 or fewer work-units
The CORRECT answer is:

    A. I, II, III   B. I, II
    C. I, III   D. II, III

22. Unit S's production fluctuated substantially from one year to another. In 2004, Unit S's production was 100% greater than in 2003. In 2005, production decreased by 25% from 2004. In 2006, Unit S's production was 10% greater than in 2005.
On the basis of this information, it is CORRECT to conclude that Unit S's production in 2006 exceeded Unit S's production in 2003 by

22.____

    A. 65%   B. 85%   C. 95%   D. 135%

23. Agency "X" is moving into a new building. It has 1500 employees presently on its staff and does not contemplate much variance from this level. The new building contains 100 available offices, each with a maximum capacity of 30 employees. It has been decided that only 2/3 of the maximum capacity of each office will be utilized. The TOTAL number of offices that will be occupied by Agency "X" is

23.____

    A. 30   B. 66   C. 75   D. 90

24. One typist completes a form letter every 5 minutes and another typist completes one every 6 minutes.
If the two typists start together, they will again start typing new letters simultaneously _____ minutes later and will have completed _____ letters by that time.

24.____

    A. 11; 30   B. 12; 24   C. 24; 12   D. 30; 11

25. During one week, a machine operator produces 10 fewer pages per hour of work than he usually does. If it ordinarily takes him six hours to produce a 300-page report, it will take him____hours LONGER to produce that same 300-page report during the week when he produces MORE slowly.

25.____

    A. $1\frac{1}{2}$ B. $1\frac{2}{3}$ C. 2   D. $2\frac{3}{4}$

KEY (CORRECT ANSWERS)

<u>Incorrect Words</u>

1.	A	stability
2.	D	obsolete
3.	D	freeze
4.	D	abrogated
5.	C	preclude

6.	C	16.	C
7.	C	17.	D
8.	B	18.	B
9.	A	19.	C
10.	D	20.	A
11.	D	21.	B
12.	C	22.	A
13.	D	23.	C
14.	C	24.	D
15.	C	25.	A

EXAMINATION SECTION
TEST 1

DIRECTIONS: Each question or incomplete statement is followed by several suggested answers or completions. Select the one that BEST answers the question or completes the statement. *PRINT THE LETTER OF THE CORRECT ANSWER IN THE SPACE AT THE RIGHT.*

1. As a supervisor in a bureau, you have been asked by the head of the bureau to recommend whether or not the work of the bureau requires an increase in the permanent staff of the bureau.
   Of the following questions, the one whose answer would MOST likely assist you in making your recommendation is: Are

    A. some permanent employees working irregular hours because they occasionally work overtime?
    B. the present permanent employees satisfied with their work assignments?
    C. temporary employees hired to handle seasonal fluctuations in work load?
    D. the present permanent employees keeping the work of the bureau current?

1.____

2. In making job assignments to his subordinates, a supervisor should follow the principle that each individual GENERALLY is capable of

    A. performing one type of work well and less capable of performing other types well
    B. learning to perform a wide variety of different types of work
    C. performing best the type of work in which he has had experience
    D. learning to perform any type of work in which he is given training

2.____

3. Assume that you are the supervisor of a large number of clerks in a unit in a city agency. Your unit has just been given an important assignment which must be completed a week from now. You know that, henceforth, your unit will be given this assignment every six months.
   You or any one of your subordinates who has been properly instructed can complete this assignment in one day. This assignment is of a routine type which is ordinarily handled by clerks. There is enough time for you to train one of your subordinates to handle the assignment and then have him do it. However, it would take twice as much time for you to take this course of action as it would for you to do the assignment yourself. The one of the following courses of action which you should take in this situation is to

    A. do the assignment yourself as soon as possible without discussing it with any of your subordinates at this time
    B. do the assignment yourself and then train one of your subordinates to handle it in the future
    C. give the assignment to one of your subordinates after training him to handle it
    D. train each of your subordinates to do the assignment on a rotating basis after you have done it yourself the first time

3.____

4. You are in charge of an office in which each member of the staff has a different set of duties, although each has the same title. No member of the staff can perform the duties of any other member of the staff without first receiving extensive training. Assume that it is necessary for one member of the staff to take on, in addition to his regular work, an assignment which any member of the staff is capable of carrying out.
The one of the following considerations which would have the MOST weight in determining which staff member is to be given the additional assignment is the

    A. quality of the work performed by the individual members of the staff
    B. time consumed by individual members of the staff in performing their work
    C. level of difficulty of the duties being performed by individual members of the staff
    D. relative importance of the duties being performed by individual members of the staff

5. The one of the following causes of clerical error which is usually considered to be LEAST attributable to faulty supervision or inefficient management is

    A. inability to carry out instructions
    B. too much work to do
    C. an inappropriate recordkeeping system
    D. continual interruptions

6. Suppose you are in charge of a large unit in which all of the clerical staff perform similar tasks.
In evaluating the relative accuracy of the clerks, the clerk who should be considered to be the LEAST accurate is the one

    A. whose errors result in the greatest financial loss
    B. whose errors cost the most to locate
    C. who makes the greatest percentage of errors in his work
    D. who makes the greatest number of errors in the unit

7. Assume that under a proposed procedure for handling employee grievances in a public agency, the first step to be taken is for the aggrieved employee to submit his grievance as soon as it arises to a grievance board set up to hear all employee grievances in the agency. The board, which is to consist of representatives of management and of rank and file employees, is to consider the grievance, obtain all necessary pertinent information, and then render a decision on the matter. Thus, the first-line supervisor would not be involved in the settlement of any of his subordinates' grievances except when asked by the board to submit information.
This proposed procedure would be generally UNDESIRABLE chiefly because the

    A. board may become a bottleneck to delay the prompt disposition of grievances
    B. aggrieved employees and their supervisors have not been first given the opportunity to resolve the grievances themselves
    C. employees would be likely to submit imaginary, as well as real, grievances to the board
    D. board will lack first-hand, personal knowledge of the factors involved in grievances

8. Sometimes jobs in private organizations and public agencies are broken down so as to permit a high degree of job specialization.
Of the following, an IMPORTANT effect of a high degree of job specialization in a public agency is that employees performing

A. highly specialized jobs may not be readily transferable to other jobs in the agency
B. similar duties may require closer supervision than employees performing unrelated functions
C. specialized duties can be held responsible for their work to a greater extent than can employees performing a wide variety of functions
D. specialized duties will tend to cooperate readily with employees performing other types of specialized duties

9. Assume that you are the supervisor of a clerical unit in an agency. One of your subordinates violates a rule of the agency, a violation which requires that the employee be suspended from his work for one day. The violated rule is one that you have found to be unduly strict, and you have recommended to the management of the agency that the rule be changed or abolished. The management has been considering your recommendation but has not yet reached a decision on the matter.
In these circumstances, you should

    9.____

A. not initiate disciplinary action but, instead, explain to the employee that the rule may be Changed shortly
B. delay disciplinary action on the violation until the management has reached a decision on changing the rule
C. modify the disciplinary action by reprimanding the employee and informing him that further action may be taken when the management has reached a decision on changing the rule
D. initiate the prescribed disciplinary action without commenting on the strictness of the rule or on your recommendation

10. Assume that a supervisor praises his subordinates for satisfactory aspects of their work only when he is about to criticize them for unsatisfactory aspects of their work.
Such a practice is UNDESIRABLE primarily because

    10.____

A. his subordinates may expect to be praised for their work even if it is unsatisfactory
B. praising his subordinates for some aspects of their work while criticizing other aspects will weaken the effects of the criticisms
C. his subordinates would be more receptive to criticism if it were followed by praise
D. his subordinates may come to disregard praise and wait for criticism to be given

11. The one of the following which would be the BEST reason for an agency to eliminate a procedure for obtaining and recording certain information is that

    11.____

A. it is no longer legally required to obtain the information
B. there is no advantage in obtaining the information
C. the information could be compiled on the basis of other information available
D. the information obtained is sometimes incorrect

12. In determining the type and number of records to be kept in an agency, it is important to recognize that records are of value PRIMARILY as

    12.____

A. raw material to be used in statistical analysis
B. sources of information about the agency's activities
C. by-products of the activities carried on by the agency
D. data for evaluating the effectiveness of the agency

13. Aside from requirements imposed by authority, the frequency with which reports are sub-   13.____
mitted or the length of the interval which they cover should depend PRINCIPALLY on the

    A. availability of the data to be included in the reports
    B. amount of time required to prepare the reports
    C. extent of the variations in the data with the passage of time
    D. degree of comprehensiveness required in the reports

14. Organizations that occupy large, general, open-area offices sometimes consider it desir-   14.____
able to build private offices for the supervisors of large bureaus.
The one of the following which is generally NOT considered to be a justification of the
use of private offices is that they

    A. lend prestige to the person occupying the office
    B. provide facilities for private conferences
    C. achieve the maximum use of office space
    D. provide facilities for performing work requiring a high degree of concentration

15. The LEAST important factor to be considered in planning the layout of an office is the   15.____

    A. relative importance of the different types of work to be done
    B. convenience with which communication can be achieved
    C. functional relationships of the activities of the office
    D. necessity for screening confidential activities from unauthorized persons

16. The one of the following which is generally considered to be the CHIEF advantage of   16.____
using data processing equipment in modern offices is to

    A. facilitate the use of a wide variety of sources of information
    B. supply management with current information quickly
    C. provide uniformity in the processing and reporting of information
    D. broaden the area in which management decisions can be made

17. In the box design of office forms, the spaces in which information is to be entered are   17.____
arranged in boxes containing captions.
Of the following, the one which is generally NOT considered to be an acceptable rule in
employing box design is that

    A. space should be allowed for the lengthiest anticipated entry in a box
    B. the caption should be located in the upper left corner of the box
    C. the boxes on a form should be of the same size and shape
    D. boxes should be aligned vertically whenever possible

18. As a management tool, the work count would generally be of LEAST assistance to a unit   18.____
supervisor in

    A. scheduling the work of his unit
    B. locating bottlenecks in the work of his unit
    C. ascertaining the number of subordinates he needs
    D. tracing the flow of work in the unit

19. Of the following, the FIRST step that should be taken in a forms simplification program is   19.____
to make a

A. detailed analysis of the items found on current forms
B. study of the amount of use made of existing forms
C. survey of the amount of each kind of form on hand
D. survey of the characteristics of the more effective forms in use

20. The work-distribution chart is a valuable tool for an office supervisor to use in conducting work'simplification programs.
Of the following questions, the one which a work-distribution chart would generally be LEAST useful in answering is:

    20.____

    A. What activities take the most time?
    B. Are the employees doing many unrelated tasks?
    C. Is work being distributed evenly among the employees?
    D. Are activities being performed in proper sequence?

21. Assume that, as a supervisor, you conduct, from time to time, work-performance studies in various sections of your agency. The units of measurement used in any study depend on the particular study and may be number of letters typed, number of papers filed, or other suitable units.
It is MOST important that the units of measurement to be used in a study conform to the units used in similar past studies when the

    21.____

    A. units of measurement to be used in the study cannot be defined sharply
    B. units of measurement used in past studies were satisfactory
    C. results of the study are to be compared with those of past studies
    D. results of the study are to be used for the same purpose as were those of past studies

22. As it is used in auditing, an internal check is a

    22.____

    A. procedure which is designed to guard against fraud
    B. periodic audit by a public accounting firm to verify the accuracy of the internal transactions of an organization
    C. document transferring funds from one section to another within an organization
    D. practice of checking documents twice before they are transmitted outside an organization

23. Of the following, the one which can LEAST be considered to be a proper function of an accounting system is to

    23.____

    A. indicate the need to curtail expenditures
    B. provide information for future fiscal programs
    C. record the expenditure of funds from special appropriations
    D. suggest methods to expedite the collection of revenues

24. Assume that a new unit is to be established in an agency. The unit is to compile and tabulate data so that it will be of the greatest usefulness to the high-level administrators in the agency in making administrative decisions. In planning the organization of this unit, the question that should be answered FIRST is:

    24.____

A. What interpretations are likely to be made of the data by the high-level administrators in making decisions?
B. At what point in the decision-making process will it be most useful to inject the data?
C. What types of data will be required by high-level administrators in making decisions?
D. What criteria will the high-level administrators use to evaluate the decisions they make?

25. The one of the following which is the CHIEF limitation of the organization chart as it is generally used in business and government is that the chart   25._____

A. engenders within incumbents feelings of rights to positions they occupy
B. reveals only formal authority relationships, omitting the informal ones
C. shows varying degrees of authority even though authority is not subject to such differentiation
D. presents organizational structure as it is rather than what it is supposed to be

26. The degree of decentralization that is effective and economical in an organization tends to vary INVERSELY with the   26._____

A. size of the organization
B. availability of adequate numbers of competent personnel
C. physical dispersion of the organization's activities
D. adequacy of the organization's communications system

27. The one of the following which usually can LEAST be considered to be an advantage of committees as they are generally used in government and business is that they   27._____

A. provide opportunities for reconciling varying points of view
B. promote coordination by the interchange of information among the members of the committee
C. act promptly in situations requiring immediate action
D. use group judgment to resolve questions requiring a wide range of experience

28. Managerial decentralization is defined as the decentralization of decision-making authority.   28._____
The degree of managerial decentralization in an organization varies INVERSELY with the

A. number of decisions made lower down the management hierarchy
B. importance of the decisions made lower down the management hierarchy
C. number of major organizational functions affected by decisions made at lower management levels
D. amount of review to which decisions made at lower management levels are subjected

29. Some policy-making commissions are composed of members who are appointed to overlapping terms.   29._____
Of the following, the CHIEF advantage of appointing members to overlapping terms in such commissions is that

A. continuity of policy is promoted
B. the likelihood of compromise policy decisions is reduced
C. responsibility for policy decisions can be fixed upon individual members
D. the likelihood of unanimity of opinion is increased

30. If a certain public agency with a fixed number of employees has a line organizational structure, then the width of the span of supervision is

    30.____

A. inversely proportional to the length of the chain of command in the organization
B. directly proportional to the complexity of tasks performed in the organization
C. inversely proportional to the competence of the personnel in the organization
D. directly proportional to the number of levels of supervision existing in the organization

31. Mr. Brown is a supervisor in charge of a section of clerical employees in an agency. The section consists of four units, each headed by a unit supervisor. From time to time, he makes tours of his section for the purpose of maintaining contact with the rank and file employees. During these tours, he discusses with these employees their work production, work methods, work problems, and other related topics. The information he obtains in this manner is often incomplete or inaccurate. At meetings with the unit supervisors, he questions them on the information acquired during his tours. The supervisors are often unable to answer the questions immediately because they are based on incomplete or inaccurate information. When the supervisors ask that they be permitted to accompany Mr. Brown on his tours and thus answer his questions on the spot, Mr. Brown refuses, explaining that a rank and file employee might be reluctant to speak freely in the presence of his supervisor. This situation may BEST be described as a violation of the principle of organization called

    31.____

A. span of control
C. specialization of work
B. delegation of authority
D. unity of command

Questions 32-36.

DIRECTIONS: Each of Questions 32 through 36 consists of a statement which contains one word that is incorrectly used because it is not in keeping with the meaning that the quotation is evidently intended to convey. For each of these questions, you are to select the INCORRECTLY used word and substitute for it one of the words lettered A, B, C, or D, which helps BEST to convey the meaning of the statement.

32. There has developed in recent years an increasing awareness of the need to measure the quality of management in all enterprises and to seek the principles that can serve as a basis for this improvement.

    32.____

A. growth   B. raise   C. efficiency   D. define

33. It is hardly an exaggeration to deny that the permanence, productivity, and humanity of any industrial system depend upon its ability to utilize the positive and constructive impulses of all who work and upon its ability to arouse and continue interest in the necessary activities.

    33.____

A. develop
C. state
B. efficiency
D. inspirational

34. The selection of managers on the basis of technical knowledge alone seems to recognize that the essential characteristic of management is getting things done through others, thereby demanding skills that are essential in coordinating the activities of subordinates.   34.____

    A. training   B. fails
    C. organization   D. improving

35. Only when it is deliberate and when it is clearly understood what impressions the ease of communication will probably create in the minds of employees and subordinate management, should top management refrain from commenting on a subject that is of general concern.   35.____

    A. obvious   B. benefit   C. doubt   D. absence

36. Scientific planning of work requires careful analysis of facts and a precise plan of action for the whims and fancies of executives that often provide only a vague indication of the work to be done.   36.____

    A. substitutes   B. development
    C. preliminary   D. comprehensive

37. Within any single level of government, as a city or a state, the administrative authority may be concentrated or dispersed.
Of the following plans of government, the one in which administrative authority would be dispersed the MOST is the _____ plan.   37.____

    A. mayor   B. mayor-council
    C. commission   D. city manager

38. In general, the courts may review a decision of an administrative agency with rule-making powers. However, the courts will usually REFUSE to review a decision of such an agency if the only question raised concerning the decision is whether or not the   38.____

    A. decision contravenes public policy
    B. agency has abused the powers conferred upon it
    C. decision deals with an issue which is within the jurisdiction of the agency
    D. agency has applied the same rules of evidence as are used in the courts

39. A legislature sometimes delegates rule-making powers to the administrators of a public agency.
Of the following, the CHIEF advantage of such delegation is that   39.____

    A. the frequency with which the legality of the agency's rules is contested in court will be reduced
    B. the agency will have the flexibility to adjust to changing conditions and problems
    C. mistakes made by the administrators or the legislature in defining the scope of the agency's program may be easily corrected
    D. the legislature will not be required to approve the rules formulated by the agency

40. Some municipalities have delegated the functions of budget preparation and personnel selection to central agencies, thus removing these functions from operating departments.
Of the following, the MOST important reason why municipalities have delegated these functions to central agencies is that   40.____

A. the performance of these functions presents problems that vary from one operating department to another
B. operating departments often lack sufficient funds to perform these functions adequately
C. the performance of these functions by a central agency produces more uniform policies than if these functions are performed by the operating departments
D. central agencies are not controlled as closely as are operating departments and so have greater freedom in formulating new policies and procedures to deal with difficult budget and personnel problems

41. Of the following, the MOST fundamental reason for the use of budgets in governmental administration is that budgets
    41.____

    A. minimize seasonal variations in work loads and expenditures of public agencies
    B. facilitate decentralization of functions performed by public agencies
    C. provide advance control on the expenditure of funds
    D. establish valid bases for comparing present governmental activities with corresponding activities in previous periods

42. In some governmental jurisdictions, the chief executive prepares the budget for a fiscal period and presents it to the legislative branch of government for adoption. In other jurisdictions, the legislative branch prepares and adopts the budget.
    Preparation of the budget by the chief executive rather than by the legislative branch is
    42.____

    A. *desirable*, primarily because the chief executive is held largely accountable by the public for the results of fiscal operations and should, therefore, be the one to prepare the budget
    B. *undesirable,* primarily because such a separation of the legislative and executive branches leads to the enactment of a budget that does not consider the overall needs of the government
    C. *desirable,* primarily because the preparation of the budget by the chief executive limits legislative review and evaluation of operating programs
    D. *undesirable,* primarily because responsibility for budget preparation should be placed in the branch that must eventually adopt the budget and appropriate the funds for it

43. The one of the following which is generally the FIRST step in the budget-making process of a municipality that has a central budget agency is
    43.____

    A. determination of available sources of revenue within the municipality
    B. establishment of tax rates at levels sufficient to achieve a balanced budget in the following fiscal period
    C. evaluation by the central budget agency of the adequacy of the municipality's previous budgets
    D. assembling by the central budget agency of the proposed expenditures of each agency in the municipality for the following fiscal period

44. It is advantageous for a municipality to issue serial bonds rather than sinking fund bonds CHIEFLY because
    44.____

A. an issue of serial bonds usually includes a wider range of maturity dates than does an issue of sinking fund bonds

B. appropriations set aside periodically to retire serial bonds as they fall due are more readily invested in long-term securities at favorable rates of interest than are appropriations earmarked for redemption of sinking fund bonds

C. serial bonds are sold at regular intervals while sinking fund bonds are issued as the need for funds arises

D. a greater variety of interest rates is usually offered in an issue of serial bonds than in an issue of sinking fund bonds

45. Studies conducted by the Regional Plan Association of the 22-county New York Metropolitan Region, comprising New York City and surrounding counties in New York, New Jersey, and Connecticut, have defined Manhattan, Brooklyn, Queens, the Bronx, and Hudson County in New Jersey as the *core*. Such studies have examined the per capita personal income of the core as a percent of the per capita personal income of the entire Region, and the population of the core as a percent of the total population of the entire Region.
These studies support the conclusion that, as a percent of the entire Region, 45.____

A. both population and per capita personal income in the core were higher in 1970 than in 1940

B. both population and per capita personal income in the core were lower in 1970 than in 1940

C. population was higher and per capita personal income was lower in the core in 1970 than in 1940

D. population was lower and per capita personal income was higher in the core in 1970 than in 1940

KEY (CORRECT ANSWERS)

1. D	11. B	21. C	31. D	41. C
2. B	12. B	22. A	32. B	42. A
3. C	13. C	23. D	33. C	43. D
4. B	14. C	24. C	34. B	44. A
5. A	15. A	25. B	35. D	45. B
6. C	16. B	26. D	36. A	
7. B	17. C	27. C	37. C	
8. A	18. D	28. D	38. D	
9. D	19. B	29. A	39. B	
10. D	20. D	30. A	40. C	

EXAMINATION SECTION
TEST 1

DIRECTIONS: Each question or incomplete statement is followed by several suggested answers or completions. Select the one that BEST answers the question or completes the statement. *PRINT THE LETTER OF THE CORRECT ANSWER IN THE SPACE AT THE RIGHT.*

1. A supervisor notices that one of his more competent subordinates has recently been showing less interest in his work. The work performed by this employee has also fallen off and he seems to want to do no more than the minimum acceptable amount of work. When his supervisor questions the subordinate about his decreased interest and his mediocre work performance, the subordinate replies: *Sure, I've lost interest in my work. I don't see any reason why I should do more than I have to. When I do a good job, nobody notices it. But, let me fall down on one minor job and the whole place knows about it! So why should I put myself out on this job?*
If the subordinate's contentions are true, it would be correct to assume that the

    A. subordinate has not received adequate training
    B. subordinate's workload should be decreased
    C. supervisor must share responsibility for this employee's reaction
    D. supervisor has not been properly enforcing work standards

1.____

2. *How many subordinates should report directly to each supervisor? While there is agreement that there are limits to the number of subordinates that a manager can supervise well, this limit is determined by a number of important factors.*
Which of the following factors is most likely to increase the number of subordinates that can be effectively supervised by one supervisor in a particular unit?

    A. The unit has a great variety of activities
    B. A staff assistant handles the supervisor's routine duties
    C. The unit has a relatively inexperienced staff
    D. The office layout is being rearranged to make room for more employees

2.____

3. Mary Smith, an Administrative Assistant, heads the Inspection Records Unit of Department Y. She is a dedicated supervisor who not only strives to maintain an efficient operation, but she also tries to improve the competence of each individual member of her staff. She keeps these considerations in mind when assigning work to her staff. Her bureau chief asks her to compile some data based on information contained in her records. She feels that any member of her staff should be able to do this job. The one of the following members of her staff who would probably be given LEAST consideration for this assignment is

    A. Jane Abel, a capable Supervising Clerk with considerable experience in the unit
    B. Kenneth Brown, a Senior Clerk recently transferred to the unit who has not had an opportunity to demonstrate his capabilities
    C. Laura Chance, a Clerk who spends full time on a single routine assignment
    D. Michael Dunn, a Clerk who works on several minor jobs but still has the lightest workload

3.____

4. *There are very few aspects of a supervisor's job that do not involve communication, either in writing or orally.*
Which of the following statements regarding oral and written orders is NOT correct?

4.____

A. Oral orders usually permit more immediate feedback than do written orders.
B. Written orders, rather than oral orders, should generally be given when the subordinate will be held strictly accountable.
C. Oral orders are usually preferable when the order contains lengthy detailed instructions.
D. Written orders, rather than oral orders, should usually be given to a subordinate who is slow to understand or is forgetful.

5. Assume that you are the head of a large clerical unit in Department R. Your department's personnel office has appointed a Clerk, Roberta Rowe, to fill a vacancy in your unit. Before bringing this appointee to your office, the personnel office has given Roberta the standard orientation on salary, fringe benefits, working conditions, attendance and the department's personnel rules. In addition, he has supplied her with literature covering these areas. Of the following, the action that you should take FIRST after Roberta has been brought to your office is to

    5.____

A. give her an opportunity to read the literature furnished by the personnel office so that she can ask you questions about it
B. escort her to the desk she will use and assign her to work with an experienced employee who will act as her trainer
C. explain the duties and responsibilities of her job and its relationship with the jobs being performed by the other employees of the unit
D. summon the employee who is currently doing the work that will be performed by Roberta and have him explain and demonstrate how to perform the required tasks

6. Your superior informs you that the employee turnover rate in your office is well above the norm and must be reduced. Which one of the following initial steps would be LEAST appropriate in attempting to overcome this problem?

    6.____

A. Decide to be more lenient about performance standards and about employee requests for time off, so that your office will gain a reputation as an easy place to work
B. Discuss the problem with a few of your key people whose judgment you trust to see if they can shed some light on the underlying causes of the problem
C. Review the records of employees who have left during the past year to see if there is a pattern that will help you understand the problem
D. Carefully review your training procedures to see whether they can be improved

7. In issuing instructions to a subordinate on a job assignment, the supervisor should ordinarily explain why the assignment is being made. Omission of such an explanation is best justified when the

    7.____

A. subordinate is restricted in the amount of discretion he can exercise in carrying out the assignment
B. assignment is one that will be unpopular with the subordinate
C. subordinate understands the reason as a result of previous similar assignments
D. assignment is given to an employee who is in need of further training

8. When a supervisor allows sufficient time for training and makes an appropriate effort in the training of his subordinates, his chief goal is to

    8.____

A. increase the dependence of one subordinate upon another in their everyday work activities
B. spend more time with his subordinates in order to become more involved in their work
C. increase the capability and independence of his subordinates in carrying out their work
D. increase his frequency of contact with his subordinates in order to better evaluate their performance

9. In preparing an evaluation of a subordinate's performance, which one of the following items is usually irrelevant?

    9.____

A. Remarks about tardiness or absenteeism
B. Mention of any unusual contributions or accomplishments
C. A summary of the employee's previous job experience
D. An assessment of the employee's attitude toward the job

10. The ability to delegate responsibility while maintaining adequate controls is one key to a supervisor's success. Which one of the following methods of control would minimize the amount of responsibility assumed by the subordinate?

    10.____

A. Asking for a monthly status report in writing
B. Asking to receive copies of important correspondence so that you can be aware of potential problems
C. Scheduling periodic project status conferences with your subordinate
D. Requiring that your subordinate confer with you before making decisions on a project

11. You wish to assign an important project to a subordinate who you think has good potential. Which one of the following approaches would be most effective in successfully completing the project while developing the subordinate's abilities?

    11.____

A. Describe the project to the subordinate in general terms and emphasize that it must be completed as quickly as possible
B. Outline the project in detail to the subordinate and emphasize that its successful completion could lead to career advancement
C. Develop a detailed project outline and timetable, discuss the details and timing with him and assign the subordinate to carry out the plan on his own
D. Discuss the project objectives and suggested approaches with the subordinate, and ask the subordinate to develop a detailed project outline and timetable of your approval

12. Research studies reveal that an important difference between high-production and low-production supervisors lies not in their interest in eliminating mistakes, but in their manner of handling mistakes. High-production supervisors are most likely to look upon mistakes as primarily

    12.____

A. an opportunity to provide training
B. a byproduct of subordinate negligence
C. an opportunity to fix blame in a situation
D. a result of their own incompetence

13. Supervisors should try to establish what has been called *positive discipline*, an atmosphere in which subordinates willingly abide by rules which they consider fair. When a supervisor notices a subordinate violating an important rule, his FIRST course of action should be to

    A. stop the subordinate and tell him what he is doing wrong
    B. wait a day or two before approaching the employee involved
    C. call a meeting of all subordinates to discuss the rule
    D. forget the matter in the hope that it will not happen again

13.____

14. The working climate is the feeling, degree of freedom, the tone and the mood of the working environment. Which of the following contributes most to determining the working climate in a unit or group?

    A. The rules set for rest periods
    B. The example set by the supervisor
    C. The rules set for morning check-in
    D. The wages paid to the employees

14.____

15. John Polk is a bright, ingenious clerk with a lot of initiative. He has made many good suggestions to his supervisor in the Training Division of Department T, where he is employed. However, last week one of his bright ideas literally *blew up*. In setting up some electronic equipment in the training classroom, he crossed some wires resulting in a damaged tape recorder and a classroom so filled with smoke that the training class had to be held in another room. When Mr. Brown, his supervisor, learned of this occurrence, he immediately summoned John to his private office. There Mr. Brown spent five minutes bawling John out, calling him an overzealous, overgrown kid, and sent him back to his job without letting John speak once. Of the following, the action of Mr. Brown that most deserves approval is that he

    A. took disciplinary action immediately without regard for past performance
    B. kept the disciplinary interview to a brief period
    C. concentrated his criticism on the root cause of the occurrence
    D. held the disciplinary interview in his private office .

15.____

16. Typically, when the technique of *supervision by results* is practiced, higher management sets down, either implicitly or explicitly, certain performance standards or goals that the subordinate is expected to meet. So long as these standards are met, management interferes very little. The most likely result of the use of this technique is that it will

    A. lead to ambiguity in terms of goals
    B. be successful only to the extent that close direct supervision is practiced
    C. make it possible to evaluate both employee and supervisory effectiveness
    D. allow for complete autonomy on the subordinate's part

16.____

17. Assume that you, an Administrative Assistant, are the supervisor of a large clerical unit performing routine clerical operations. One of your clerks consistently produces much less work than other members of your staff performing similar tasks. Of the following, the action you should take FIRST is to

    A. ask the clerk if he wants to be transferred to another unit

17.____

B. reprimand the clerk for his poor performance and warn him that further disciplinary action will be taken if his work does not improve
C. quietly ask the clerk's co-workers whether they know why his performance is poor
D. discuss this matter with the clerk to work out plans for improving his performance

18. When making written evaluations and reviews of the performance of subordinates, it is usually advisable to   18.____

A. avoid informing the employee of the evaluation if it is critical because it may create hard feelings
B. avoid informing the employee of the evaluation whether critical or favorable because it is tension-producing
C. permit the employee to see the evaluation but not to discuss it with him because the supervisor cannot be certain where the discussion might lead
D. discuss the evaluation openly with the employee because it helps the employee understand what is expected of him

19. There are a number of well-known and respected human relations principles that successful supervisors have been using for years in building good relationships with their employees. Which of the following does NOT illustrate such a principle?   19.____

A. Give clear and complete instructions
B. Let each person know how he is getting along
C. Keep an open-door policy
D. Make all relationships personal ones

20. Assume that it is your responsibility as an Administrative Assistant to maintain certain personnel records that are continually being updated. You have three senior clerks assigned specifically to this task. Recently you have noticed that the volume of work has increased substantially, and the processing of personnel records by the clerks is backlogged. Your supervisor is now receiving complaints due to the processing delay. Of the following, the best course of action for you to take FIRST is to   20.____

A. have a meeting with the clerks, advise them of the problem, and ask that they do their work faster; then confirm your meeting in writing for the record
B. request that an additional position be authorized for your unit
C. review the procedures being used for processing the work, and try to determine if you can improve the flow of work
D. get the system moving faster by spending some of your own time processing the backlog

21. Assume that you are in charge of a payroll unit consisting of four clerks. It is Friday, November 14. You have just arrived in the office after a conference. Your staff is preparing a payroll that must be forwarded the following Monday. Which of the following new items on your desk should you attend to FIRST?   21.____

A. A telephone message regarding very important information needed for the statistical summary of salaries paid for the month of November
B. A memorandum regarding a new procedure that should be followed in preparing the payroll
C. A telephone message from an employee who is threatening to endorse his paycheck *Under Protest* because he is dissatisfied with the amount

D. A memorandum from your supervisor reminding you to submit the probationary period report on a new employee

22. You are an Administrative Assistant in charge of a unit that orders and issues supplies. On a particular day you are faced with the following four situations. Which one should you take care of FIRST?

    22.____

    A. One of your employees who is in the process of taking the quarterly inventory of supplies has telephoned and asked that you return his call as soon as possible
    B. A representative of a company that is noted for producing excellent office supplies will soon arrive with samples for you to distribute to the various offices in your agency
    C. A large order of supplies which was delivered this morning has been checked and counted and a deliveryman is waiting for you to sign the receipt
    D. A clerk from the purchase division asks you to search for a bill you failed to send to them which is urgently needed in order for them to complete a report due this morning

23. As an Administrative Assistant, assume that it is necessary for you to give an unpleasant assignment to one of your subordinates. You expect this employee to raise some objections to this assignment. The most appropriate of the following actions for you to take FIRST is to issue the assignment

    23.____

    A. orally, with the further statement that you will not listen to any complaints
    B. in writing, to forestall any complaints by the employee
    C. orally, permitting the employee to express his feelings
    D. in writing, with a note that any comments should be submitted in writing

24. Assume that you are an Administrative Assistant supervising the Duplicating and Reproduction Unit of Department B. One of your responsibilities is to prepare a daily schedule showing when and on which of your unit's four duplicating machines jobs are to be run off. Of the following, the factor that should be given LEAST consideration in preparing the schedule is the

    24.____

    A. priority of each of the jobs to be run off
    B. production speed of the different machines that will be used
    C. staff available to operate the machines
    D. date on which the job order was received

25. *Cycling is an arrangement where papers are processed throughout a period according to an orderly plan rather than as a group all at one time. This technique has been used for a long time by public utilities in their cycle billing.* Of the following practices, the one that best illustrates this technique is that in which

    25.____

    A. paychecks for per annum employees are issued bi-weekly and those for per diem employees are issued weekly
    B. field inspectors report in person to their offices one day a week, on Fridays, when they do all their paperwork and also pick up their paychecks
    C. the dates for issuing relief checks to clients vary depending on the last digit of the clients' social security numbers
    D. the last day for filing and paying income taxes is the same for Federal, State and City income taxes

26. The employees in your division have recently been given an excellent up-to-date office manual, but you find that a good number of employees are not following the procedures outlined in it. Which one of the following would be most likely to ensure that employees begin using the manual effectively?

    A. Require each employee to keep a copy of the manual in plain sight on his desk
    B. Issue warnings periodically to those employees who deviate most from procedures prescribed in the manual
    C. Tell an employee to check his manual when he does not follow the proper procedures
    D. Suggest to the employees that the manual be studied thoroughly

26.____

27. The one of the following factors which should be considered FIRST in the design of office forms is the

    A. information to be included in the form
    B. sequence of the information
    C. purpose of the form
    D. persons who will be using the form

27.____

28. *Window envelopes are being used to an increasing extent by government and private industry.* The one of the following that is NOT an advantage of window envelopes is that they

    A. cut down on addressing costs
    B. eliminate the need to attach envelopes to letters being sent forward for signature by a superior
    C. are less costly to buy than regular envelopes
    D. reduce the risk of having letters placed in wrong envelopes

28.____

29. Your bureau head asks you to prepare the office layouts for several of his units being moved to a higher floor in your office building. Of the following possibilities, the one that you should AVOID in preparing the layouts is to

    A. place the desks of the first-line supervisors near those of the staffs they supervise
    B. place the desks of employees whose work is most closely related near one another
    C. arrange the desks so that employees do not face one another
    D. locate desks with many outside visitors farthest from the office entrance

29.____

30. Which one of the following conditions would be LEAST important in considering a change of the layout in a particular office?

    A. Installation of a new office machine
    B. Assignment of five additional employees to your office
    C. Poor flow of work
    D. Employees' personal preferences of desk location

30.____

31. Suppose Mr. Bloom, an Administrative Assistant, is dictating a letter to a stenographer. His dictation begins with the name of the addressee and continues to the body of the letter. However, Mr. Bloom does not dictate the address of the recipient of the letter. He expects the stenographer to locate it. The use of this practice by Mr. Bloom is

    A. acceptable, especially if he gives the stenographer the letter to which he is responding

31.____

B. acceptable, especially if the letter is lengthy and detailed
C. unacceptable, because it is not part of a stenographer's duties to search for information
D. unacceptable, because he should not rely on the accuracy of the stenographer

32. Assume that there are no rules, directives or instructions concerning the filing of materials in your office or the retention of such files. A system is now being followed of placing in *inactive files any materials that are more than one year old. Of the following, the most appropriate thing to do with material that has been in an inactive* file in your office for more than one year is to

    A. inspect the contents of the files to decide how to dispose of them
    B. transfer the material to a remote location, where it can be obtained if necessary
    C. keep the material intact for a minimum of another three years
    D. destroy the material which has not been needed for at least a year

32.____

33. Suppose you, an Administrative Assistant, have just returned to your desk after engaging in an all-morning conference. Joe Burns, a Clerk, informs you that Clara McClough, an administrator in another agency, telephoned during the morning and that, although she requested to speak with you, he was able to give her the desired information. Of the following, the most appropriate action for you to take in regard to Mr. Burns' action is to

    A. thank him for assisting Ms. McClough in your absence
    B. explain to him the proper telephone practice to use in the future
    C. reprimand him for not properly channeling Ms. McClough's call
    D. issue a memo to all clerical employees regarding proper telephone practices

33.____

34. *When interviewing subordinates with problems, supervisors frequently find that asking direct questions of the employee results only in evasive responses. The supervisor may therefore resort to the non-directive interview technique. In this technique the supervisor avoids pointed questions; he leads the employee to continue talking freely uninfluenced by the supervisor's preconceived notions. This technique often enables the employee to bring his problem into sharp focus and to reach a solution to his problem.*
Suppose that you are a supervisor interviewing a subordinate about his recent poor attendance record. On calling his attention to his excessive lateness record, he replies:
I just don't seem to be able to get up in the morning. Frankly, I've lost interest in this job. I don't care about it. When I get up in the morning, I have to skip breakfast and I'm still late. I don't care about this job.
If you are using the *non-directive* technique in this interview, the most appropriate of the following responses for you to make is

    A. *You don't care about this job?*
    B. *Don't you think you are letting your department down?*
    C. *Are you having trouble at home?*
    D. *Don't you realize your actions are childish?*

34.____

35. An employee in a work group made the following comment to a co-worker: *It's great to be a lowly employee instead of an Administrative Assistant because you can work without thinking. The Administrative Assistant is getting paid to plan, schedule and think. Let him see to it that you have a productive day.*
Which one of the following statements about this quotation best reflects an understanding of good personnel management techniques and the role of the supervising Administrative Assistant?

35.____

A. The employee is wrong in attitude and in his perception of the role of the Administrative Assistant
B. The employee is correct in attitude but is wrong in his perception of the role of the Administrative Assistant
C. The employee is correct in attitude and in his perception of the role of the Administrative Assistant
D. The employee is wrong in attitude but is right in his perception of the role of the Administrative Assistant

---

KEY (CORRECT ANSWERS)

1.	C	11.	D	26.	C
2.	B	12.	A	27.	C
3.	A	13.	A	28.	C
4.	C	14.	B	29.	D
5.	C	15.	D	30.	D
6.	A	16.	C/D	31.	A
7.	C	17.	D	32.	A/B
8.	C	18.	D	33.	A
9.	C	19.	D	34.	A
10.	D	20.	C	35.	D
		21.	B		
		22.	C		
		23.	C		
		24.	D		
		25.	C		

TEST 2

DIRECTIONS: Each question or incomplete statement is followed by several suggested answers or completions. Select the one that BEST answers the question or completes the statement. *PRINT THE LETTER OF THE CORRECT ANSWER IN THE SPACE AT THE RIGHT.*

Questions 1 through 5 are to be answered solely on the basis of the following passage:

General supervision, in contrast to close supervision, involves a high degree of delegation of authority and requires some indirect means to ensure that employee behavior conforms to management needs. Not everyone works well under general supervision, however. General supervision works best where subordinates desire responsibility. General supervision also works well where individuals in work groups have strong feelings about the quality of the finished work products. Strong identification with management goals is another trait of persons who work well under general supervision. There are substantial differences in the amount of responsibility people are willing to accept on the job. One person may flourish under supervision that another might find extremely restrictive.

Psychological research provides evidence that the nature of a person's personality affects his attitude toward supervision. There are some employees with a low need for achievement and high fear of failure who shy away from challenges and responsibilities. Many seek self-expression off the job and ask only to be allowed to daydream on it. There are others who have become so accustomed to the authoritarian approach in their culture, family and previous work experience that they regard general supervision as no supervision at all. They abuse the privileges it bestows on them and refuse to accept the responsibilities it demands.

Different groups develop different attitudes toward work. Most college graduates, for example, expect a great deal of responsibility and freedom. People with limited education, on the other hand, often have trouble accepting the concept that people should make decisions for themselves, particularly decisions concerning work. Therefore, the extent to which general supervision will be effective varies greatly with the subordinates involved.

1. According to the above passage, which one of the following is a necessary part of management policy regarding general supervision?   1.____

    A. Most employees should formulate their own work goals
    B. Deserving employees should be rewarded periodically
    C. Some controls on employee work patterns should be established
    D. Responsibility among employees should generally be equalized

2. It can be inferred from the above passage that an employee who avoids responsibilities and challenges is most likely to   2.____

    A. gain independence under general supervision
    B. work better under close supervision than under general supervision
    C. abuse the liberal guidelines of general supervision
    D. become more restricted and cautious under general supervision

3. Based on the above passage, employees who succeed under general supervision are most likely to   3.____

    A. have a strong identification with people and their problems
    B. accept work obligations without fear
    C. seek self-expression off the job
    D. value the intellectual aspects of life

4. Of the following, the best title for the passage is　　　　　　　　　　　　　　　4._____

    A. Benefits and Disadvantages of General Supervision
    B. Production Levels of Employees Under General Supervision
    C. Employee Attitudes Toward Work and the Work Environment
    D. Employee Background and Personality as a Factor in Utilizing General Supervision

5. It can be inferred from the above passage that the one of the following employees who is　　5._____
most likely to work best under general supervision is one who

    A. is a part-time graduate student
    B. was raised by very strict parents
    C. has little self-confidence
    D. has been closely supervised in past jobs

Questions 6 through 10 are to be answered solely on the basis of the information in the following passage:

The concept of *program management* was first developed in order to handle some of the complex projects undertaken by the U.S. Department of Defense in the 1950's. Program management is an administrative system combining planning and control techniques to guide and coordinate all the activities which contribute to one overall program or project. It has been used by the federal government to manage space exploration and other programs involving many contributing organizations. It is also used by state and local governments and by some large firms to provide administrative integration of work from a number of sources, be they individuals, departments or outside companies.

One of the specific administrative techniques for program management is Program Evaluation Review Technique (PERT). PERT begins with the assembling of a list of all the activities needed to accomplish an overall task. The next step consists of arranging these activities in a sequential network showing both how much time each activity will take and which activities must be completed before others can begin. The time required for each activity is estimated by simple statistical techniques by the persons who will be responsible for the work, and the time required to complete the entire string of activities along each sequential path through the network is then calculated. There may be dozens or hundreds of these paths, so the calculation is usually done by computer. The longest path is then labeled the *critical path* because no matter how quickly events not on this path are completed, the events along the longest path must be finished before the project can be terminated. The overall starting and completion dates are then pinpointed, and target dates are established for each task. Actual progress can later be checked by comparison to the network plan.

6. Judging from the information in the above passage, which one of the following projects is　　6._____
most suitable for handling by a program management technique?

    A. Review and improvement of the filing system used by a city office
    B. Computerization of accounting data already on file in an office
    C. Planning and construction of an urban renewal project
    D. Announcing a change in city tax regulations to thousands of business firms

7. The passage indicates that program management methods are now in wide use by various　　7._____
kinds of organizations. Which one of the following organizations would you LEAST
expect to make much use of such methods today?

    A.   An automobile manufacturer
    B.   A company in the aerospace business
    C.   The government of a large city
    D.   A library reference department

8.   In making use of the PERT technique, the first step is to determine   8._____

    A.   every activity that must take place in order to complete the project
    B.   a target date for completion of the project
    C.   the estimated time required to complete each activity which is related to the whole
    D.   which activities will make up the longest path on the chart

9.   Who estimates the time required to complete a particular activity in a PERT program?   9._____

    A.   The people responsible for the particular activity
    B.   The statistician assigned to the program
    C.   The organization that has commissioned the project
    D.   The operator who programs the computer

10.   Which one of the following titles best describes the contents of the passage?   10._____

    A.   *The Need For Computers in Today's Projects*
    B.   *One Technique For Program Management*
    C.   *Local Governments Can Now Use Space-Age Techniques*
    D.   *Why Planning Is Necessary For Complex Projects*

11.   An Administrative Assistant has been criticized for the low productivity in the group which   11._____
he supervises. Which of the following best reflects an understanding of supervisory
responsibilities in the area of productivity? An Administrative Assistant should be held
responsible for

    A.   his own individual productivity and the productivity of the group he supervises,
        because he is in a position where he maintains or increases production through
        others
    B.   his own personal productivity only, because the supervisor is not likely to have any
        effect on the productivity of subordinates
    C.   his own individual productivity but only for a drop in the productivity of the group he
        supervises, since subordinates will receive credit for increased productivity individ-
        ually
    D.   his own personal productivity only, because this is how he would be evaluated if he
        were not a supervisor

12.   A supervisor has held a meeting in his office with an employee about the employee's   12._____
grievance. The grievance concerned the sharp way in which the supervisor reprimanded
the employee for an error the employee made in the performance of a task assigned to
him. The problem was not resolved. Which one of the following statements about this
meeting best reflects an understanding of good supervisory techniques?

    A.   It is awkward for a supervisor to handle a grievance involving himself. The supervi-
        sor should not have held the meeting.
    B.   It would have been better if the supervisor had held the meeting at the employee's
        workplace, even though there would have been frequent distractions, because the
        employee would have been more relaxed.

C. The resolution of a problem is not the only sign of a successful meeting. The achievement of communication was worthwhile.

D. The supervisor should have been forceful. There is nothing wrong with raising your voice to an employee every once in a while.

13. John Hayden, the owner of a single-family house, complains that he submitted an application for reduction of assessment that obviously was not acted upon before his final assessment notice was sent to him. The timely receipt of the application has been verified in a departmental log book. As the supervisor of the clerical unit through which this application was processed and where this delay occurred, you should be LEAST concerned with   13._____

A. what happened
C. why it happened

B. who is responsible
D. what can be learned from it

14. The one of the following that applies most appropriately to the role of the first-line supervisor is that usually he is   14._____

A. called upon to help determine agency policy
B. involved in long-range agency planning
C. responsible for determining some aspects of basic organization structure
D. a participant in developing procedures and methods

15. Sally Jones, an Administrative Assistant, gives clear and precise instructions to Robert Warren, a Senior Clerk. In these instructions, Ms. Jones clearly delegates authority to Mr. Warren to undertake a well-defined task. In this situation Ms. Jones should expect Mr. Warren to   15._____

A. come to her to check out details as he progresses with the task
B. come to her only with exceptional problems
C. ask her permission if he wishes to use his delegated authority
D. use his authority to redefine the task and its related activities

16. Planning involves establishing departmental goals and programs and determining ways of reaching them. The main advantage of such planning is that   16._____

A. there will be no need for adjustments once a plan is put into operation
B. it ensures that everyone is working on schedule
C. it provides the framework for an effective operation
D. unexpected work problems are easily overcome

17. As a result of reorganization, the jobs in a large clerical unit were broken down into highly specialized tasks. Each specialized task was then assigned to a particular employee to perform. This action will probably lead to an increase in   17._____

A. flexibility
C. need for coordination

B. job satisfaction
D. employee initiative

18. Your office carries on a large volume of correspondence concerned with the purchase of supplies and equipment for city offices. You use form letters to deal with many common situations. In which one of the following situations would use of a form letter be LEAST appropriate?   18._____

A. Informing suppliers of a change in city regulations concerning purchase contracts
B. Telling a new supplier the standard procedures to be followed in billing
C. Acknowledging receipt of a complaint and saying that the complaint will be investigated
D. Answering a city councilman's request for additional information on a particular regulation affecting suppliers

19. Assume that you are an Administrative Assistant heading a large clerical unit. Because of the great demands being made on your time, you have designated Tom Smith, a Supervising Clerk, to be your assistant and to assume some of your duties. Of the following duties performed by you, the most appropriate one to assign to Tom Smith is to   19._____

    A. conduct the on-the-job training of new employees
    B. prepare the performance appraisal reports on your staff members
    C. represent your unit in dealings with the heads of other units
    D. handle matters that require exception to general policy

20. In establishing rules for his subordinates, a superior should be primarily concerned with   20._____

    A. creating sufficient flexibility to allow for exceptions
    B. making employees aware of the reasons for the rules and the penalties for infractions
    C. establishing the strength of his own position in relation to his subordinates
    D. having his subordinates know that such rules will be imposed in a personal manner

21. The practice of conducting staff training sessions on a periodic basis is generally considered   21._____

    A. poor; it takes employees away from their work assignments
    B. poor; all staff training should be done on an individual basis
    C. good; it permits the regular introduction of new methods and techniques
    D. good; it ensures a high employee productivity rate

22. Suppose, as an Administrative Assistant, you have just announced at a staff meeting with your subordinates that a radical reorganization of work will take place next week. Your subordinates at the meeting appear to be excited, tense and worried. Of the following, the best action for you to take at that time is to   22._____

    A. schedule private conferences with each subordinate to obtain his reaction to the meeting
    B. close the meeting and tell your subordinates to return immediately to their work assignments
    C. give your subordinates some time to ask questions and discuss your announcement
    D. insist that your subordinates do not discuss your announcement among themselves or with other members of the agency

23. Suppose that as an Administrative Assistant you were recently placed in charge of the Duplicating and Stock Unit of Department Y. From your observation of the operations of your unit during your first week as its head, you get the impression that there are inefficiencies in its operations causing low productivity. To obtain an increase in its productivity, the FIRST of the following actions you should take is to   23._____

A. seek the advice of your immediate superior on how he would tackle this problem
B. develop plans to correct any unsatisfactory conditions arising from other than man-power deficiencies
C. identify the problems causing low productivity
D. discuss your productivity problem with other unit heads to find out how they handled similar problems

24. Assume that you are an Administrative Assistant recently placed in charge of a large clerical unit. At a meeting, the head of another unit tells you, *My practice is to give a worker more than he can finish. In that way you can be sure that you are getting the most out of him.* For you to adopt this practice would be   24.____

   A. advisable, since your actions would be consistent with those practiced in your agency
   B. inadvisable, since such a practice is apt to create frustration and lower staff morals
   C. advisable, since a high goal stimulates people to strive to attain it
   D. inadvisable, since management may, in turn, set too high a productivity goal for the unit

25. Suppose that you are the supervisor of a unit in which there is an increasing amount of friction among several of your staff members. One of the reasons for this friction is that the work of some of these staff members cannot be completed until other staff members complete related work. Of the following, the most appropriate action for you to take is to   25.____

   A. summon these employees to a meeting to discuss the responsibilities each has and to devise better methods of coordination
   B. have a private talk with each employee involved and make each understand that there must be more cooperation among the employees
   C. arrange for interviews with each of the employees involved to determine what his problems are
   D. shift the assignments of these employees so that each will be doing a job different from his current one

26. An office supervisor has a number of responsibilities with regard to his subordinates. Which one of the following functions should NOT be regarded as a basic responsibility of the office supervisor?   26.____

   A. Telling employees how to solve personal problems that may be interfering with their work
   B. Training new employees to do the work assigned to them
   C. Evaluating employees' performance periodically and discussing the evaluation with each employee
   D. Bringing employee grievances to the attention of higher-level administrators and seeking satisfactory resolutions

27. One of your most productive subordinates frequently demonstrates a poor attitude toward his job. He seems unsure of himself, and he annoys his co-workers because he is continually belittling himself and the work that he is doing. In trying to help him overcome this problem, which of the following approaches is LEAST likely to be effective?   27.____

A. Compliment him on his work and assign him some additional responsibilities, telling him that he is being given these responsibilities because of his demonstrated ability
B. Discuss with him the problem of his attitude, and warn him that you will have to report it on his next performance evaluation
C. Assign him a particularly important and difficult project, stressing your confidence in his ability to complete it successfully
D. Discuss with him the problem of his attitude, and ask him for suggestions as to how you can help him overcome it

28. You come to realize that a personality conflict between you and one of your subordinates is adversely affecting his performance. Which one of the following would be the most appropriate FIRST step to take?   28.____

A. Report the problem to your superior and request assistance. His experience may be helpful in resolving this problem.
B. Discuss the situation with several of the subordinate's co-workers to see if they can suggest any remedy.
C. Suggest to the subordinate that he get professional counseling or therapy.
D. Discuss the situation candidly with the subordinate, with the objective of resolving the problem between yourselves.

29. Assume that you are an Administrative Assistant supervising the Payroll Records Section in Department G. Your section has been requested to prepare and submit to the department's budget officer a detailed report giving a breakdown of labor costs under various departmental programs and sub-programs. You have assigned this task to a Supervising Clerk, giving him full authority for seeing that this job is performed satisfactorily. You have given him a written statement of the job to be done and explained the purpose and use of this report. The next step that you should take in connection with this delegated task is to   29.____

A. assist the Supervising Clerk in the step-by-step performance of the job
B. assure the Supervising Clerk that you will be understanding of mistakes if made at the beginning
C. require him to receive your approval for interim reports submitted at key points before he can proceed further with his task
D. give him a target date for the completion of this report

30. Assume that you are an Administrative Assistant heading a unit staffed with six clerical employees. One Clerk, John Snell, is a probationary employee appointed four months ago. During the first three months, John learned his job quickly, performed his work accurately and diligently, and was cooperative and enthusiastic in his attitude. However, during the past few weeks his enthusiasm seems dampened, he is beginning to make mistakes and at times appears bored. Of the following, the most appropriate action for you to take is to   30.____

A. check with John's co-workers to find out whether they can explain John's change in attitude and work habits
B. wait a few more weeks before taking any action, so that John will have an opportunity to make the needed changes on his own initiative
C. talk to John about the change in his work performance and his decreased enthusiasm

D. change John's assignment since this may be the basic cause of John's change in attitude and performance

31. The supervisor of a clerical unit, on returning from a meeting, finds that one of his subordinates is performing work not assigned by him. The subordinate explains that the group supervisor had come into the office while the unit supervisor was out and directed the employee to work on an urgent assignment. This is the first time the group supervisor had bypassed the unit supervisor. Of the following, the most appropriate action for the unit supervisor to take is to

31.____

A. explain to the group supervisor that bypassing the unit supervisor is an undesirable practice
B. have the subordinate stop work on the assignment until the entire matter can be clarified with the group supervisor
C. raise the matter of bypassing a supervisor at the next staff conference held by the group supervisor
D. forget about the incident

32. Assume that you are an Administrative Assistant in charge of the Mail and Records Unit of Department K. On returning from a meeting, you notice that Jane Smith is not at her regular work location. You learn that another employee, Ruth Reed, had become faint, and that Jane took Ruth outdoors for some fresh air. It is a long-standing rule in your unit that no employee is to leave the building during office hours except on official business or with the unit head's approval. Only a few weeks ago, John Duncan was reprimanded by you for going out at 10:00 a.m. for a cup of coffee. With respect to Jane Smith's violation of this rule, the most appropriate of the following actions for you to take is to

32.____

A. issue a reprimand to Jane Smith, with an explanation that all employees must be treated in exactly the same way
B. tell Jane that you should reprimand her, but you will not do so in this instance
C. overlook this rule violation in view of the extenuating circumstances
D. issue the reprimand with no further explanation, treating her in the same manner that you treated John Duncan

33. Assume that you are an Administrative Assistant recently assigned as supervisor of Department X's Mail and Special Services Unit. In addition to processing your department's mail, your clerical employees are often sent on errands in the city. You have learned that, while on such official errands, these clerks sometimes take care of their own personal matters or those of their co-workers. The previous supervisor had tolerated this practice even though it violated a departmental personnel rule. The most appropriate of the following actions for you to take is to

33.____

A. continue to tolerate this practice so long as it does not interfere with the work of your unit
B. take no action until you have proof that an employee has violated this rule; then give a mild reprimand
C. wait until an employee has committed a gross violation of this rule; then bring him up on charges
D. discuss this rule with your staff and caution them that its violation might necessitate disciplinary action

34. Supervisors who exercise 'close supervision' over their subordinates usually check up on   34.____
their employees frequently, give them frequent instructions and, in general, limit their
freedom to do their work in their own way. Those who exercise 'general supervision' usually set forth the objectives of a job, tell their subordinates what they want accomplished,
fix the limits within which the subordinates can work and let the employees (if they are
capable) decide how the job is to be done. Which one of the following conditions would
contribute LEAST to the success of the general supervision approach in an organizational unit?

   A. Employees in the unit welcome increased responsibilities
   B. Work assignments in the unit are often challenging
   C. Work procedures must conform with those of other units
   D. Staff members support the objectives of the unit

35. Assume that you are an Administrative Assistant assigned as supervisor of the Clerical   35.____
Services Unit of a large agency's Labor Relations Division. A member of your staff
comes to you with a criticism of a policy followed by the Labor Relations Division. You
also have similar views regarding this policy. Of the following, the most appropriate action
for you to take in response to his criticism is to

   A. agree with him, but tell him that nothing can be done about it at your level
   B. suggest to him that it is not wise for him to express criticism of policy
   C. tell the employee that he should direct his criticism to the head of your agency if he
      wants quick action
   D. ask the employee if he has suggestions for revising the policy

---

KEY (CORRECT ANSWERS)

1.	C	11.	A	26.	A
2.	B	12.	C	27.	B
3.	B	13.	B	28.	D
4.	D	14.	D	29.	D
5.	A	15.	B	30.	C
6.	C	16.	C	31.	D
7.	D	17.	C	32.	C
8.	A	18.	D	33.	D
9.	A	19.	A	34.	C
10.	B	20.	B	35.	D
		21.	C		
		22.	C		
		23.	C		
		24.	B		
		25.	A		

TEST 3

DIRECTIONS: Each question or incomplete statement is followed by several suggested answers or completions. Select the one that BEST answers the question or completes the statement. *PRINT THE LETTER OF THE CORRECT ANSWER IN THE SPACE AT THE RIGHT.*

1. At the request of your bureau head you have designed a simple visitor's referral form.   1.____
   The form will be cut from 8-1/2" x 11" stock.
   Which of the following should be the dimensions of the form if you want to be sure that there is no waste of paper?

   A. 2-3/4" x 4-1/4"   B. 3-1/4" x 4-3/4"
   C. 3-3/4" x 4-3/4"   D. 4-1/2" x 5-1/2"

2. An office contains six file cabinets, each containing three drawers. One of your responsi-   2.____
   bilities as a new Administrative Assistant is to see that there is sufficient filing space. At
   the present time, 1/4 of the file space contains forms, 2/9 contains personnel records,
   1/3 contains reports, and 1/7 of the remaining space contains budget records.
   If each drawer may contain more than one type of record, how much drawer space is
   now *empty*?

   A. 0 drawers   B. 13/14 of a drawer
   C. 3 drawers   D. 3-1/2 drawers

3. Assume that there were 21 working days in March. The five clerks in your unit had the   3.____
   following number of absences in March:
   Clerk H - 2 absences
   Clerk J - 1 absence
   Clerk K - 6 absences
   Clerk L - 0 absences
   Clerk M - 10 absences

   To the nearest day, what was the *average* attendance in March for the five clerks in
   your unit?

   A. 4   B. 17   C. 18   D. 21

Questions 4-12

DIRECTIONS: Questions 4 through 12 each consist of a sentence which may or may not be an example of good English usage. Consider grammar, punctuation, spelling, capitalization, verbosity, awkwardness, etc. Examine each sentence, and then choose the correct statement about it from the four choices below it. If the English usage in the sentence is better as given than with any of the changes suggested in options B, C or D, choose option A.

4. The stenographers who are secretaries to commissioners have more varied duties than   4.____
   the stenographic pool.

   A. This is an example of effective writing.
   B. In this sentence there would be a comma after *commissioners* in order to break up
      the sentence into clauses.
   C. In this sentence the words *stenographers in* should be inserted after the word *than*.
   D. In this sentence the word *commissioners* is misspelled.

5. A person who becomes an administrative assistant will be called upon to provide leader-   5.____
   ship, to insure proper quantity and quality of production, and many administrative chores
   must be performed.

   A. This sentence is an example of effective writing.
   B. The sentence should be divided into three separate sentences, each describing a
      duty.
   C. The words *many administrative chores must be performed* should be changed to
      to perform many administrative chores.
   D. The words *to provide leadership* should be changed to *to be a leader.*

6. A complete report has been submitted by our branch office, giving details about this   6.____
   transaction.

   A. This sentence is an example of effective writing.
   B. The phrase *giving details about this transaction* should be placed between the
      words *report* and *has.*
   C. A semi-colon should replace the comma after the word *office* to indicate indepen-
      dent clauses.
   D. A colon should replace the comma after the word *office* since the second clause
      provides further explanation.

7. The report was delayed because of the fact that the writer lost his rough draft two days   7.____
   before the deadline.

   A. This sentence is an example of effective writing.
   B. In this sentence the words *of the fact that* are unnecessary and should be deleted.
   C. In this sentence the words *because of the fact that* should be shortened to *due to.*
   D. In this sentence the word *before* should be replaced by *prior to.*

8. Included in this offer are a six months' guarantee, a complete set of instructions, and one   8.____
   free inspection of the equipment.

   A. This sentence is an example of effective writing.
   B. The word *is* should be substituted for the word *are.*
   C. The word *months* should have been spelled *month's.*
   D. The word *months* should be spelled *months.*

9. Certain employees come to the attention of their employers. Especially those with poor   9.____
   work records and excessive absences.

   A. This sentence is an example of effective writing.
   B. The period after the word *employers* should be changed to a comma, and the first
      letter of the word *Especially* should be changed to a small *e.*
   C. The period after the word *employers* should be changed to a semicolon, and the
      first letter of the word *Especially* should be changed to a small *e.*
   D. The period after the word *employers* should be changed to a colon.

10. The applicant had decided to decline the appointment by the time he was called for the   10.____
    interview.

A. This sentence is an example of effective writing.
B. In this sentence the word *had* should be deleted.
C. In this sentence the phrase *was called* should be replaced by *had been called.*
D. In this sentence the phrase *had decided to decline* should be replaced by *declined.*

11. There are two elevaters, each accommodating ten people.　　　　　　　11.____

A. This sentence is correct.
B. In this sentence the word *elevaters* should be spelled *elevators.*
C. In this sentence the word *each* should be replaced by the word *both.*
D. In this sentence the word *accommodating* should be spelled *accomodating.*

12. With the aid of a special device, it was possible to alter the letterhead on the depart-　12.____
ment's stationary.

A. This sentence is correct.
B. The word *aid* should be spelled *aide.*
C. The word *device* should be spelled *devise.*
D. The word *stationary* should be spelled *stationery.*

13. Examine the following sentence and then choose from the options below the correct　　13.____
word to be inserted in the blank space.
Everybody in both offices _____ involved in the project.

A. are　　　　　　　　　B. feel　　　　　　　　　C. is

Questions 14-18

DIRECTIONS:　Answer questions 14 through 18 SOLELY on the basis of the information in the
following passage.
A new way of looking at job performance promises to be a major advance in measuring
and increasing a person's true effectiveness in business. The fact that individuals differ enor-
mously in their judgment of when a piece of work is actually finished is significant. It is
believed that more than half of all people in the business world are defective in the *sense of
closure,* that is they do not know the proper time to throw the switch that turns off their effort in
one direction and diverts it to a new job. Only a minority of workers at any level have the
required judgment and the feeling of responsibility to work on a job to the point of maximum
effectiveness. The vast majority let go of each task far short of the completion point.
Very often, a defective sense of closure exists in an entire staff. When that occurs, it usually stems from a long-standing laxness on the part of higher management. A low degree of
responsibility has been accepted and it has come to be standard. Combating this requires
implementation of a few basic policies. Firstly, it is important to make each responsibility completely clear and to set certain guideposts as to what constitutes complete performance. Secondly, excuses for delays and failures should not be dealt with too sympathetically, but
interest should be shown in the encountered obstacles. Lastly, a checklist should be used
periodically to determine whether new levels of expectancy and new closure values have
been set.

14. According to the above passage, a *majority of* people in the business world　　14.____

A. do not complete their work on time

B. cannot properly determine when a particular job is completed
C. make lame excuses for not completing a job on time
D. can adequately judge their own effectiveness at work

15. It can be *inferred from* the above passage that when a poor sense of closure is observed   15.____
among all the employees in a unit, the responsibility for raising the performance level
belongs to

A. non-supervisory employees
B. the staff as a whole
C. management
D. first-line supervisors

16. It is *implied by* the above passage that, by the establishment of work guideposts, employ-   16.____
ees may develop a

A. better understanding of expected performances
B. greater interest in their work relationships
C. defective sense of closure
D. lower level of performance

17. It can be inferred from the above passage that an individual's idea of whether a job is fin-   17.____
ished is *most closely* associated with his

A. loyalty to management
B. desire to overcome obstacles
C. ability to recognize his own defects
D. sense of responsibility

18. Of the following, the BEST heading for the above passage is   18.____

A. Management's Role in a Large Bureaucracy
B. Knowing When a Job is Finished
C. The Checklist, a Supervisor's Tool for Effectiveness
D. Supervisory Techniques

Questions 19-25

DIRECTIONS: Answer questions 19 through 25 assuming that you are in charge of public
information for an office which issues reports and answers questions from
other offices and from the public on changes in land use. The charts below
represent comparative land use in four neighborhoods. The area of each
neighborhood is expressed in city blocks. Assume that all city blocks are the
same size.

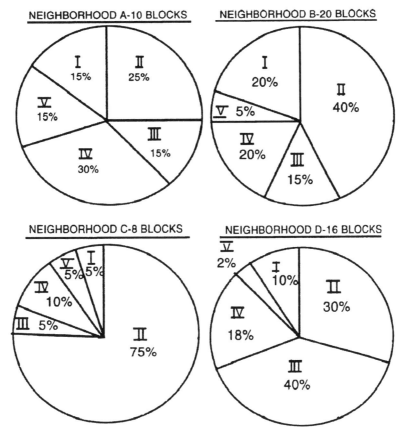

NEIGHBORHOOD A-10 BLOCKS

NEIGHBORHOOD B-20 BLOCKS

NEIGHBORHOOD C-8 BLOCKS

NEIGHBORHOOD D-16 BLOCKS

KEY: I - One- and two-family houses
      II - Apartment buildings
      III - Office buildings
      IV - Retail stores
      V - Factories and warehouses

19. In how many of these neighborhoods does residential use (categories I and II together) account for *more than 50%* of the land use?

    A. 1   B. 2   C. 3   D. 4

19._____

20. How many of the neighborhoods have an area of land occupied by apartment buildings which is *greater than* the area of land occupied by apartment buildings in Neighborhood C?

    A. none   B. 1   C. 2   D. 3

20._____

21. Which neighborhood has the LARGEST land area occupied by factories and warehouses?

    A. A   B. B   C. C   D. D

21._____

22. In which neighborhood is the LARGEST percentage of the land devoted to *both* office buildings and retail stores?

    A. A   B. B   C. C   D. D

22._____

23. What is the difference, to the nearest city block, between the amount of land devoted to one- and two-family houses in Neighborhood A and the amount devoted to similar use in Neighborhood C?   23.____

    A. 1 block   B. 2 blocks   C. 5 blocks   D. 10 blocks

24. Which one of the following types of buildings occupies the same amount of land area in Neighborhood B as the amount of land area occupied by retail stores in Neighborhood A?   24.____

    A. Apartment buildings
    B. Office buildings
    C. Retail stores
    D. Factories and warehouses

25. Based on the information in the charts, which one of the following statements must be TRUE?   25.____

    A. Factories and warehouses are gradually disappearing from all the neighborhoods except Neighborhood A.
    B. Neighborhood B has more land area occupied by retail stores than any of the other neighborhoods.
    C. There are more apartment dwellers living in Neighborhood C than in any of the other neighborhoods.
    D. All four of these neighborhoods are predominantly residential.

KEY (CORRECT ANSWERS)

1.	A		11.	B
2.	C		12.	D
3.	B		13.	C
4.	C		14.	B
5.	C		15.	C
6.	B		16.	A
7.	B		17.	D
8.	A		18.	B
9.	B		19.	B
10.	A		20.	B

21.	A
22.	D
23.	A
24.	B
25.	B

EXAMINATION SECTION
TEST 1

DIRECTIONS: Each question or incomplete statement is followed by several suggested answers or completions. Select the one that BEST answers the question or completes the statement. *PRINT THE LETTER OF THE CORRECT ANSWER IN THE SPACE AT THE RIGHT.*

1. Professional staff members in large organizations are sometimes frustrated by a lack of vital work-related information because of the failure of some middle-management supervisors to pass along unrestricted information from top management.
All of the following are considered to be reasons for such failure to pass along information EXCEPT the supervisors'

    A. belief that information affecting procedures will be ignored unless they are present to supervise their subordinates
    B. fear that specific information will require explanation or justification
    C. inclination to regard the possession of information as a symbol of higher status
    D. tendency to treat information as private property

1.____

2. Increasingly in government, employees' records are being handled by automated data processing systems. However, employees frequently doubt a computer's ability to handle their records properly.
Which of the following is the BEST way for management to overcome such doubts?

    A. Conduct a public relations campaign to explain the savings certain to result from the use of computers
    B. Use automated data processing equipment made by the firm which has the best repair facilities in the industry
    C. Maintain a clerical force to spot check on the accuracy of the computer's record-keeping
    D. Establish automated data processing systems that are objective, impartial, and take into account individual factors as far as possible

2.____

3. Some management experts question the usefulness of offering cash to individual employees for their suggestions.
Which of the following reasons for opposing cash awards is MOST valid?

    A. Emphasis on individual gain deters cooperative effort.
    B. Money spent on evaluating suggestions may outweigh the value of the suggestions.
    C. Awards encourage employees to think about unusual methods of doing work.
    D. Suggestions too technical for ordinary evaluation are usually presented.

3.____

4. The use of outside consultants, rather than regular staff, in studying and recommending improvements in the operations of public agencies has been criticized.
Of the following, the BEST argument in favor of using regular staff is that such staff can better perform the work because they

    A. are more knowledgeable about operations and problems
    B. can more easily be organized into teams consisting of technical specialists
    C. may wish to gain additional professional experience
    D. will provide reports which will be more interesting to the public since they are more experienced

4.____

5. One approach to organizational problem-solving is to have all problem-solving authority   5.___
centralized at the top of the organization.
However, from the viewpoint of providing maximum service to the public, this practice
is UNWISE chiefly because it

   A. reduces the responsibility of the decision-makers
   B. produces delays
   C. reduces internal communications
   D. requires specialists

6. Research has shown that problem-solving efficiency is optimal when the motivation of   6.___
the problem-solver is at a moderate rather than an extreme level.
Of the following, probably the CHIEF reason for this is that the problem-solver

   A. will cause confusion among his subordinates when his motivation is too high
   B. must avoid alternate solutions that tend to lead him up blind alleys
   C. can devote his attention to both the immediate problem as well as to other relevant
      problems in the general area
   D. must feel the need to solve the problem but not so urgently as to direct all his atten-
      tion to the need and none to the means of solution

7. Don't be afraid to make mistakes. Many organizations are paralyzed from the fear of   7.___
making mistakes. As a result, they don't do the things they should; they don't try new and
different ideas.
For the effective supervisor, the MOST valid implication of this statement is that

   A. mistakes should not be encouraged, but there are some unavoidable risks in deci-
      sion-making
   B. mistakes which stem from trying new and different ideas are usually not serious
   C. the possibility of doing things wrong is limited by one's organizational position
   D. the fear of making mistakes will prevent future errors

8. The duties of an employee under your supervision may be either routine, problem-solv-   8.___
ing, innovative, or creative. Which of the following BEST describes duties which are both
innovative and creative?

   A. Checking to make sure that work is done properly
   B. Applying principles in a practical manner
   C. Developing new and better methods of meeting goals
   D. Working at two or more jobs at the same time

9. According to modern management theory, a supervisor who uses as little authority as   9.___
possible and as much as is necessary would be considered to be using a mode that is

   A. autocratic   B. inappropriate
   C. participative   D. directive

10. Delegation involves establishing and maintaining effective working arrangements   10.____
between a supervisor and the persons who report to him.
Delegation is MOST likely to have taken place when the

     A. entire staff openly discusses common problems in order to reach solutions satis-
factory to the supervisor
     B. performance of specified work is entrusted to a capable person, and the expected
results are mutually understood
     C. persons assigned to properly accomplish work are carefully evaluated and given a
chance to explain shortcomings
     D. supervisor provides specific written instructions in order to prevent anxiety on the
part of inexperienced persons

11. Supervisors often are not aware of the effect that their behavior has on their subordi-   11.____
nates.
The one of the following training methods which would be BEST for changing such
supervisory behavior is

     A. essential skills training
     B. off-the-job training
     C. sensitivity training
     D. developmental training

12. A supervisor, in his role as a trainer, may have to decide on the length and frequency of   12.____
training sessions.
When the material to be taught is new, difficult, and lengthy, the trainer should be
guided by the principle that for BEST results in such circumstances, sessions should
be

     A. longer, relatively fewer in number, and held on successive days
     B. shorter, relatively greater in number, and spaced at intervals of several days
     C. of average length, relatively fewer in number, and held at intermittent intervals
     D. of random length and frequency, but spaced at fixed intervals

13. Employee training which is based on realistic simulation, sometimes known as *game*   13.____
play or *role play*, is sometimes preferable to learning from actual experience on the
job. Which of the following is NOT a correct statement concerning the value of simulation
to trainees?

     A. Simulation allows for practice in decision-making without any need for subsequent
discussion.
     B. Simulation is intrinsically motivating because it offers a variety of challenges.
     C. Compared to other, more traditional training techniques, simulation is dynamic.
     D. The simulation environment is nonpunitive as compared to real life.

14. Programmed instruction as a method of training has all of the following advantages   14.____
EXCEPT:

     A. Learning is accomplished in an optimum sequence of distinct steps
     B. Trainees have wide latitude in deciding what is to be learned within each program
     C. The trainee takes an active part in the learning process
     D. The trainee receives immediate knowledge of the results of his response

15. In a work-study program, trainees were required to submit weekly written performance reports in order to insure that work assignments fulfilled the program objectives. Such reports would also assist the administrator of the work-study program PRIMARILY to

    A. eliminate personal counseling for the trainees
    B. identify problems requiring prompt resolution
    C. reduce the amount of clerical work for all concerned
    D. estimate the rate at which budgeted funds are being expended

15.____

16. Which of the following would be MOST useful in order to avoid misunderstanding when preparing correspondence or reports?

    A. Use vocabulary which is at an elementary level
    B. Present each sentence as an individual paragraph
    C. Have someone other than the writer read the material for clarity
    D. Use general words which are open to interpretation

16.____

17. Which of the following supervisory methods would be MOST likely to train subordinates to give a prompt response to memoranda in an organizational setting where most transactions are informal?

    A. Issue a written directive setting forth a schedule of strict deadlines
    B. Let it be known, informally, that those who respond promptly will be rewarded
    C. Follow up each memorandum by a personal inquiry regarding the receiver's reaction to it
    D. Direct subordinates to furnish a precise explanation for ignoring memos

17.____

18. Conferences may fail for a number of reasons. Still, a conference that is an apparent failure may have some benefit.
Which of the following would LEAST likely be such a benefit? It may

    A. increase for most participants their possessiveness about information they have
    B. produce a climate of good will and trust among many of the participants
    C. provide most participants with an opportunity to learn things about the others
    D. serve as a unifying force to keep most of the individuals functioning as a group

18.____

19. Assume that you have been assigned to study and suggest improvements in an operating unit of a delegate agency whose staff has become overwhelmed with problems, has had inadequate resources, and has become accustomed to things getting worse. The staff is indifferent to cooperating with you because they see no hope of improvement. Which of the following steps would be LEAST useful in carrying out your assignment?

    A. Encourage the entire staff to make suggestions to you for change
    B. Inform the staff that management is somewhat dissatisfied with their performance
    C. Let staff know that you are fully aware of their problems and stresses
    D. Look for those problem areas where changes can be made quickly

19.___

20. Which of the following statements about employer-employee relations is NOT considered to be correct by leading managerial experts?   20._____

    A. An important factor in good employer-employee relations is treating workers respectfully.
    B. Employer-employee relations are profoundly influenced by the fundamentals of human nature.
    C. Good employer-employee relations must stem from top management and reach downward.
    D. Employee unions are usually a major obstacle to establishing good employer-employee relations.

21. In connection with labor relations, the term *management rights* GENERALLY refers to   21._____

    A. a managerial review level in a grievance system
    B. statutory prohibitions that bar monetary negotiations
    C. the impact of collective bargaining on government
    D. those subjects which management considers to be non-negotiable

22. Barriers may exist to the utilization of women in higher level positions. Some of these barriers are attitudinal in nature.   22._____
Which of the following is MOST clearly attitudinal in nature?

    A. Advancement opportunities which are vertical in nature and thus require seniority
    B. Experience which is inadequate or irrelevant to the needs of a dynamic and progressive organization
    C. Inadequate means of early identification of employees with talent and potential for advancement
    D. Lack of self-confidence on the part of some women concerning their ability to handle a higher position

23. Because a reader reacts to the meaning he associates with a word, we can never be sure what emotional impact a word may carry or how it may affect our readers.   23._____
The MOST logical implication of this statement for employees who correspond with members of the public is that

    A. a writer should try to select a neutral word that will not bias his writing by its hidden emotional meaning
    B. simple language should be used in writing letters denying requests so that readers are not upset by the denial
    C. every writer should adopt a writing style which he finds natural and easy
    D. whenever there is any doubt as to how a word is defined, the dictionary should be consulted

24. A public information program should be based on clear information about the nature of actual public knowledge and opinion. One way of learning about the views of the public is through the use of questionnaires.   24._____
Which of the following is of LEAST importance in designing a questionnaire?

    A. A respondent should be asked for his name and address.
    B. A respondent should be asked to choose from among several statements the one which expresses his views.
    C. Questions should ask for responses in a form suitable for processing.
    D. Questions should be stated in familiar language.

25. Assume that you have accepted an invitation to speak before an interested group about 25.____
a problem. You have brought with you for distribution a number of booklets and other informational material.
Of the following, which would be the BEST way to use this material?

   A. Distribute it before you begin talking so that the audience may read it at their leisure.
   B. Distribute it during your talk to increase the likelihood that it will be read.
   C. Hold it until the end of your talk, then announce that those who wish may take or examine the material.
   D. Before starting the talk, leave it on a table in the back of the room so that people may pick it up as they enter.

————————

KEY (CORRECT ANSWERS)

1.	A	11.	C
2.	D	12.	B
3.	A	13.	A
4.	A	14.	B
5.	B	15.	B
6.	D	16.	C
7.	A	17.	C
8.	C	18.	A
9.	C	19.	B
10.	B	20.	D

21.	D
22.	D
23.	A
24.	A
25.	C

————————

TEST 2

1. Of the following, the FIRST step in planning an operation is to   1._____

   A. obtain relevant information
   B. identify the goal to be achieved
   C. consider possible alternatives
   D. make necessary assignments

2. A supervisor who is extremely busy performing routine tasks is MOST likely making   2._____
   INCORRECT use of what basic principle of supervision?

   A. Homogeneous Assignment   B. Span of Control
   C. Work Distribution   D. Delegation of Authority

3. Controls help supervisors to obtain information from which they can determine whether   3._____
   their staffs are achieving planned goals.
   Which one of the following would be LEAST useful as a control device?

   A. Employee diaries   B. Organization charts
   C. Periodic inspections   D. Progress charts

4. A certain employee has difficulty in effectively performing a particular portion of his rou-   4._____
   tine assignments, but his overall productivity is average.
   As the direct supervisor of this individual, your BEST course of action would be to

   A. attempt to develop the man's capacity to execute the problematical facets of his
      assignments
   B. diversify the employee's work assignments in order to build up his confidence
   C. reassign the man to less difficult tasks
   D. request in a private conversation that the employee improve his work output

5. A supervisor who uses persuasion as a means of supervising a unit would GENERALLY   5._____
   also use which of the following practices to supervise his unit?

   A. Supervise and control the staff with an authoritative attitude to indicate that he is a
      take-charge individual
   B. Make significant changes in the organizational operations so as to improve job effi-
      ciency
   C. Remove major communication barriers between himself, subordinates, and man-
      agement
   D. Supervise everyday operations while being mindful of the problems of his subordi-
      nates

6. Whenever a supervisor in charge of a unit delegates a routine task to a capable subordi-   6._____
   nate, he tells him exactly how to do it.
   This practice is GENERALLY

   A. *desirable,* chiefly because good supervisors should be aware of the traits of their
      subordinates and delegate responsibilities to them accordingly
   B. *undesirable,* chiefly because only non-routine tasks should be delegated
   C. *desirable,* chiefly because a supervisor should frequently test the willingness of his
      subordinates to perform ordinary tasks
   D. *undesirable,* chiefly because a capable subordinate should usually be allowed to
      exercise his own discretion in doing a routine job

7. The one of the following activities through which a supervisor BEST demonstrates leadership ability is by 　　　　7.___

    A. arranging periodic staff meetings in order to keep his subordinates informed about professional developments in the field
    B. frequently issuing definite orders and directives which will lessen the need for subordinates to make decisions in handling any tasks assigned to them
    C. devoting the major part of his time to supervising subordinates so as to stimulate continuous improvement
    D. setting aside time for self-development and research so as to improve the skills, techniques, and procedures of his unit

8. The following three statements relate to the supervision of employees: 　　　　8.___
    I. The assignment of difficult tasks that offer a challenge is more conducive to good morale than the assignment of easy tasks
    II. The same general principles of supervision that apply to men are equally applicable to women
    III. The best retraining program should cover all phases of an employee's work in a general manner

Which of the following choices list ALL of the above statements that are generally correct?

    A. II, III   B. I
    C. I, II   D. I, II, III

9. Which of the following examples BEST illustrates the application of the *exception principle* as a supervisory technique? 　　　　9.___

    A. A complex job is divided among several employees who work simultaneously to complete the whole job in a shorter time.
    B. An employee is required to complete any task delegated to him to such an extent that nothing is left for the superior who delegated the task except to approve it.
    C. A superior delegates responsibility to a subordinate but retains authority to make the final decisions.
    D. A superior delegates all work possible to his subordinates and retains that which requires his personal attention or performance.

10. Assume that you are a supervisor. Your immediate superior frequently gives orders to your subordinates without your knowledge. 　　　　10.___
Of the following, the MOST direct and effective way for you to handle this problem is to

    A. tell your subordinates to take orders only from you
    B. submit a report to higher authority in which you cite specific instances
    C. discuss it with your immediate superior
    D. find out to what extent your authority and prestige as a supervisor have been affected

11. In an agency which has as its primary purpose the protection of the public against fraudulent business practices, which of the following would GENERALLY be considered an *auxiliary* or *staff* rather than a *line* function? 　　　　11.___

    A. Interviewing victims of frauds and advising them about their legal remedies
    B. Daily activities directed toward prevention of fraudulent business practices
    C. Keeping records and statistics about business violations reported and corrected
    D. Follow-up inspections by investigators after corrective action has been taken

12. A supervisor can MOST effectively reduce the spread of false rumors through the *grapevine* by   12._____

    A. identifying and disciplining any subordinate responsible for initiating such rumors
    B. keeping his subordinates informed as much as possible about matters affecting them
    C. denying false rumors which might tend to lower staff morale and productivity
    D. making sure confidential matters are kept secure from access by unauthorized employees

13. A supervisor has tried to learn about the background, education, and family relationships of his subordinates through observation, personal contact, and inspection of their personnel records.
These supervisory actions are GENERALLY   13._____

    A. *inadvisable,* chiefly because they may lead to charges of favoritism
    B. *advisable,* chiefly because they may make him more popular with his subordinates
    C. *inadvisable,* chiefly because his efforts may be regarded as an invasion of privacy
    D. *advisable,* chiefly because the information may enable him to develop better understanding of each of his subordinates

14. In an emergency situation, when action must be taken immediately, it is BEST for the supervisor to give orders in the form of   14._____

    A. direct commands which are brief and precise
    B. requests, so that his subordinates will not become alarmed
    C. suggestions which offer alternative courses of action
    D. implied directives, so that his subordinates may use their judgment in carrying them out

15. When demonstrating a new and complex procedure to a group of subordinates, it is ESSENTIAL that a supervisor   15._____

    A. go slowly and repeat the steps involved at least once
    B. show the employees common errors and the consequences of such errors
    C. go through the process at the usual speed so that the employees can see the rate at which they should work
    D. distribute summaries of the procedure during the demonstration and instruct his subordinates to refer to them afterwards

16. After a procedures manual has been written and distributed,   16._____

    A. continuous maintenance work is necessary to keep the manual current
    B. it is best to issue new manuals rather than make changes in the original manual
    C. no changes should be necessary
    D. only major changes should be considered

17. Of the following, the MOST important criterion of effective report writing is   17.____

    A. eloquence of writing style
    B. the use of technical language
    C. to be brief and to the point
    D. to cover all details

18. The use of electronic data processing   18.____

    A. has proven unsuccessful in most organizations
    B. has unquestionable advantages for all organizations
    C. is unnecessary in most organizations
    D. should be decided upon only after careful feasibility studies by individual organizations

19. The PRIMARY purpose of work measurement is to   19.____

    A. design and install a wage incentive program
    B. determine who should be promoted
    C. establish a yardstick to determine extent of progress
    D. set up a spirit of competition among employees

20. The action which is MOST effective in gaining acceptance of a study by the agency which is being studied is   20.____

    A. a directive from the agency head to install a study based on recommendations included in a report
    B. a lecture-type presentation following approval of the procedures
    C. a written procedure in narrative form covering the proposed system with visual presentations and discussions
    D. procedural charts showing the *before* situation, forms, steps, etc., to the employees affected

21. Which organization principle is MOST closely related to procedural analysis and improvement?   21.____

    A. Duplication, overlapping, and conflict should be eliminated.
    B. Managerial authority should be clearly defined.
    C. The objectives of the organization should be clearly defined.
    D. Top management should be freed of burdensome detail.

22. Which one of the following is the MAJOR objective of operational audits?   22.____

    A. Detecting fraud
    B. Determining organization problems
    C. Determining the number of personnel needed
    D. Recommending opportunities for improving operating and management practices

23. Of the following, the formalization of organization structure is BEST achieved by   23.____

    A. a narrative description of the plan of organization
    B. functional charts
    C. job descriptions together with organization charts
    D. multi-flow charts

24. Budget planning is MOST useful when it achieves   24.____

    A. cost control   B. forecast of receipts
    C. performance review   D. personnel reduction

25. GENERALLY, in applying the principle of delegation in dealing with subordinates, a   25.____
supervisor

    A. allows his subordinates to set up work goals and to fix the limits within which they
        can work
    B. allows his subordinates to set up work goals and then gives detailed orders as to
        how they are to be achieved
    C. makes relatively few decisions by himself and frames his orders in broad, general
        terms
    D. provides externalized motivation for his subordinates

KEY (CORRECT ANSWERS)

1.	B		11.	C
2.	D		12.	B
3.	B		13.	D
4.	A		14.	A
5.	D		15.	A
6.	D		16.	A
7.	C		17.	C
8.	C		18.	D
9.	D		19.	C
10.	C		20.	C

21.	A
22.	D
23.	C
24.	A
25.	C

EXAMINATION SECTION
TEST 1

DIRECTIONS: Each question or incomplete statement is followed by several suggested answers or completions. Select the one that BEST answers the question or completes the statement. *PRINT THE LETTER OF THE CORRECT ANSWER IN THE SPACE AT THE RIGHT.*

1. At times there may be a conflict between employees' needs and agency goals. A supervisor's MAIN role in motivating employees in such circumstances is to try to

    A. develop good work habits among the employees whom he supervises
    B. emphasize the importance of material rewards such as merit increases
    C. keep careful records of employees' performance for possible disciplinary action
    D. reconcile employees' objectives with those of the public agency

1._____

2. Organizations cannot function effectively without policies. However, when an organization imposes excessively detailed policy restrictions, it is MOST likely to lead to

    A. conflicts among individual employees
    B. a lack of adequate supervision
    C. a reduction of employee initiative
    D. a reliance on punitive discipline

2._____

3. The PRIMARY responsibility for establishing good employee relations in the public service USUALLY rests with

    A. employees   B. management
    C. civil service organizations   D. employee organizations

3._____

4. At times, certain off-the-job conduct of public employees may be of concern to management. This concern stems from the fact that

    A. agency programs could be harmed by adverse publicity if employees' conduct is considered detrimental by the public
    B. fairness to all concerned is usually the major consideration in disciplinary cases
    C. public employees must meet higher standards than employees working in private industry
    D. public employees have high ethical standards and may participate in social action programs

4._____

5. At one time or another, most employees ask for, or expect, special treatment. For a supervisor faced with this problem, the one of the following which is the MOST valid guideline is:

    A. According to the rules, a supervisor must give identical treatment to all his subordinates, regardless of the circumstances.
    B. Although all employees have equal rights, it is sometimes necessary to give an employee special treatment to meet an individual need.
    C. It would damage morale if any employee were to receive special treatment, regardless of circumstances.
    D. Since each employee has different needs, there is little reason to maintain general rules.

5._____

6. Mental health problems exist in many parts of our society and may also be found in the work setting. The BASIC role of the supervisor in relation to the mental health problems of his subordinates is to

    A. restrict himself solely to the taking of disciplinary measures, if warranted, and follow up carefully
    B. avoid involvement in personal matters
    C. identify mental health problems as early as possible
    D. resolve mental health problems through personal counseling

6.____

7. Supervisory expectation of high levels of employee performance, where such performance is possible, is MOST likely to lead to employees'

    A. expecting frequent praise and encouragement
    B. gaining a greater sense of satisfaction
    C. needing less detailed instructions then previously
    D. reducing their quantitative output

7.____

8. In public agencies, as elsewhere, supervisors sometimes compete with one another to increase their units' productivity. Of the following, the MAJOR disadvantage of such competition, from the general viewpoint of providing good public service, is that

    A. while individual employee effort will increase, unit productivity will decrease
    B. employees will be discouraged from sincere interest in their work
    C. the supervisors' competition may hinder the achievement of agency goals
    D. total payroll costs will increase as the activities of each unit increase

8.____

9. If employees are motivated primarily by material compensation, the amount of effort an individual employee will put into performing his work effectively will depend MAINLY upon how he perceives

    A. cooperation to be tied to successful effort
    B. the association between good work and increased compensation
    C. the public status of his particular position
    D. the supervisor's behavior in work situations

9.___

10. Cash awards to individual employees are sometimes used to encourage useful suggestions. However, some management experts believe that awards should involve some form of employee recognition other than cash. Which of the following reasons BEST supports opposition to using cash as a reward for worthwhile suggestions?

    A. Cash awards cause employees to expend excessive time in making suggestions.
    B. Taxpayer opposition to cash awards has increased following generous salary increases for public employees in recent years.
    C. Public funds expended on awards lead to a poor image of public employees.
    D. The use of cash awards raises the problem of deciding tne monetary value of suggestions.

10.__

11. The BEST general rule for a supervisor to follow in giving praise and criticism is to

    A. criticize and praise publicly
    B. criticize publicly and praise privately
    C. praise and criticize privately
    D. praise publicly and criticize privately

11.__

12. An important step in designing an error-control policy is to determine the maximum number of errors that can be considered acceptable for the entire organization. Of the following, the MOST important factor in making such a decision is the   12.____

    A. number of clerical staff available to check for errors
    B. frequency of errors by supervisors
    C. human and material costs of errors
    D. number of errors that will become known to the public

13. When a supervisor tries to correct a situation where errors have been widespread, he should concentrate his efforts, and those of the employees involved, on   13.____

    A. avoiding future mistakes   B. fixing appropriate blame
    C. preparing a written report   D. determining fair penalties

14. When delegating work to a subordinate, a supervisor should ALWAYS tell the subordinate   14.____

    A. each step in the procedure for doing the work
    B. how much time to expend
    C. what is to be accomplished
    D. whether reports are necessary

15. The responsibilities of all employees should be clearly defined and understood. In addition, in order for employees to successfully fulfill their responsibilities, they should also GENERALLY be given   15.____

    A. written directives   B. close supervision
    C. corresponding authority   D. daily instructions

16. The one of the following types of training in which positive transfer of training to the actual work situation is MOST likely to take place is   16.____

    A. conference training   B. demonstration training
    C. classroom training   D. on-the-job training

17. The type of training or instruction in which the subject matter is presented in small units called frames is known as   17.____

    A. programmed instruction   B. reinforcement
    C. remediation   D. skills training

18. In order to bring about maximum learning in a training situation, a supervisor acting as a trainer should attempt to create a setting in which   18.____

    A. all trainees experience a large amount of failure as an incentive
    B. all trainees experience a small amount of failure as an incentive
    C. each trainee experiences approximately the same amounts of success and failure
    D. each trainee experiences as much success and as little failure as possible

19. Assume that, in a training course given by an agency, the instructor conducts a brief quiz, on paper, toward the close of each session. From the point of view of maximizing learning, it would be BEST for the instructor to

    A. wait until the last session to provide the correct answers
    B. give the correct answers aloud immediately after each quiz
    C. permit trainees to take the questions home with them so that they can look up the answers
    D. wait until the next session to provide the correct answers

19.____

20. A supervisor, in the course of evaluating employees, should ALWAYS determine whether

    A. employees realize that their work is under scrutiny
    B. the ratings will be included in permanent records
    C. employees meet standards of performance
    D. his statements on the rating form are similar to those made by the previous supervisor

20.____

21. All of the following are legitimate objectives of employee performance reporting systems EXCEPT

    A. serving as a check on personnel policies such as job qualification requirements and placement techniques
    B. determining who is the least efficient worker among a large number of employees
    C. improving employee performance by identifying strong and weak points in individual performance
    D. developing standards of satisfactory performance

21.____

22. Studies of existing employee performance evaluation schemes have revealed a common tendency to construct guides in order to measure _inferred_ traits. Of the following, the BEST example of an inferred trait is

    A. appearance   B. loyalty   C. accuracy   D. promptness

22.____

23. Which of the following is MOST likely to be a positive influence in promoting common agreement at a staff conference?

    A. A mature, tolerant group of participants
    B. A strong chairman with firm opinions
    C. The normal differences of human personalities
    D. The urge to forcefully support one's views

23.____

24. Before holding a problem-solving conference, the conference leader sent to each invitee an announcement on which he listed the names of all invitees. His action in listing the names was

    A. _wise,_ mainly because all invitees will know who has been invited, and can, if necessary, plan a proper approach
    B. _unwise,_ mainly because certain invitees could form factions prior to the conference
    C. _unwise,_ mainly because invitees might come to the conference in a belligerent mood if they had had interpersonal conflicts with other invitees
    D. _wise,_ mainly because invitees who are antagonistic to each other could decide not to attend

24.____

25. Methods analysis is a detailed study of existing or proposed work methods for the pur-   25.____
    pose of improving agency operations. Of the following, it is MOST accurate to say that
    this type of study

    A. can sometimes be made informally by the experienced supervisor who can identify
       problems and suggest solutions
    B. is not suitable for studying the operations of a public agency
    C. will be successfully accomplished only if an outside organization reviews agency
       operations
    D. usually costs more to complete than is justified by the potential economies to be
       realized

KEY (CORRECT ANSWERS)

1.	D		11.	D
2.	C		12.	C
3.	B		13.	A
4.	A		14.	C
5.	B		15.	C
6.	C		16.	D
7.	B		17.	A
8.	C		18.	D
9.	B		19.	B
10.	D		20.	C

21.	B
22.	B
23.	A
24.	A
25.	A

TEST 2

DIRECTIONS: Each question or incomplete statement is followed by several suggested answers or completions. Select the one that BEST answers the question or completes the statement. *PRINT THE LETTER OF THE CORRECT ANSWER IN THE SPACE AT THE RIGHT.*

1. Present-day managerial practices advocate that adequate hierarchical levels of commu-   1.___
   nication be maintained among all levels of management. Of the following, the BEST way
   to accomplish this is with

   A. interdepartmental memoranda only
   B. interdepartmental memoranda only
   C. periodic staff meetings, interdepartmental and interdepartmental memoranda
   D. interdepartmental and interdepartmental memoranda

2. It is generally agreed upon that it is important to have effective communications in the   2.___
   unit so that everyone knows exactly what is expected of him. Of the following, the communications system which can assist in fulfilling this objective BEST is one which consists of

   A. written policies and procedures for administrative functions and verbal policies and
      procedures for professional functions
   B. written policies and procedures for professional and administrative functions
   C. verbal policies and procedures for professional and administrative functions
   D. verbal policies and procedures for professional functions

3. If a department manager wishes to build an effective department, he MOST generally   3.___
   must

   A. be able to hire and fire as he feels necessary
   B. consider the total aspects of his job, his influence and the effects of his decisions
   C. have access to reasonable amounts of personnel and money with which to build
      his programs
   D. attend as many professional conferences as possible so that he can keep up-to-
      date with all the latest advances in the field

4. Of the following, the factor which generally contributes MOST effectively to the perfor-   4.___
   mance of the unit is that the supervisor

   A. personally inspect the work of all employees
   B. fill orders at a faster rate than his subordinates
   C. have an exact knowledge of theory
   D. implement a program of professional development for his staff

5. Administrative policies relate MOST closely to   5.___

   A. control of commodities and personnel
   B. general policies emanating from the central office
   C. fiscal management of the department only
   D. handling and dispensing of funds

6. Part of being a good supervisor is to be able to develop an attitude towards employees   6._____
which will motivate them to do their best on the job. The GOOD supervisor, therefore,
should

    A. take an interest in subordinates, but not develop an all-consuming attitude in this
area
    B. remain in an aloof position when dealing with employees
    C. be as close to subordinates as possible on the job
    D. take a complete interest in all the activities of subordinates, both on and off the job

7. The practice of a supervisor assigning an experienced employee to train new employees   7._____
instead of training them himself, is, GENERALLY, considered

    A. *undesirable*; the more experienced employee will resent being taken away from his
regular job
    B. *desirable*; the supervisor can then devote more time to his regular duties
    C. *undesirable*; the more experienced employee is not working at the proper level to
train new employees
    D. *desirable*; the more experienced employee is probably a better trainer than the
supervisor

8. It is generally agreed that on-the-job training is MOST effective when new employees are   8._____

    A. provided with study manuals, standard operating procedures and other written
materials to be studied for at least two weeks before the employees attempt to do
the job
    B. shown how to do the job in detail, and then instructed to do the work under close
supervision
    C. trained by an experienced worker for at least a week to make certain that the
employees can do the job
    D. given work immediately which is checked at the end of each day

9. Employees sometimes form small informal groups, commonly called cliques. With regard   9._____
to the effect of such groups on processing of the workload, the attitude a supervisor
should take towards these cliques is that of

    A. *acceptance*, since they take the employees' minds off their work without wasting
too much time
    B. *rejection*, since those workers inside the clique tend to do less work than the out-
siders
    C. *acceptance*, since the supervisor is usually included in the clique
    D. *rejection*, since they are usually disliked by higher management

10. Of the following, the BEST statement regarding rules and regulations in a unit is that they   10._____

    A. are "necessary evils" to be tolerated by those at and above the first supervisory
level only
    B. are stated in broad, indefinite terms so as to allow maximum amount of leeway in
complying with them
    C. must be understood by all employees in the unit
    D. are primarily for management's needs since insurance regulations mandate them

11. It is sometimes considered desirable for a supervisor to survey the opinions of his employees before taking action on decisions affecting them. Of the following, the greatest DISADVANTAGE of following this approach is that the employees might

    A. use this opportunity to complain rather than to make constructive suggestions
    B. lose respect for their supervisor whom they feel cannot make his own decisions
    C. regard this as an attempt by the supervisor to get ideas for which he can later claim credit
    D. be resentful if their suggestions are not adopted

11.___

12. Of the following, the MOST important reason for keeping statements of duties of employees up-to-date is to

    A. serve as a basis of information for other governmental jurisdictions
    B. enable the department of personnel to develop job-related examinations
    C. differentiate between levels within the occupational groups
    D. enable each employee to know what his duties are

12.___

13. Of the following, the BEST way to evaluate the progress of a new subordinate is to

    A. compare the output of the new employee from week to week as to quantity and quality
    B. obtain the opinions of the new employee's co-workers
    C. test the new employee periodically to see how much he has learned
    D. hold frequent discussions with the employee focusing on his work

13.___

14. Of the following, a supervisor is LEAST likely to contribute to good morale in the unit if he

    A. encourages employees to increase their knowledge and proficiency in their work on their own time
    B. reprimands subordinates uniformly when infractions are committed
    C. refuses to accept explanations for mistakes regardless of who has made them or how serious they are
    D. compliments subordinates for superior work performance in the presence of their peers

14.___

15. The practice of promoting supervisors from within a given unit only, rather than from within the entire agency, may BEST be described as

    A. *desirable*, because the type of work in each unit generally is substantially different from all other units
    B. *undesirable*, since it will severely reduce the number of eligibles from which to select a supervisor
    C. *desirable*, since it enables each employee to know in advance the precise extent of promotion opportunities in his unit
    D. *undesirable*, because it creates numerous administrative and budgetary difficulties

15.___

16. Of the following, the BEST way for a supervisor to make assignments GENERALLY is to

    A. give the easier assignments to employees with greater seniority
    B. give the difficult assignments to the employees with greater seniority
    C. make assignments according to the ability of each employee
    D. rotate the assignments among the employees

16.___

17. Assume that a supervisor makes a proposal through appropriate channels which would delegate final authority and responsibility to a subordinate employee for a major control function within the agency. According to current management theory, this proposal should be

    A. *adopted,* since this would enable the supervisor to devote more time to non-routine tasks
    B. *rejected,* since final responsibility for this high-level assignment may not properly be delegated to a subordinate employee
    C. *adopted,* since the assignment of increased responsibility to subordinate employees is a vital part of their development and training
    D. *rejected,* since the morale of the subordinate employees not selected for this assignment would be adversely affected

17.____

18. If it becomes necessary for a supervisor to improve the performance of a subordinate to assure the achievement of results according to plans, the BEST course of action, of the following, generally, would be to

    A. emphasize the subordinate's strengths and try to motivate the employee to improve on those factors
    B. emphasize the subordinate's weak areas of performance and try to bring them up to an acceptable standard
    C. issue a memorandum to all employees warning that if performance does not improve, disciplinary measures will be taken
    D. transfer the subordinate to another section engaged in different work

18.____

19. A supervisor who specifies each phase of a job in detail, supervises closely and permits very little discretion in performance of tasks, GENERALLY

    A. provides motivation for his staff to produce more work
    B. finds that his subordinates make fewer mistakes than those with minimal supervision
    C. finds that his subordinates have little or no incentive to work any harder than necessary
    D. provides superior training opportunities for his employees

19.____

20. Assume that you supervise two employees who do not get along well with each other. Their relationship has been continuously deteriorating. You decide to take steps to solve this problem by first determining the reason for their inability to get along well with each other. This course of action is

    A. *desirable,* because their work is probably adversely affected by their differences
    B. *undesirable,* because your inquiries might be is-interpreted by the employees and cause resentment
    C. *desirable,* because you could then learn who is at fault for causing the deteriorating relationship and take appropriate disciplinary measures
    D. *undesirable,* because it is best to let them work their differences out between themselves

20.____

21. Routine procedures that have worked well in the past should be reviewed periodically by a supervisor MAINLY because   21.____

    A. they may have become outdated or in need of revision
    B. employees may dislike the procedures even though they have proven successful in the past
    C. these reviews are the main part of a supervisor's job
    D. this practice serves to give the supervisor an idea of how productive his subordinates are

22. Assume that an employee tells his supervisor about a grievance he has against a co-worker. The supervisor assures the employee that he will immediately take action to eliminate the grievance. The supervisor's attitude should be considered   22.____

    A. *correct*; because a good supervisor is one who can come to a quick decision
    B. *incorrect*; because the supervisor should have told the employee that he will investigate the grievance and then determine a future course of action
    C. *correct*; because the employee's morale will be higher, resulting in greater productivity
    D. *incorrect*; because the supervisor should remain uninvolved and let the employees settle grievances between themselves

23. If an employee's work output is low and of poor quality due to faulty work habits, the MOST constructive of the following ways for a supervisor to correct this situation, GENERALLY, is to   23.____

    A. discipline the employee
    B. transfer the employee to another unit
    C. provide additional training
    D. check the employee's work continuously

24. Assume that it becomes necessary for a supervisor to ask his staff to work overtime. Which one of the following techniques is MOST likely to win their willing cooperation to do this?   24.____

    A. Point out that this is part of their job specification entitled "performs related work"
    B. Explain the reason it is necessary for the employees to work overtime
    C. Promise the employees special consideration regarding future leave matters
    D. Warn that if the employees do not work overtime, they will face possible disciplinary action

25. If an employee's work performance has recently fallen below established minimum standards for quality and quantity, the threat of demotion or other disciplinary measures as an attempt to improve this employee's performance would probably be the MOST acceptable and effective course of action   25.____

    A. *only* after other more constructive measures have failed
    B. *if* applied uniformly to all employees as soon as performance falls below standard
    C. *only* if the employee understands that the threat will not actually be carried out
    D. *if* the employee is promised that, as soon as his work performance improves, he will be reinstated to his previous status

KEY (CORRECT ANSWERS)

1.	C	11.	D
2.	B	12.	D
3.	B	13.	A
4.	D	14.	C
5.	A	15.	B
6.	A	16.	C
7.	B	17.	B
8.	B	18.	B
9.	A	19.	C
10.	C	20.	A

21.	A
22.	B
23.	C
24.	B
25.	A

TEST 3

DIRECTIONS: Each question or incomplete statement is followed by several suggested answers or completions. Select the one that BEST answers the question or completes the statement. *PRINT THE LETTER OF THE CORRECT ANSWER IN THE SPACE AT THE RIGHT.*

1. If, as a supervisor, it becomes necessary for you to assign an employee to supervise your unit during your vacation, it would generally be BEST to select the employee who

    A. is the best technician on the staff
    B. can get the work out smoothly, without friction
    C. has the most seniority
    D. is the most popular with the group

1.____

2. Assume that, as a supervisor, your own work has accumulated to the point where you decide that it is desirable for you to delegate in order to meet your deadlines. The one of the following tasks which would be MOST appropriate to delegate to a subordinate is

    A. checking the work of the employees for accuracy
    B. attending a staff conference at which implementation of a new departmental policy will be discussed
    C. preparing a final report including a recommendation on purchase of expensive new laboratory equipment
    D. preparing final budget estimates for next year's budget

2.____

3. Of the following actions, the one LEAST appropriate for you to take during an *initial* interview with a new employee is to

    A. find out about the experience and education of the new employee
    B. attempt to determine for what job in your unit the employee would best be suited
    C. tell the employee about his duties and responsibilities
    D. ascertain whether the employee will make good promotion material

3.____

4. If it becomes necessary to reprimand a subordinate employee, the BEST of the following ways to do this is to

    A. ask the employee to stay after working hours and then reprimand him
    B. reprimand the employee immediately after the infraction has been committed
    C. take the employee aside and speak to him privately during regular working hours
    D. write a short memo to the employee warning that strict adherence to departmental policy and procedures is required of all employees

4.____

5. If you, as a supervisor, believe that one of your subordinate employees has a serious problem, such as alcoholism or an emotional disturbance, which is adversely affecting his work, the BEST way to handle this situation *initially* would be to

    A. urge him to seek proper professional help before he is dismissed from his job
    B. ignore it and let the employee work out the problem himself
    C. suggest that the employee take an extended leave of absence until he can again function effectively
    D. frankly tell the employee that unless his work improves, you will take disciplinary measures against him

5.____

6. Of the following, the BEST way to develop a subordinate's potential is to　　　6._____

    A. give him a fair chance to learn by doing
    B. assign him more than his share of work
    C. criticize only his work
    D. urge him to do his work rapidly

7. During a survey, an employee from another agency asks you to assist him on a job which　　　7._____
would require a full day of your time. Of the following, the BEST immediate action for you
to take is to

    A. refuse to assist him
    B. ask for compensation before doing it
    C. assist him promptly
    D. notify his department head

8. Of the following, the BEST way to handle an overly talkative subordinate is to　　　8._____

    A. have your superior talk to him about it
    B. have a subordinate talk to him about it
    C. talk to him about it in a group conference
    D. talk to him about it in private

9. While you are making a survey, a citizen questions you about the work you are doing. Of　　　9._____
the following, the BEST thing to do is to

    A. answer the questions tactfully
    B. refuse to answer any questions
    C. advise him to write a letter to the main office
    D. answer the questions in double-talk

10. Respect for a supervisor is MOST likely to increase if he is　　　10._____

    A. morose   B. sporadic   C. vindictive   D. zealous

11. A subordinate who continuously bypasses his immediate supervisor for technical infor-　　　11._____
mation should be

    A. reprimanded by his immediate supervisor
    B. ignored by his immediate supervisor
    C. given more difficult work to do
    D. given less difficult work to do

12. Complicated instructions should NOT be written　　　12._____

    A. accurately   B. lucidly   C. factually   D. verbosely

13. Of the following, the MOST important reason for checking a report is to　　　13._____

    A. check accuracy   B. eliminate unnecessary sections
    C. catch mistakes   D. check for delineation

14. Two subordinates under your supervision dislike each other to the extent that production   14.____
is cut down. Your BEST action as a supervisor is to

    A. ignore the matter and hope for the best
    B. transfer the more aggressive man
    C. cut down on the work load
    D. talk to them together about the matter

15. One of the following characteristics which a supervisor should NOT display while explain-   15.____
ing a job to a subordinate is

    A. enthusiasm   B. confidence
    C. apathy   D. determination

16. Of the following, for BEST production of work, it should be assigned according to a per-   16.____
son's

    A. attitude toward the work   B. ability to do the work
    C. salary   D. seniority

17. You receive an anonymous written complaint from a citizen about a subordinate who   17.____
used abusive language. Of the following, your BEST course of action is to

    A. ignore the letter
    B. report it to your supervisor
    C. discuss the complaint with the subordinate privately
    D. keep the subordinate in the office

18. A supervisor should recognize that the way to get the BEST results from his instructions   18.____
and assignments to the staff is to use

    A. a suggestive approach after he has decided exactly what is to be done and how
    B. the willing and cooperative staff members and avoid the hard-to-handle people
    C. care to select the persons most capable of carrying out the assignments
    D. an authoritative, non-nonsense tone when issuing instructions or giving assign-
       ments

19. As the supervisor of a unit, you find that you are spending too much of your time on rou-   19.___
tine tasks and not enough on coordinating the work of the staff or preparing necessary
reports. Of the following, it would be MOST advisable for you to

    A. discard a great portion of the routine jobs done in the unit
    B. give some of the routine jobs to other members of the staff
    C. postpone the routine jobs and concentrate on coordinating the work of the staff
    D. delegate the job of coordinating the work to the most capable member of the staff

20. At times a supervisor may be called upon to train new employees. Suppose that you are   20.___
giving such training in several sessions to be held on different days. During the first session, a trainee interrupts everal times to ask questions at key points in your discussion.
Of the following, the BEST way to handle this trainee is to

    A. advise him to pay closer attention so he can avoid asking too many questions
    B. tell him to listen without interrupting and he'll hear his questions answered

C. answer his questions to show him that you know your field, but make a mental note that this trainee is a troublemaker
D. answer each question fully and make certain he understands the answers

21. Employee errors can be reduced to a minimum by effective supervision and by training. Which of the following approaches used by a supervisor would usually be MOST effective in handling an employee who has made an avoidable and serious error for the first time?   21._____

    A. Tell the worker how other employees avoid making errors
    B. Analyze with the employee the situation leading to the error and then take whatever administrative or training steps are needed to avoid such errors
    C. Use this error as the basis for a staff meeting at which the employee's error is disclosed and discussed in an effort to improve the performance
    D. Urge the employee to modify his behavior in light of his mistake

22. Suppose that a particular staff member, formerly one of your most regular workers, has recently fallen into the habit of arriving a bit late to work several times a week. You feel that such a habit can grow consistently worse and spread to other staff members unless it is checked. Of the following, the BEST action for you to take, as the supervisor in charge of the unit, is to   22._____

    A. go immediately to your own supervisor, present the facts, and have this employee disciplined
    B. speak privately to this tardy employee, advise him of the need to improve his punctuality, and inform him that he'll be disciplined if late again
    C. talk to the co-worker with whom this late employee is most friendly and ask the friend to help him solve his tardiness problem
    D. speak privately with this employee, and try to discover and deal with the reasons for the latenesses

23. A supervisor may make an assignment in the form of a request, a command, or a call for volunteers. It is LEAST desirable to make an assignment in the form of a request when   23._____

    A. an employee does not like the particular kind of assignment to be given
    B. the assignment requires working past the regular closing day
    C. an emergency has come up
    D. the assignment is not particularly pleasant for anybody

24. When you give a certain task that you normally perform yourself to one of your employees, it is MOST important that you   24._____

    A. lead the employee to believe that he has been chosen above others to perform this job
    B. describe the job as important even though it is merely a routine task
    C. explain the job that needs to be accomplished, but always let the employee decide how to do it
    D. tell the employee why you are delegating the job to him and explain exactly what he is to do

25. A supervisor when instructing new trainees in the routine of his unit should include a description of the department's overall objectives and programs in order to   25.___

    A. insure that individual work assignments will be completed satisfactorily
    B. create a favorable impression of his supervisory capabilities
    C. develop a better understanding of the purposes behind work assignments
    D. produce an immediate feeling of group cooperation

KEY (CORRECT ANSWERS)

1.	B	11.	A
2.	A	12.	D
3.	D	13.	C
4.	C	14.	D
5.	A	15.	C
6.	A	16.	B
7.	A	17.	C
8.	D	18.	C
9.	A	19.	B
10.	D	20.	D

21.	B
22.	D
23.	A
24.	D
25.	C

TEST 4

DIRECTIONS: Each question or incomplete statement is followed by several suggested answers or completions. Select the one that BEST answers the question or completes the statement. *PRINT THE LETTER OF THE CORRECT ANSWER IN THE SPACE AT THE RIGHT.*

1. An integral part of every supervisor's job is getting his ideas or instructions across to his staff. The extent of his success, if he has a reasonably competent staff, is PRIMARILY dependent on the   1.____

    A. interest of the employee
    B. intelligence of the employee
    C. reasoning behind the ideas or instructions
    D. presentation of the ideas or instructions

2. Generally, what is the FIRST action the supervisor should take when an employee approaches him with a complaint?   2.____

    A. Review the employee's recent performance with him
    B. Use the complaint as a basis to discuss improvement of procedures
    C. Find out from the employee the details of the complaint
    D. Advise the employee to take his complaint to the head of the department

3. Of the following, which is NOT usually considered one of the purposes of counseling an employee after an evaluation of his performance?   3.____

    A. Explaining the performance standards used by the supervisor
    B. Discussing necessary disciplinary action to be taken
    C. Emphasizing the employee's strengths and weaknesses
    D. Planning better utilization of the employee's strengths

4. Assume that a supervisor, when reviewing a decision reached by one of his subordinates, finds the decision incorrect. Under these circumstances, it would be MOST desirable for the supervisor to   4.____

    A. correct the decision and inform the subordinate of this at a staff meeting
    B. correct the decision and suggest a more detailed analysis in the future
    C. help the employee find the reason for the correct decision
    D. refrain from assigning this type of a problem to the employee

5. An IMPORTANT characteristic of a good supervisor is his ability to   5.____

    A. be a stern disciplinarian
    B. put off the settling of grievances
    C. solve problems   D. find fault in individuals

6. A new supervisor will BEST obtain the respect of the men assigned to him if he   6.____

    A. makes decisions rapidly and sticks to them, regardless of whether they are right or wrong
    B. makes decisions rapidly and then changes them just as rapidly if the decisions are wrong
    C. does not make any decisions unless he is absolutely sure that they are right
    D. makes his decisions after considering carefully all available information

7. A newly appointed worker is operating at a level of performance below that of the other employees. In this situation, a supervisor should FIRST

    A. lower the acceptable standard for the new man
    B. find out why the new man cannot do as well as the others
    C. advise the new worker he will be dropped from the payroll at the end of the probationary period
    D. assign another new worker to assist the first man

7.____

8. Assume that you have to instruct a new man on a specific departmental operation. The new man seems unsure of what you have said. Of the following, the BEST way for you to determine whether the man has understood you is to

    A. have the man explain the operation to you in his own words
    B. repeat your explanation to him slowly
    C. repeat your explanation to him, using simpler wording
    D. emphasize the important parts of the operation to him

8.____

9. A supervisor realizes that he has taken an instanteous dislike to a new worker assigned to him. The BEST course of action for the supervisor to take in this case is to

    A. be especially observant of the new worker's actions
    B. request that the new worker be reassigned
    C. make a special effort to be fair to the new worker
    D. ask to be transferred himself

9.____

10. A supervisor gives detailed instructions to his men as to how a certain type of job is to be done. One ADVANTAGE of this practice is that this will

    A. result in a more flexible operation
    B. standardize operations
    C. encourage new men to learn
    D. encourage initiative in the men

10.____

11. Of the following, the one that would MOST likely be the result of poor planning is:

    A. Omissions are discovered after the work is completed.
    B. During the course of normal inspection, a meter is found to be inaccessible.
    C. An inspector completes his assignments for that day ahead of schedule.
    D. A problem arises during an inspection and prevents an inspector from completing his day's assignments.

11.____

12. Of the following, the BEST way for a supervisor to maintain good employee morale is for the supervisor to

    A. avoid correcting the employee when he makes mistakes
    B. continually praise the employee's work even when it is of average quality
    C. show that he is willing to assist in solving the employee's problems
    D. accept the employee's excuses for failure even though the excuses are not valid

12.___

13. A supervisor takes time to explain to his men why a departmental order has been issued.   13.____
This practice is

     A. *good,* mainly because without this explanation the men will not be able to carry out the order
     B. *bad,* mainly because time will be wasted for no useful purpose
     C. *good,* because understanding the reasons behind an order will lead to more effective carrying out of the order
     D. *bad,* because men will then question every order that they receive

14. Of the following, the MOST important responsibility of a supervisor in charge of a section   14.____
is to

     A. establish close personal relationships with each of his subordinates in the section
     B. insure that each subordinate in the section knows the full range of his duties and responsibilities
     C. maintain friendly relations with his immediate supervisor
     D. protect his subordinates from criticism from any source

15. The BEST way to get a good work output from employees is to   15.____

     A. hold over them the threat of disciplinary action or removal
     B. maintain a steady, unrelenting pressure on them
     C. show them that you can do anything they can do faster and better
     D. win their respect and liking, so they want to work for you

———

KEY (CORRECT ANSWERS)

1.	A		6.	D
2.	C		7.	B
3.	A		8.	A
4.	C		9.	C
5.	C		10.	B

11.	A
12.	C
13.	C
14.	B
15.	D

———

WORD SUBSTITUTION
EXAMINATION SECTION
TEST 1

DIRECTIONS: Each question or incomplete statement is followed by several suggested answers or completions. Select the one that BEST answers the question or completes the statement. *PRINT THE LETTER OF THE CORRECT ANSWER IN THE SPACE AT THE RIGHT.*

Questions 1-5.

DIRECTIONS: Each of Questions 1 through 5 consists of a statement which contains one word that is INCORRECTLY used because it is not in keeping with the meaning that the statement is evidently intended to convey. Determine which word is incorrectly used. Select from the choices lettered A, B, C, and D the word which, when substituted for the incorrectly used word, would BEST help to convey the meaning of the statement.

1. A complex society like our own, after all, depends on the skills of the individuals composing it. Concerns of human safety, convenience, and the quality of our collective life are of as great consequence as our concern for equal protection of the laws. We do want a qualified surgeon when we need an operation. We assume a skilled pilot, especially when it is we who are on the plane. We want the telephone to work, and our mail to come to us, and not to someone down the street. We want competent teachers for our children. In universities, we want high standards of scholarship and research.
Our existence places us at the mercy of persons, never invisible to us, who are certified for their qualities. While we may argue about the manner in which, in real life, skill and competence are elicited and ascertained, we can hardly argue that there are no such things as skill and competence or that there is no way of measuring them. But there are those among us who do make this argument and those who also accept it, and its spreading influence may well constitute the single greatest threat to the quality of our lives today.

    A. little   B. quibble
    C. gullibility   D. often

1____

2. If strategy or policy does not further plans or make enterprise procedures more attainable, it has not done its job. No manager should ever be able to say: There's no good reason why we do it, it is just our policy! While many policies and some strategies are, in effect, permanent, it should never be assumed that they represent natural laws engraved on stone. If goals, premises, or major plans change, strategies and policies should be reconsidered to meet the new situation.

    A. objectives   B. exclaim
    C. diverge   D. reinforced

2____

3. To some extent, the attitude that experience is the best teacher is justifiable. The very 3____
fact that the manager has reached his position appears to justify his decisions. Moreover,
the reasoning process of thinking problems through, making decisions, and seeing programs succeed or fail, does make for a degree of good judgment (at times bordering on
the intuitive). Many people, however, do not profit by their errors, and there are managers
who seen never to gain the seasoned judgment required by modern enterprise.
There is danger, however, in relying on one's past experience as a guide for future
action. In the first place, it is an unusual human being who recognizes the obvious reasons for his mistakes or failures. In the second place, the lessons of experience may
be entirely unsuitable to new problems. Good decisions must be evaluated against
future events, while experience belongs to the past.

   A. poorest   B. underlying
   C. principle   D. quantified

4. A bit of thinking will give a clue to the variety of disciplines which are involved in the 4____
range of the personnel function. In staffing - from initial entry to promotion and transfer
the field of psychological measurement is brought into play. Compensation decisions
require economists and statisticians. Job analysis calls for skills in research and administrative procedure. Training draws upon adult education specialists and other occupas-
tions. Health and safety measures demand the employment of medical doctors, nurses,
and safety engineers. Operating a retirement system necessitates expertise in the insurance field and actuarial mathematics. Dealing with employees corporately requires
knowledge in labor relations. Interpretation of rules and adjudication of claims and complaints call for the skills of lawyers. And all the elements of leadership, budgeting, incentive, evaluation, and discipline, on which the personnel program is expected to provide
the principal guidance, can be fortified only by a liberal understanding of such social sciences as social psychology and sociology, to say nothing of a healthy dose of that conventional wisdom known as common sense.

   A. supervision   B. physiological
   C. economic   D. purchasing

5. Another means of increasing participation is what has been called *grass roots* budgeting. 5____
Instead of a budget for operations or capital expenditures being prepared at the top or
departmental level, the smallest organization units prepare their budgets and submit
them upward. Naturally, to be effective, these units must be aware of objectives, policies,
and programs which affect their operations, must above all be given clear planning preri-
ises, and be furnished factors enabling them to convert work load into requirements for
men, material, and money. If these budget requests are reviewed and coordinated by
departmental management, and if the budget makers are required to expend their budgets, this means of planning participation becomes real and purposeful. There probably
exist no greater incentive to planning and no stronger sense of participation than those
created in developing, defending, and selling a course of action over which the manager
has control and for which he bears responsibility.

   A. intermediate   B. productivity
   C. defend   D. cut

KEY (CORRECT ANSWERS)

1. D
2. A
3. B
4. A
5. C

———

TEST 2

Questions 1-5.

DIRECTIONS: Each of Questions 1 through 5 consists of a paragraph which contains one word that is incorrectly used because it is not in keeping with the meaning that the paragraph is evidently intended to convey. This word will be found in that portion of the paragraph which is underlined. Read the entire paragraph. Then determine which word is incorrectly used. Select from the choices lettered A, B, C, and D the word which, when substituted for the incorrectly used word, would BEST help to convey the meaning of the quotation.

1.   In plotting its manpower course, an organization has to make assumptions about   1____
     changes ahead in the next 5, 10, 15, or 20 years. The most profound changes will occur
     in people themselves, particularly in young people. The fact is that today's young people
     are much better educated than their counterparts of 20 and 30 years ago, are much
     more likely to react negatively to blind authority and to have different ideas about trans-
     portation to work. While the transformation may not show up as readily in young busi-
     ness managers, they must be taken into account because they most certainly will have a
     profound effect upon management style and management potential in the next 20 years.

     A.   contemporary   B.   evolve
     C.   favorably   D.   motivation

2.   The need for flexibility has an important bearing on the time span that programs should   2____
     cover. The very existence of a program inhibits some loss of flexibility. By reason of hav-
     ing adopted it, the agency reduces its freedom, to do something different in future years,
     since a conscious act of revision is required. On the other hand investment projects, to
     say nothing of research and development, undertaken now must be based on some view
     of a highly uncertain future. Time spans should be long enough but not unnecessarily
     long. The dilemma could be partially resolved if programs could be expressed in terms of
     ranges rather than single figures. If the ranges included genuine upper and lower limits, it
     would become clear that projection beyond a limited period was not operationally mean-
     ingful.

     A.   counteracts   B.   lag
     C.   accelerated   D.   implies

3. The tendency to delude ourselves into believing that organizations largely run themselves is why there are so many counterfeits in the management ranks. Such persons are glib, intelligent, persuasive, personable, and even charming. But once on the executive staff they will produce little and destroy more. Sometimes a counterfeit manager can get by for years in a company by the simple device of not remaining in the same job for more than two years. Long-range effects usually are felt first in the intervening variables such as employee loyalties, attitudes, and motivations. These variables affect the end-result variables such as productivity and earnings much more slowly, so that the outcome is difficult to trace back to a specific manager. Managerial effectiveness becomes, therefore, an explicit quality, greatly to be desired but difficult to pinpoint. Advances in the behavioral sciences are making inroads. We now know that only certain types of personalities have the talent to achieve excellence in management positions.

3____

    A. concomitant   B. elusive
    C. encroachments   D. simulated

4. The implementation of appropriation decisions without distortion or deceit is an important element in the maintenance of democratic institutions. The people must control the public purse through the judgments of their elected representatives and the performance of their civil servants. This is the foundation of public confidence and trust. However, honest and faithful execution of appropriation decisions is not enough. What about the preparation of those decisions whose undeviating performance has been guaranteed? Is a democracy effectively administered if it does not clearly identify its objectives and its resources and rationally allocate scarce means to ensure achievement of these objectives? A budget appropriately designed to meet the requirements of a rational decision-making process will not, of course, automatically ensure the making of rational decisions. But it can be a powerful influence in that direction.

4____

    A. approval   B. recognize
    C. adherence   D. quality

5. How effective is a program in attaining its intended objective? Can existing program results be accomplished at lower cost? These questions attempt to draw a distinction between the *effectiveness* of a program in achieving its objective and the *efficiency* with which it is carried out. For instance, if it is possible to consider the effectiveness of the rent control program under the present organization of the office, it should also be possible to decide whether the same results could be more efficiently achieved by reorganization. Efficiency might be increased by having fewer senior attorneys and more assistants, or vice versa. The distinction between effectiveness and efficiency must, however, be used with extreme care. Measures that purport to increase efficiency generally have a negligible effect, good or bad, on effectiveness. Government economy campaigns, for instance, often greatly reduce effectiveness in the guise of merely increasing office efficiency.

5____

    A. augment   B. pronounced
    C. purposefully   D. improving

———

KEY (CORRECT ANSWERS)

1. D
2. D
3. B
4. D
5. B

———

READING COMPREHENSION
UNDERSTANDING AND INTERPRETING WRITTEN MATERIAL
EXAMINATION SECTION
TEST 1

DIRECTIONS: Each question or incomplete statement is followed by several suggested answers or completions. Select the one that BEST answers the question or completes the statement. *PRINT THE LETTER OF THE CORRECT ANSWER IN THE SPACE AT THE RIGHT.*

Questions 1-5.

DIRECTIONS: Questions 1 through 5 are to be answered SOLELY on the basis of the following passage.

The most effective control mechanism to prevent gross incompetence on the part of public employees is a good personnel program. The personnel officer in the line departments and the central personnel agency should exert positive leadership to raise levels of performance. Although the key factor is the quality of the personnel recruited, staff members other than personnel officers can make important contributions to efficiency. Administrative analysts, now employed in many agencies, make detailed studies of organization and procedures, with the purpose of eliminating delays, waste, and other inefficiencies. Efficiency is, however, more than a question of good organization and procedures; it is also the product of the attitudes and values of the public employees. Personal motivation can provide the will to be efficient. The best management studies will not result in substantial improvement of the performance of those employees who feel no great urge to work up to their abilities.

1. The above passage indicates that the KEY factor in preventing gross incompetence of public employees is the

    A. hiring of administrative analysts to assist personnel people
    B. utilization of effective management studies
    C. overlapping of responsibility
    D. quality of the employees hired

1.____

2. According to the above passage, the central personnel agency staff SHOULD

    A. work more closely with administrative analysts in the line departments than with personnel officers
    B. make a serious effort to avoid jurisdictional conflicts with personnel officers in line departments
    C. contribute to improving the quality of work of public employees
    D. engage in a comprehensive program to change the public's negative image of public employees

2.____

3. The above passage indicates that efficiency in an organization can BEST be brought about by

    A. eliminating ineffective control mechanisms
    B. instituting sound organizational procedures

3.____

    C.   promoting competent personnel
    D.   recruiting people with desire to do good work

4.   According to the above passage, the purpose of administrative analysis in a public agency is to   4._____

    A.   prevent injustice to the public employee
    B.   promote the efficiency of the agency
    C.   protect the interests of the public
    D.   ensure the observance of procedural due process

5.   The above passage implies that a considerable rise in the quality of work of public employees can be brought about by   5._____

    A.   encouraging positive employee attitudes toward work
    B.   controlling personnel officers who exceed their powers
    C.   creating warm personal associations among public employees in an agency
    D.   closing loopholes in personnel organization and procedures

Questions 6-8.

DIRECTIONS: Questions 6 through 8 are to be answered SOLELY on the basis of the following passage on Employee Needs.

EMPLOYEE NEEDS

The greatest waste in industry and in government may be that of human resources. This waste usually derives not from employees' unwillingness or inability, but from management's ineptness to meet the maintenance and motivational needs of employees. Maintenance needs refer to such needs as providing employees with safe places to work, written work rules, job security, adequate salary, employer-sponsored social activities, and with knowledge of their role in the overall framework of the organization. However, of greatest significance to employees are the motivational needs of job growth, achievement, responsibility, and recognition.

Although employee dissatisfaction may stem from either poor maintenance or poor motivation factors, the outward manifestation of the dissatisfaction may be very much alike, i.e., negativism, complaints, deterioration of performance, and so forth. The improvement in the lighting of an employee's work area or raising his level of pay won't do much good if the source of the dissatisfaction is the absence of a meaningful assignment. By the same token, if an employee is dissatisfied with what he considers inequitable pay, the introduction of additional challenge in his work may simply make matters worse.

It is relatively easy for an employee to express frustration by complaining about pay, washroom conditions, fringe benefits, and so forth; but most people cannot easily express resentment in terms of the more abstract concepts concerning job growth, responsibility, and achievement.

It would be wrong to assume that there is no interaction between maintenance and motivational needs of employees. For example, conditions of high motivation often overshadow poor maintenance conditions. If an organization is in a period of strong growth and expansion, opportunities for job growth, responsibility, recognition, and achievement are usually abundant, but the rapid growth may have outrun the upkeep of maintenance factors. In this situation, motivation may be high, but only if employees recognize the poor maintenance conditions as unavoidable and temporary. The subordination of maintenance factors cannot go on indefinitely, even with the highest motivation.

Both maintenance and motivation factors influence the behavior of all employees, but employees are not identical and, furthermore, the needs of any individual do not remain constant. However, a broad distinction can be made between employees who have a basic orientation toward maintenance factors and those with greater sensitivity toward motivation factors.

A highly maintenance-oriented individual, preoccupied with the factors peripheral to his job rather than the job itself, is more concerned with comfort than challenge. He does not get deeply involved with his work but does with the condition of his work area, toilet facilities, and his time for going to lunch. By contrast, a strongly motivation-oriented employee is usually relatively indifferent to his surroundings and is caught up in the pursuit of work goals.

Fortunately, there are few people who are either exclusively maintenance-oriented or purely motivation-oriented. The former would be deadwood in an organization, while the latter might trample on those around him in his pursuit to achieve his goals.

6. With respect to employee motivational and maintenance needs, the management policies of an organization which is growing rapidly will probably result   6._____

    A. more in meeting motivational needs rather than maintenance needs
    B. more in meeting maintenance needs rather than motivational needs
    C. in meeting both of these needs equally
    D. in increased effort to define the motivational and maintenance needs of its employees

7. In accordance with the above passage, which of the following CANNOT be considered as an example of an employee maintenance need for railroad clerks?   7._____

    A. Providing more relief periods
    B. Providing fair salary increases at periodic intervals
    C. Increasing job responsibilities
    D. Increasing health insurance benefits

8. Most employees in an organization may be categorized as being interested in   8._____

    A. maintenance needs *only*
    B. motivational needs *only*
    C. both motivational and maintenance needs
    D. money only, to the exclusion of all other needs

Questions 9-11.

DIRECTIONS: Questions 9 through 11 are to be answered SOLELY on the basis of the following passage on Good Employee Practices.

GOOD EMPLOYEE PRACTICES

As a city employee, you will be expected to take an interest in your work and perform the duties of your job to the best of your ability and in a spirit of cooperation. Nothing shows an interest in your work more than coming to work on time, not only at the start of the day but also when returning from lunch. If it is necessary for you to keep a personal appointment at lunch hour which might cause a delay in getting back to work on time, you should explain the situation to your supervisor and get his approval to come back a little late before you leave for lunch.

You should do everything that is asked of you willingly and consider important even the small jobs that your supervisor gives you. Although these jobs may seem unimportant, if you forget to do them or if you don't do them right, trouble may develop later.

Getting along well with your fellow workers will add much to the enjoyment of your work. You should respect your fellow workers and try to see their side when a disagreement arises. The better you get along with your fellow workers and your supervisor, the better you will like your job and the better you will be able to do it.

9. According to the above passage, in your job as a city employee, you are expected to   9.____

    A.   show a willingness to cooperate on the job
    B.   get your supervisor's approval before keeping any personal appointments at lunch hour
    C.   avoid doing small jobs that seem unimportant
    D.   do the easier jobs at the start of the day and the more difficult ones later on

10. According to the above passage, getting to work on time shows that you   10.____

    A.   need the job
    B.   have an interest in your work
    C.   get along well with your fellow workers
    D.   like your supervisor

11. According to the above passage, the one of the following statements that is NOT true is   11.____

    A.   if you do a small job wrong, trouble may develop
    B.   you should respect your fellow workers
    C.   if you disagree with a fellow worker, you should try to see his side of the story
    D.   the less you get along with your supervisor, the better you will be able to do your job

Questions 12-15.

DIRECTIONS: Questions 12 through 15 are to be answered SOLELY on the basis of the following passage on Employee Suggestions.

EMPLOYEE SUGGESTIONS

To increase the effectiveness of the city government, the city asks its employees to offer suggestions when they feel an improvement could be made in some government operation. The Employees' Suggestions Program was started to encourage city employees to do this.

Through this Program, which is only for city employees, cash awards may be given to those whose suggestions are submitted and approved. Suggestions are looked for not only from supervisors but from all city employees as any city employee may get an idea which might be approved and contribute greatly to the solution of some problem of city government

Therefore, all suggestions for improvement are welcome, whether they be suggestions on how to improve working conditions, or on how to increase the speed with which work is done, or on how to reduce or eliminate such things as waste, time losses, accidents or fire hazards. There are, however, a few types of suggestions for which cash awards cannot be given. An example of this type would be a suggestion to increase salaries or a suggestion to change the regulations about annual leave or about sick leave. The number of suggestions sent in has increased sharply during the past few years. It is hoped that it will keep increasing in the future in order to meet the city's needs for more ideas for improved ways of doing things.

12. According to the above passage, the MAIN reason why the city asks its employees for suggestions about government operations is to   12._____

    A. increase the effectiveness of the city government
    B. show that the Employees' Suggestion Program is working well
    C. show that everybody helps run the city government
    D. have the employee win a prize

13. According to the above passage, the Employees' Suggestion Program can approve awards ONLY for those suggestions that come from   13._____

    A. city employees
    B. city employees who are supervisors
    C. city employees who are not supervisors
    D. experienced employees of the city

14. According to the above passage, a cash award cannot be given through the Employees' Suggestion Program for a suggestion about   14._____

    A. getting work done faster
    B. helping prevent accidents on the job
    C. increasing the amount of annual leave for city employees
    D. reducing the chance of fire where city employees work

15. According to the above passage, the suggestions sent in during the past few years have   15._____

    A. all been approved
    B. generally been well written
    C. been mostly about reducing or eliminating waste
    D. been greater in number than before

Questions 16-18.

DIRECTIONS: Questions 16 through 18 are to be answered SOLELY on the basis of the following passage.

The supervisor will gain the respect of the members of his staff and increase his influence over them by controlling his temper and avoiding criticizing anyone publicly. When a mistake is made, the good supervisor will talk it over with the employee quietly and privately. The supervisor will listen to the employee's story, suggest the better way of doing the job, and offer help so the mistake won't happen again. Before closing the discussion, the supervisor should try to find something good to say about other parts of the employee's work. Some praise and appreciation, along with instruction, is more likely to encourage an employee to improve in those areas where he is weakest.

16. A good title that would show the meaning of the above passage would be   16.__

   A. HOW TO CORRECT EMPLOYEE ERRORS
   B. HOW TO PRAISE EMPLOYEES
   C. MISTAKES ARE PREVENTABLE
   D. THE WEAK EMPLOYEE

17. According to the above passage, the work of an employee who has made a mistake is   17.__
    more likely to improve if the supervisor

   A. avoids criticizing him
   B. gives him a chance to suggest a better way of doing the work
   C. listens to the employee's excuses to see if he is right
   D. praises good work at the same time he corrects the mistake

18. According to the above passage, when a supervisor needs to correct an employee's mis-   18.__
    take, it is important that he

   A. allow some time to go by after the mistake is made
   B. do so when other employees are not present
   C. show his influence with his tone of voice
   D. tell other employees to avoid the same mistake

Questions 19-23.

DIRECTIONS: Questions 19 through 23 are to be answered SOLELY on the basis of the fol-
              lowing passage.

In studying the relationships of people to the organizational structure, it is absolutely necessary to identify and recognize the informal organizational structure. These relationships are
necessary when coordination of a plan is attempted. They may be with the boss, line supervisors, staff personnel, or other representatives of the formal organization's hierarchy, and they
may include the liaison men who serve as the leaders of the informal organization. An
acquaintanceship with the people serving in these roles in the organization, and its formal
counterpart, permits a supervisor to recognize sensitive areas in which it is simple to get a
conflict reaction. Avoidance of such areas, plus conscious efforts to inform other people of his
own objectives for various plans, will usually enlist their aid and support. Planning without
people can lead to disaster because the individuals who must act together to make any plan
a success are more important than the plans themselves.

19. Of the following titles, the one that MOST clearly describes the above passage is   19.__

   A. COORDINATION OF A FUNCTION
   B. AVOIDANCE OF CONFLICT
   C. PLANNING WITH PEOPLE
   D. PLANNING OBJECTIVES

20. According to the above passage, attempts at coordinating plans may fail unless   20.____

    A. the plan's objectives are clearly set forth
    B. conflict between groups is resolved
    C. the plans themselves are worthwhile
    D. informal relationships are recognized

21. According to the above passage, conflict   21.____

    A. may, in some cases, be desirable to secure results
    B. produces more heat than light
    C. should be avoided at all costs
    D. possibilities can be predicted by a sensitive supervisor

22. The above passage implies that   22.____

    A. informal relationships are more important than formal structure
    B. the weakness of a formal structure depends upon informal relationships
    C. liaison men are the key people to consult when taking formal and informal structures into account
    D. individuals in a group are at least as important as the plans for the group

23. The above passage suggests that   23.____

    A. some planning can be disastrous
    B. certain people in sensitive areas should be avoided
    C. the supervisor should discourage acquaintanceships in the organization
    D. organizational relationships should be consciously limited

Questions 24-25.

DIRECTIONS: Questions 24 and 25 are to be answered SOLELY on the basis of the following passage.

Good personnel relations of an organization depend upon mutual confidence, trust, and good will. The basis of confidence is understanding. Most troubles start with people who do not understand each other. When the organization's intentions or motives are misunderstood, or when reasons for actions, practices, or policies are misconstrued, complete cooperation from individuals is not forthcoming. If management expects full cooperation from employees, it has a responsibility of sharing with them the information which is the foundation of proper understanding, confidence, and trust. Personnel management has long since outgrown the days when it was the vogue to *treat them rough and tell them nothing.* Up-to-date personnel management provides all possible information about the activities, aims, and purposes of the organization. It seems altogether creditable that a desire should exist among employees for such information which the best-intentioned executive might think would not interest them and which the worst-intentioned would think was none of their business.

24. The above passage implies that one of the causes of the difficulty which an organization   24.____ might have with its personnel relations is that its employees

    A. have not expressed interest in the activities, aims, and purposes of the organization
    B. do not believe in the good faith of the organization

C. have not been able to give full cooperation to the organization
D. do not recommend improvements in the practices and policies of the organization

25. According to the above passage, in order for an organization to have good personnel relations, it is NOT essential that   25.____

A. employees have confidence in the organization
B. the purposes of the organization be understood by the employees
C. employees have a desire for information about the organization
D. information about the organization be communicated to employees

---

KEY (CORRECT ANSWERS)

1.	D	11.	D
2.	C	12.	A
3.	D	13.	A
4.	B	14.	C
5.	A	15.	D
6.	A	16.	A
7.	C	17.	D
8.	C	18.	B
9.	A	19.	C
10.	B	20.	D

21.	D
22.	D
23.	A
24.	B
25.	C

TEST 2

DIRECTIONS: Questions 1 through 8 are to be answered SOLELY on the basis of the following passage.

Important figures in education and in public affairs have recommended development of a private organization sponsored in part by various private foundations which would offer installment payment plans to full-time matriculated students in accredited colleges and universities in the United States and Canada. Contracts would be drawn to cover either tuition and fees, or tuition, fees, room and board in college facilities, from one year up to and including six years. A special charge, which would vary with the length of the contract, would be added to the gross repayable amount. This would be in addition to interest at a rate which would vary with the income of the parents. There would be a 3% annual interest charge for families with total income, before income taxes, of $50,000 or less. The rate would increase by 1/10 of 1% for every $1,000 of additional net income in excess of $50,000 up to a maximum of 10% interest. Contracts would carry an insurance provision on the life of the parent or guardian who signs the contract; all contracts must have the signature of a parent or guardian. Payment would be scheduled in equal monthly installments.

1. Which of the following students would be eligible for the payment plan described in the above passage? A

    A. matriculated student taking six semester hours toward a graduate degree
    B. matriculated student taking seventeen semester hours toward an undergraduate degree
    C. graduate matriculated at the University of Mexico taking eighteen semester hours toward a graduate degree
    D. student taking eighteen semester hours in a special pre-matriculation program

1.____

2. According to the above passage, the organization described would be sponsored in part by

    A. private foundations
    B. colleges and universities
    C. persons in the field of education
    D. persons in public life

2.____

3. Which of the following expenses could NOT be covered by a contract with the organization described in the above passage?

    A. Tuition amounting to $20,000 per year
    B. Registration and laboratory fees
    C. Meals at restaurants near the college
    D. Rent for an apartment in a college dormitory

3.____

4. The total amount to be paid would include ONLY the

    A. principal
    B. principal and interest
    C. principal, interest, and special charge
    D. principal, interest, special charge, and fee

4.____

5. The contract would carry insurance on the   5.__

    A. life of the student
    B. life of the student's parents
    C. income of the parents of the student
    D. life of the parent who signed the contract

6. The interest rate for an annual loan of $25,000 from the organization described in the   6.__
   above passage for a student whose family's net income was $55,000 should be

    A. 3%   B. 3.5%   C. 4%   D. 4.5%

7. The interest rate for an annual loan of $35,000 from the organization described in the   7.__
   above passage for a student whose family's net income was $100,000 should be

    A. 5%   B. 8%   C. 9%   D. 10%

8. John Lee has submitted an application for the installment payment plan described in the   8.__
   above passage. John's mother and father have a store which grossed $500,000 last
   year, but the income which the family received from the store was $90,000 before taxes.
   They also had $5,000 income from stock dividends. They paid $10,000 in income taxes.
   The amount of income upon which the interest should be based is

    A. $85,000   B. $90,000   C. $95,000   D. $105,000

Questions 9-13.

DIRECTIONS: Questions 9 through 13 are to be answered SOLELY on the basis of the follow-
                 ing passage.

    Since an organization chart is pictorial in nature, there is a tendency for it to be drawn in
an artistically balanced and appealing fashion, regardless of the realities of actual organizational structure. In addition to being subject to this distortion, there is the difficulty of communicating in any organization chart the relative importance or the relative size of various
component parts of an organizational structure. Furthermore, because of the need for sim-
plicity of design, an organization chart can never indicate the full extent of the interrelationships among the component parts of an organization.

    These interrelationships are often just as vital as the specifications which an organization
chart endeavors to indicate. Yet, if an organization chart were to be drawn with all the wide
variety of criss-crossing communication and cooperation networks existent within a typical
organization, the chart would probably be much more confusing than informative. It is also
obvious that no organization chart as such can prove or disprove that the organizational
structure it represents is effective in realizing the objectives of the organization. At best, an
organization chart can only illustrate some of the various factors to be taken into consideration in understanding, devising, or altering organizational arrangements.

9. According to the above passage, an organization chart can be expected to portray the   9.__

    A. structure of the organization along somewhat ideal lines
    B. relative size of the organizational units quite accurately
    C. channels of information distribution within the organization graphically
    D. extent of the obligation of each unit to meet the organizational objectives

10. According to the above passage, those aspects of internal functioning which are NOT shown on an organization chart   10._____

    A. can be considered to have little practical application in the operations of the organization
    B. might well be considered to be as important as the structural relationships which a chart does present
    C. could be the cause of considerable confusion in the operations of an organization which is quite large
    D. would be most likely to provide the information needed to determine the overall effectiveness of an organization

11. In the above passage, the one of the following conditions which is NOT implied as being a defect of an organization chart is that an organization chart may   11._____

    A. present a picture of the organizational structure which is different from the structure that actually exists
    B. fail to indicate the comparative size of various organizational units
    C. be limited in its ability to convey some of the meaningful aspects of organizational relationships
    D. become less useful over a period of time during which the organizational facts which it illustrated have changed

12. The one of the following which is the MOST suitable title for the above passage is   12._____

    A. THE DESIGN AND CONSTRUCTION OF AN ORGANIZATION CHART
    B. THE INFORMAL ASPECTS OF AN ORGANIZATION CHART
    C. THE INHERENT DEFICIENCIES OF AN ORGANIZATION CHART
    D. THE UTILIZATION OF A TYPICAL ORGANIZATION CHART

13. It can be INFERRED from the above passage that the function of an organization chart is to   13._____

    A. contribute to the comprehension of the organization form and arrangements
    B. establish the capabilities of the organization to operate effectively
    C. provide a balanced picture of the operations of the organization
    D. eliminate the need for complexity in the organization's structure

Questions 14-16.

DIRECTIONS: Questions 14 through 16 are to be answered SOLELY on the basis of the following passage.

In dealing with visitors to the school office, the school secretary must use initiative, tact, and good judgment. All visitors should be greeted promptly and courteously. The nature of their business should be determined quickly and handled expeditiously. Frequently, the secretary should be able to handle requests, receipts, deliveries, or passes herself. Her judgment should determine when a visitor should see members of the staff or the principal. Serious problems or doubtful cases should be referred to a supervisor.

14. In general, visitors should be handled by the   14.___

    A. school secretary   B. principal
    C. appropriate supervisor   D. person who is free

15. It is wise to obtain the following information from visitors: 15.___

    A. Name   B. Nature of business
    C. Address   D. Problems they have

16. All visitors who wish to see members of the staff should   16.___

    A. be permitted to do so
    B. produce identification
    C. do so for valid reasons only
    D. be processed by a supervisor

Questions 17-19.

DIRECTIONS: Questions 17 through 19 are to be answered SOLELY on the basis of the following passage.

Information regarding payroll status, salary differentials, promotional salary increments, deductions, and pension payments should be given to all members of the staff who have questions regarding these items. On occasion, if the secretary is uncertain regarding the information, the staff member should be referred to the principal or the appropriate agency. No question by a staff member regarding payroll status should be brushed aside as immaterial or irrelevant. The school secretary must always try to handle the question or pass it on to the person who can handle it.

17. If a teacher is dissatisfied with information regarding her salary status, as given by the school secretary, the matter should be   17.___

    A. dropped
    B. passed on to the principal
    C. passed on by the secretary to proper agency or the principal
    D. made a basis for grievance procedures

18. The following is an adequate summary of the above passage: 18.___

    A. The secretary must handle all payroll matters
    B. The secretary must handle all payroll matters or know who can handle them
    C. The secretary or the principal must handle all payroll matters
    D. Payroll matters too difficult to handle must be followed up until they are solved

19. The above passage implies that   19.___

    A. many teachers ask immaterial questions regarding payroll status
    B. few teachers ask irrelevant pension questions
    C. no teachers ask immaterial salary questions
    D. no question regarding salary should be considered irrelevant

Questions 20-22:

DIRECTIONS: Questions 20 through 22 are to be answered SOLELY on the basis of the following passage.

The necessity for good speech on the part of the school secretary cannot be overstated.
The school secretary must deal with the general public, the pupils, the members of the staff,
and the school supervisors. In every situation which involves the general public, the secretary
serves as a representative of the school. In dealing with pupils, the secretary's speech must
serve as a model from which students may guide themselves. Slang, colloquialisms, mala-
propisms, and local dialects must be avoided.

20.   The above passage implies that the speech pattern of the secretary must be   20._____

A.   perfect
B.   very good
C.   average
D.   on a level with that of the pupils

21.   The last sentence indicates that slang   21._____

A.   is acceptable
B.   occurs in all speech
C.   might be used occasionally
D.   should be shunned

22.   The above passage implies that the speech of pupils   22._____

A.   may be influenced   B.   does not change readily
C.   is generally good   D.   is generally poor

Questions 23-25.

DIRECTIONS: Questions 23 through 25 are to be answered SOLELY on the basis of the following passage.

The school secretary who is engaged in the task of filing records and correspondence
should follow a general set of rules. Items which are filed should be available to other secretaries or to supervisors quickly and easily by means of the application of a modicum of common sense and good judgment. Items which, by their nature, may be difficult to find should be
cross-indexed. Folders and drawers should be neatly and accurately labeled. There should
never be a large accumulation of papers which have not been filed.

23.   A good general rule to follow in filing is that materials should be   23._____

A.   placed in folders quickly
B.   neatly stored
C.   readily available
D.   cross-indexed

24.   Items that are filed should be available to   24._____

A.   the secretary charged with the task of filing
B.   secretaries and supervisors
C.   school personnel
D.   the principal

25. A modicum of common sense means _____ common sense.

    A. an average amount of   B. a great deal of
    C. a little   D. no

25._____

———————

KEY (CORRECT ANSWERS)

1.	B	11.	D
2.	A	12.	C
3.	C	13.	A
4.	C	14.	A
5.	D	15.	B
6.	B	16.	C
7.	B	17.	C
8.	C	18.	B
9.	A	19.	D
10.	B	20.	B

21.	D
22.	A
23.	C
24.	B
25.	C

———————

TEST 3

DIRECTIONS: Questions 1 through 4 are to be answered SOLELY on the basis of the following passage.

The proposition that administrative activity is essentially the same in all organizations appears to underlie some of the practices in the administration of private higher education. Although the practice is unusual in public education, there are numerous instances of industrial, governmental, or military administrators being assigned to private institutions of higher education and, to a lesser extent, of college and university presidents assuming administrative positions in other types of organizations. To test this theory that administrators are interchangeable, there is a need for systematic observation and classification. The myth that an educational administrator must first have experience in the teaching profession is firmly rooted in a long tradition that has historical prestige. The myth is bound up in the expectations of the public and personnel surrounding the administrator. Since administrative success depends significantly on how well an administrator meets the expectations others have of him, the myth may be more powerful than the special experience in helping the administrator attain organizational and educational objectives. Educational administrators who have risen through the teaching profession have often expressed nostalgia for the life of a teacher or scholar, but there is no evidence that this nostalgia contributes to administrative success

1. Which of the following statements as completed is MOST consistent with the above passage? The greatest number of administrators has moved from 1.____

   A. industry and the military to government and universities
   B. government and universities to industry and the military
   C. government, the armed forces, and industry to colleges and universities
   D. colleges and universities to government, the armed forces, and industry

2. Of the following, the MOST reasonable inference from the above passage is that a specific area requiring further research is the 2.____

   A. place of myth in the tradition and history of the educational profession
   B. relative effectiveness of educational administrators from inside and outside the teaching profession
   C. performance of administrators in the administration of public colleges
   D. degree of reality behind the nostalgia for scholarly pursuits often expressed by educational administrators

3. According to the above passage, the value to an educational administrator of experience in the teaching profession 3.____

   A. lies in the firsthand knowledge he has acquired of immediate educational problems
   B. may lie in the belief of his colleagues, subordinates, and the public that such experience is necessary
   C. has been supported by evidence that the experience contributes to administrative success in educational fields
   D. would be greater if the administrator were able to free himself from nostalgia for his former duties

4. Of the following, the MOST suitable title for the above passage is 4.____

   A. EDUCATIONAL ADMINISTRATION, ITS PROBLEMS
   B. THE EXPERIENCE NEEDED FOR EDUCATIONAL ADMINISTRATION
   C. ADMINISTRATION IN HIGHER EDUCATION
   D. EVALUATING ADMINISTRATIVE EXPERIENCE

Questions 5-6.

DIRECTIONS: Questions 5 and 6 are to be answered SOLELY on the basis of the following passage.

Management by objectives (MBO) may be defined as the process by which the superior and the subordinate managers of an organization jointly define its common goals, define each individual's major areas of responsibility in terms of the results expected of him and use these measures as guides for operating the unit and assessing the contribution of each of its members.

The MBO approach requires that after organizational goals are established and communicated, targets must be set for each individual position which are congruent with organizational goals. Periodic performance reviews and a final review using the objectives set as criteria are also basic to this approach.

Recent studies have shown that MBO programs are influenced by attitudes and perceptions of the boss, the company, the reward-punishment system, and the program itself. In addition, the manner in which the MBO program is carried out can influence the success of the program. A study done in the late sixties indicates that the best results are obtained when the manager sets goals which deal with significant problem areas in the organizational unit, or with the subordinate's personal deficiencies. These goals must be clear with regard to what is expected of the subordinate. The frequency of feedback is also important in the success of a management-by-objectives program. Generally, the greater the amount of feedback, the more successful the MBO program.

5. According to the above passage, the expected output for individual employees should be determined 5.____

   A. after a number of reviews of work performance
   B. after common organizational goals are defined
   C. before common organizational goals are defined
   D. on the basis of an employee's personal qualities

6. According to the above passage, the management-by-objectives approach requires 6.____

   A. less feedback than other types of management programs
   B. little review of on-the-job performance after the initial setting of goals
   C. general conformance between individual goals and organizational goals
   D. the setting of goals which deal with minor problem areas in the organization

Questions 7-10.

DIRECTIONS: Questions 7 through 10 are to be answered SOLELY on the basis of the following passage.

Management, which is the function of executive leadership, has as its principal phases the planning, organizing, and controlling of the activities of subordinate groups in the accomplishment of organizational objectives. Planning specifies the kind and extent of the factors, forces, and effects, and the relationships among them, that will be required for satisfactory accomplishment. The nature of the objectives and their requirements must be known before determinations can be made as to what must be done, how it must be done and why, where actions should take place, who should be responsible, and similar problems pertaining to the formulation of a plan. Organizing, which creates the conditions that must be present before the execution of the plan can be undertaken successfully, cannot be done intelligently without knowledge of the organizational objectives. Control, which has to do with the constraint and regulation of activities entering into the execution of the plan, must be exercised in accordance with the characteristics and requirements of the activities demanded by the plan.

7. The one of the following which is the MOST suitable title for the above passage is   7.____

   A. THE NATURE OF SUCCESSFUL ORGANIZATION
   B. THE PLANNING OF MANAGEMENT FUNCTIONS
   C. THE IMPORTANCE OF ORGANIZATIONAL FUNCTIONS
   D. THE PRINCIPLE ASPECTS OF MANAGEMENT

8. It can be inferred from the above passage that the one of the following functions whose   8.____
   existence is essential to the existence of the other three is the

   A. regulation of the work needed to carry out a plan
   B. understanding of what the organization intends to accomplish
   C. securing of information of the factors necessary for accomplishment of objectives
   D. establishment of the conditions required for successful action

9. The one of the following which would NOT be included within any of the principal phases   9.____
   of the function of executive leadership as defined in the above passage is

   A. determination of manpower requirements
   B. procurement of required material
   C. establishment of organizational objectives
   D. scheduling of production

10. The conclusion which can MOST reasonably be drawn from the above passage is that   10.____
    the control phase of managing is most directly concerned with the

    A. influencing of policy determinations
    B. administering of suggestion systems
    C. acquisition of staff for the organization
    D. implementation of performance standards

Questions 11-12.

DIRECTIONS: Questions 11 and 12 are to be answered SOLELY on the basis of the following passage.

Under an open-and-above-board policy, it is to be expected that some supervisors will gloss over known shortcomings of subordinates rather than face the task of discussing them face-to-face. It is also to be expected that at least some employees whose job performance is below par will reject the supervisor's appraisal as biased and unfair. Be that as it may, these are inescapable aspects of any performance appraisal system in which human beings are involved. The supervisor who shies away from calling a spade a spade, as well as the employee with a chip on his shoulder, will each in his own way eventually be revealed in his true light--to the benefit of the organization as a whole.

11. The BEST of the following interpretations of the above passage is that   11.____

    A.   the method of rating employee performance requires immediate revision to improve employee acceptance
    B.   substandard performance ratings should be discussed with employees even if satisfactory ratings are not
    C.   supervisors run the risk of being called unfair by their subordinates even though their appraisals are accurate
    D.   any system of employee performance rating is satisfactory if used properly

12. The BEST of the following interpretations of the above passage is that   12.____

    A.   supervisors generally are not open-and-above-board with their subordinates
    B.   it is necessary for supervisors to tell employees objectively how they are performing
    C.   employees complain when their supervisor does not keep them informed
    D.   supervisors are afraid to tell subordinates their weaknesses

Questions 13-15.

DIRECTIONS: Questions 13 through 15 are to be answered SOLELY on the basis of the following passage.

During the last decade, a great deal of interest has been generated around the phenomenon of *organizational development,* or the process of developing human resources through conscious organization effort. Organizational development (OD) stresses improving interpersonal relationships and organizational skills, such as communication, to a much greater degree than individual training ever did. The kind of training that an organization should emphasize depends upon the present and future structure of the organization. If future organizations are to be unstable, shifting coalitions, then individual skills and abilities, particularly those emphasizing innovativeness, creativity, flexibility, and the latest technological knowledge, are crucial and individual training is most appropriate.

But if there is to be little change in organizational structure, then the main thrust of training should be group-oriented or organizational development. This approach seems better designed for overcoming hierarchical barriers, for developing a degree of interpersonal relationships which make communication along the chain of command possible, and for retaining a modicum of innovation and/or flexibility.

13. According to the above passage, group-oriented training is MOST useful in   13.____

    A.   developing a communications system that will facilitate understanding through the chain of command
    B.   highly flexible and mobile organizations
    C.   preventing the crossing of hierarchical barriers within an organization
    D.   saving energy otherwise wasted on developing methods of dealing with rigid hierarchies

14. The one of the following conclusions which can be drawn MOST appropriately from the   14.____
above passage is that

    A. behavioral research supports the use of organizational development training meth-
ods rather than individualized training
    B. it is easier to provide individualized training in specific skills than to set up sensitiv-
ity training programs
    C. organizational development eliminates innovative or flexible activity
    D. the nature of an organization greatly influences which training methods will be
most effective

15. According to the above passage, the one of the following which is LEAST important for   15.____
large-scale organizations geared to rapid and abrupt change is

    A. current technological information
    B. development of a high degree of interpersonal relationships
    C. development of individual skills and abilities
    D. emphasis on creativity

Questions 16-18.

DIRECTIONS: Questions 16 through 18 are to be answered SOLELY on the basis of the following passage.

    The increase in the extent to which each individual is personally responsible to others is
most noticeable in a large bureaucracy. No one person *decides* anything; each decision of
any importance, is the product of an intricate process of brokerage involving individuals inside
and outside the organization who feel some reason to be affected by the decision, or who
have special knowledge to contribute to it. The more varied the organization's constituency,
the more outside *veto-groups* will need to be taken into account. But even if no outside con-
sultations were involved, sheer size would produce a complex process of decision. For a
large organization is a deliberately created system of tensions into which each individual is
expected to bring work-ways, viewpoints, and outside relationships markedly different from
those of his colleagues. It is the administrator's task to draw from these disparate forces the
elements of wise action from day to day, consistent with the purposes of the organization as a
whole.

16. The above passage is essentially a description of decision making as   16.____

    A. an organization process
    B. the key responsibility of the administrator
    C. the one best position among many
    D. a complex of individual decisions

17. Which one of the following statements BEST describes the responsibilities of an adminis-   17.____
trator?

    A. He modifies decisions and goals in accordance with pressures from within and out-
side the organization.
    B. He creates problem-solving mechanisms that rely on the varied interests of his
staff and *veto-groups*.
    C. He makes determinations that will lead to attainment of his agency's objectives.
    D. He obtains agreement among varying viewpoints and interests.

18. In the context of the operations of a central public personnel agency, a *veto group* would LEAST likely consist of

    18.___

    A. employee organizations
    B. professional personnel societies
    C. using agencies
    D. civil service newspapers

Questions 19-25.

DIRECTIONS: Questions 19 through 25 are to be answered SOLELY on the basis of the following passage, which is an extract from a report prepared for Department X, which outlines the procedure to be followed in the case of transfers of employees.

Every transfer, regardless of the reason therefore, requires completion of the record of transfer, Form DT 411. To denote consent to the transfer, DT 411 should contain the signatures of the transferee and the personnel officer(s) concerned, except that, in the case of an involuntary transfer, the signatures of the transferee's present and prospective supervisors shall be entered in Boxes 8A and 8B, respectively, since the transferee does not consent. Only a permanent employee may request a transfer; in such cases, the employee's attendance record shall be duly considered with regard to absences, latenesses, and accrued overtime balances. In the case of an inter-district transfer, the employee's attendance record must be included in Section 8A of the transfer request, Form DT 410, by the personnel officer of the district from which the transfer is requested. The personnel officer of the district to which the employee requested transfer may refuse to accept accrued overtime balances in excess of ten days.

An employee on probation shall be eligible for transfer. If such employee is involuntarily transferred, he shall be credited for the period of time already served on probation. However, if such transfer is voluntary, the employee shall be required to serve the entire period of his probation in the new position. An employee who has occurred a disability which prevents him from performing his normal duties may be transferred during the period of such disability to other appropriate duties. A disability transfer requires the completion of either Form DT 414 if the disability is job-connected, or Form DT 415 if it is not a job-connected disability. In either case, the personnel officer of the district from which the transfer is made signs in Box 6A of the first two copies and the personnel officer of the district to which the transfer is made signs in Box 6B of the last two copies, or, in the case of an intra-district disability transfer, the personnel officer must sign in Box 6A of the first two copies and Box 6B of the last two copies.

19. When a personnel officer consents to an employee's request for transfer from his district, this procedure requires that the personnel officer sign Form(s)

    19._

    A. DT 411
    B. DT 410 and DT 411
    C. DT 411 and either Form DT 414 or DT 415
    D. DT 410 and DT 411, and either Form DT 414 or DT 415

20. With respect to the time record of an employee transferred against his wishes during his probationary period, this procedure requires that

    20._

    A. he serve the entire period of his probation in his present office
    B. he lose his accrued overtime balance

C. his attendance record be considered with regard to absences and latenesses
D. he be given credit for the period of time he has already served on probation

21. Assume you are a supervisor and an employee must be transferred into your office against his wishes. According to the this procedure, the box you must sign on the record of transfer is

    A. 6A   B. 8A   C. 6B   D. 8B

21._____

22. Under this procedure, in the case of a disability transfer, when must Box 6A on Forms DT 414 and DT 415 be signed by the personnel officer of the district to which the transfer is being made?

    A. In all cases when either Form DT 414 or Form DT 415 is used
    B. In all cases when Form DT 414 is used and only under certain circumstances when Form DT 415 is used
    C. In all cases when Form DT 415 is used and only under certain circumstances when Form DT 414 is used
    D. Only under certain circumstances when either Form DT 414 or Form DT 415 is used

22._____

23. From the above passage, it may be inferred MOST correctly that the number of copies of Form DT 414 is

    A. no more than 2
    B. at least 3
    C. at least 5
    D. more than the number of copies of Form DT 415

23._____

24. A change in punctuation and capitalization only which would change one sentence into two and possibly contribute to somewhat greater ease of reading this report extract would be MOST appropriate in the

    A. 2nd sentence, 1st paragraph
    B. 3rd sentence, 1st paragraph
    C. next to he last sentence, 2nd paragraph
    D. 2nd sentence, 2nd paragraph

24._____

25. In the second paragraph, a word that is INCORRECTLY used is

    A. *shall* in the 1st sentence
    B. *voluntary* in the 3rd sentence
    C. *occurred* in the 4th sentence
    D. *intra-district* in the last sentence

25._____

KEY (CORRECT ANSWERS)

1.	C		11.	C
2.	B		12.	B
3.	B		13.	A
4.	B		14.	D
5.	B		15.	B
6.	C		16.	A
7.	D		17.	C
8.	B		18.	B
9.	C		19.	A
10.	D		20.	D

21.	D
22.	D
23.	B
24.	B
25.	C

PREPARING WRITTEN MATERIAL

PARAGRAPH REARRANGEMENT
COMMENTARY

The sentences which follow are in scrambled order. You are to rearrange them in proper order and indicate the letter choice containing the correct answer at the space at the right.

Each group of sentences in this section is actually a paragraph presented in scrambled order. Each sentence in the group has a place in that paragraph; no sentence is to be left out. You are to read each group of sentences and decide upon the best order in which to put the sentences so as to form as well-organized paragraph.

The questions in this section measure the ability to solve a problem when all the facts relevant to its solution are not given.

More specifically, certain positions of responsibility and authority require the employee to discover connections between events sometimes, apparently, unrelated. In order to do this, the employee will find it necessary to correctly infer that unspecified events have probably occurred or are likely to occur. This ability becomes especially important when action must be taken on incomplete information.

Accordingly, these questions require competitors to choose among several suggested alternatives, each of which presents a different sequential arrangement of the events. Competitors must choose the MOST logical of the suggested sequences.

In order to do so, they may be required to draw on general knowledge to infer missing concepts or events that are essential to sequencing the given events. Competitors should be careful to infer only what is essential to the sequence. The plausibility of the wrong alternatives will always require the inclusion of unlikely events or of additional chains of events which are NOT essential to sequencing the given events.

It's very important to remember that you are looking for the best of the four possible choices, and that the best choice of all may not even be one of the answers you're given to choose from.

There is no one right way to solve these problems. Many people have found it helpful to first write out the order of the sentences, as they would have arranged them, on their scrap paper before looking at the possible answers. If their optimum answer is there, this can save them some time. If it isn't, this method can still give insight into solving the problem. Others find it most helpful to just go through each of the possible choices, contrasting each as they go along. You should use whatever method feels comfortable, and works, for you.

While most of these types of questions are not that difficult, we've added a higher percentage of the difficult type, just to give you more practice. Usually there are only one or two questions on this section that contain such subtle distinctions that you're unable to answer confidently, and you then may find yourself stuck deciding between two possible choices, neither of which you're sure about.

EXAMINATION SECTION
TEST 1

DIRECTIONS: The sentences that follow are in scrambled order. You are to rearrange them in proper order and indicate the letter choice containing the correct answer. *PRINT THE LETTER OF THE CORRECT ANSWER IN THE SPACE AT THE RIGHT.*

1. Below are four statements labeled W., X., Y., and Z.   1._____
    W.   He was a strict and fanatic drillmaster.
    X.   The word is always used in a derogatory sense and generally shows resentment and anger on the part of the user.
    Y.   It is from the name of this Frenchman that we derive our English word, martinet.
    Z.   Jean Martinet was the Inspector-General of Infantry during the reign of King Louis XIV.
    The *PROPER* order in which these sentences should be placed in a paragraph is:

    A.   X, Z, W, Y   B.   X, Z, Y, W   C.   Z, W, Y, X   D.   Z, Y, W, X

2. In the following paragraph, the sentences which are numbered, have been jumbled.   2._____
    1.   Since then it has undergone changes.
    2.   It was incorporated in 1955 under the laws of the State of New York.
    3.   Its primary purpose, a cleaner city, has, however, remained the same.
    4.   The Citizens Committee works in cooperation with the Mayor's Inter-departmental Committee for a Clean City.
    The order in which these sentences should be arranged to form a well-organized paragraph is:

    A.   2, 4, 1, 3   B.   3, 4, 1, 2   C.   4, 2, 1, 3   D.   4, 3, 2, 1

Questions 3-5.

DIRECTIONS: The sentences listed below are part of a meaningful paragraph but they are not given in their proper order. You are to decide what would be the *best order* in which to put the sentences so as to form a well-organized paragraph. Each sentence has a place in the paragraph; there are no extra sentences. You are then to answer questions 3 to 5 inclusive on the basis of your rearrangements of these scrambled sentences into a properly organized paragraph.

In 1887 some insurance companies organized an Inspection Department to advise their clients on all phases of fire prevention and protection. Probably this has been due to the smaller annual fire losses in Great Britain than in the United States. It tests various fire prevention devices and appliances and determines manufacturing hazards and their safeguards. Fire research began earlier in the United States and is more advanced than in Great Britain. Later they established a laboratory specializing in electrical, mechanical, hydraulic, and chemical fields.

3. When the five sentences are arranged in proper order, the paragraph starts with the sentence which begins

    A. "In 1887..."   B. "Probably this ..."   C. "It tests ..."
    D. "Fire research ..."   E. "Later they ..."

3.____

4. In the last sentence listed above, "they" refers to

    A. insurance companies
    B. the United States and Great Britain
    C. the Inspection Department
    D. clients
    E. technicians

4.____

5. When the above paragraph is properly arranged, it ends with the words

    A. "... and protection."   B. "... the United States."
    C. "... their safeguards."   D. "... in Great Britain."
    E. "... chemical fields."

5.____

KEY (CORRECT ANSWERS)

    1. C
    2. C
    3. D
    4. A
    5. C

TEST 2

DIRECTIONS: In each of the questions numbered 1 through 5, several sentences are given. For each question, choose as your answer the group of numbers that represents the *most logical* order of these sentences if they were arranged in paragraph form. *PRINT THE LETTER OF THE CORRECT ANSWER IN THE SPACE AT THE RIGHT.*

1. 1. It is established when one shows that the landlord has prevented the tenant's enjoyment of his interest in the property leased.
    2. Constructive eviction is the result of a breach of the covenant of quiet enjoyment implied in all leases.
    3. In some parts of the United States, it is not complete until the tenant vacates within a reasonable time.
    4. Generally, the acts must be of such serious and permanent character as to deny the tenant the enjoyment of his possessing rights.
    5. In this event, upon abandonment of the premises, the tenant's liability for that ceases.

    The CORRECT answer is:

    A. 2, 1, 4, 3, 5   B. 5, 2, 3, 1, 4   C. 4, 3, 1, 2, 5
    D. 1, 3, 5, 4, 2

    1.____

2. 1. The powerlessness before private and public authorities that is the typical experience of the slum tenant is reminiscent of the situation of blue-collar workers all through the nineteenth century.
    2. Similarly, in recent years, this chapter of history has been reopened by anti-poverty groups which have attempted to organize slum tenants to enable them to bargain collectively with their landlords about the conditions of their tenancies.
    3. It is familiar history that many of the workers remedied their condition by joining together and presenting their demands collectively.
    4. Like the workers, tenants are forced by the conditions of modern life into substantial dependence on these who possess great political arid economic power.
    5. What's more, the very fact of dependence coupled with an absence of education and self-confidence makes them hesitant and unable to stand up for what they need from those in power.

    The CORRECT answer is:

    A. 5, 4, 1, 2, 3   B. 2, 3, 1, 5, 4   C. 3, 1, 5, 4, 2
    D. 1, 4, 5, 3, 2

    2.____

3. 1. A railroad, for example, when not acting as a common carrier may contract away responsibility for its own negligence.
    2. As to a landlord, however, no decision has been found relating to the legal effect of a clause shifting the statutory duty of repair to the tenant.
    3. The courts have not passed on the validity of clauses relieving the landlord of this duty and liability.
    4. They have, however, upheld the validity of exculpatory clauses in other types of contracts.
    5. Housing regulations impose a duty upon the landlord to maintain leased premises in safe condition.

    3.____

153

6. As another example, a bailee may limit his liability except for gross negligence, willful acts, or fraud.

The CORRECT answer is:

A. 2, 1, 6, 4, 3, 5   B. 1, 3, 4, 5, 6, 2   C. 3, 5, 1, 4, 2, 6
D. 5, 3, 4, 1, 6, 2

4.   1. Since there are only samples in the building, retail or consumer sales are generally   4._____
eschewed by mart occupants, and in some instances, rigid controls are maintained
to limit entrance to the mart only to those persons engaged in retailing.
   2. Since World War I, in many larger cities, there has developed a new type of
property, called the mart building.
   3. It can, therefore, be used by wholesalers and jobbers for the display of sample
merchandise.
   4. This type of building is most frequently a multi-storied, finished interior property
which is a cross between a retail arcade and a loft building.
   5. This limitation enables the mart occupants to ship the orders from another location after the retailer or dealer makes his selection from the samples.

The CORRECT answer is:

A. 2, 4, 3, 1, 5   B. 4, 3, 5, 1, 2   C. 1, 3, 2, 4, 5
D. 1, 4, 2, 3, 5

5.   1. In general, staff-line friction reduces the distinctive contribution of staff personnel.   5._____
   2. The conflicts, however, introduce an uncontrolled element into the managerial
system.
   3. On the other hand, the natural resistance of the line to staff innovations probably
usefully restrains over-eager efforts to apply untested procedures on a large
scale.
   4. Under such conditions, it is difficult to know when valuable ideas are being sacri-
ficed.
   5. The relatively weak position of staff, requiring accommodation to the line, tends
to restrict their ability to engage in free, experimental innovation.

The CORRECT answer is:

A. 4, 2, 3, 1, 3   B. 1, 5, 3, 2, 4   C. 5, 3, 1, 2, 4
D. 2, 1, 4, 5, 3

KEY (CORRECT ANSWERS)

1. A
2. D
3. D
4. A
5. B

TEST 3

DIRECTIONS: Questions 1 through 4 consist of six sentences which can be arranged in a logical sequence. For each question, select the choice which places the numbered sentences in the *most logical* sequence. *PRINT THE LETTER OF THE CORRECT ANSWER IN THE SPACE AT THE RIGHT.*

1. 1. The burden of proof as to each issue is determined before trial and remains upon the same party throughout the trial.
    2. The jury is at liberty to believe one witness' testimony as against a number of contradictory witnesses.
    3. In a civil case, the party bearing the burden of proof is required to prove his contention by a fair preponderance of the evidence.
    4. However, it must be noted that a fair preponderance of evidence does not necessarily mean a greater number of witnesses.
    5. The burden of proof is the burden which rests upon one of the parties to an action to persuade the trier of the facts, generally the jury, that a proposition he asserts is true.
    6. If the evidence is equally balanced, or if it leaves the jury in such doubt as to be unable to decide the controversy either way, judgment must be given against the party upon whom the burden of proof rests.

    The CORRECT answer is:

    A. 3, 2, 5, 4, 1, 6   B. 1, 2, 6, 5, 3, 4   C. 3, 4, 5, 1, 2, 6
    D. 5, 1, 3, 6, 4, 2

    1.____

2. 1. If a parent is without assets and is unemployed, he cannot be convicted of the crime of non-support of a child.
    2. The term "sufficient ability" has been held to mean sufficient financial ability.
    3. It does not matter if his unemployment is by choice or unavoidable circumstances.
    4. If he fails to take any steps at all, he may be liable to prosecution for endangering the welfare of a child.
    5. Under the penal law, a parent is responsible for the support of his minor child only if the parent is "of sufficient ability."
    6. An indigent parent may meet his obligation by borrowing money or by seeking aid under the provisions of the Social Welfare Law.

    The CORRECT answer is:

    A. 6, 1, 5, 3, 2, 4   B. 1, 3, 5, 2, 4, 6   C. 5, 2, 1, 3, 6, 4
    D. 1, 6, 4, 5, 2, 3

    2.____

3.
1. Consider, for example, the case of a rabble rouser who urges a group of twenty people to go out and break the windows of a nearby factory.
2. Therefore, the law fills the indicated gap with the crime of inciting to riot.
3. A person is considered guilty of inciting to riot when he urges ten or more persons to engage in tumultuous and violent conduct of a kind likely to create public alarm.
4. However, if he has not obtained the cooperation of at least four people, he cannot be charged with unlawful assembly.
5. The charge of inciting to riot was added to the law to cover types of conduct which cannot be classified as either the crime of "riot" or the crime of "unlawful assembly."
6. If he acquires the acquiescence of at least four of them, he is guilty of unlawful assembly even if the project does not materialize.

The CORRECT answer is:

A. 3, 5, 1, 6, 4, 2   B. 5, 1, 4, 6, 2, 3   C. 3, 4, 1, 5, 2, 6
D. 5, 1, 4, 6, 3, 2

3.____

4.
1. If, however, the rebuttal evidence presents an issue of credibility, it is for the jury to determine whether the presumption has, in fact, been destroyed.
2. Once sufficient evidence to the contrary is introduced, the presumption disappears from the trial.
3. The effect of a presumption is to place the burden upon the adversary to come forward with evidence to rebut the presumption.
4. When a presumption is overcome and ceases to exist in the case, the fact or facts which gave rise to the presumption still remain.
5. Whether a presumption has been overcome is ordinarily a question for the court.
6. Such information may furnish a basis for a logical inference.

The CORRECT answer is:

A. 4, 6, 2, 5, 1, 3   B. 3, 2, 5, 1, 4, 6   C. 5, 3, 6, 4, 2, 1
D. 5, 4, 1, 2, 6, 3

4.____

KEY (CORRECT ANSWERS)

1. D
2. C
3. A
4. B

PREPARING WRITTEN MATERIAL
EXAMINATION SECTION
TEST 1

DIRECTIONS: The following groups of sentences need to be arranged in an order that makes sense. Select the letter preceding the sequence that represents the *BEST sentence order. PRINT THE LETTER OF THE CORRECT ANSWER IN THE SPACE AT THE RIGHT.*

1.   1._____

   I.   A large Naval station on Alameda Island, near Oakland, held many warships in port, and the War Department was worried that if the bridge were to be blown up by the enemy, passage to and from the bay would be hopelessly blocked.

   II.   Though many skeptics were opposed to the idea of building such an enormous bridge, the most vocal opposition came from a surprising source: the United States War Department.

   III. The War Department's concerns led to a showdown at San Francisco City Hall between Strauss and the Secretary of War, who demanded to know what would happen if a military enemy blew up the bridge.

   IV. In 1933, by submitting a construction cost estimate of $17 million, an engineer named Joseph Strauss won the contract to build the Golden Gate Bridge of San Francisco, which would then become one of the world's largest bridges.

   V.   Strauss quickly ended the debate by explaining that the Golden Gate Bridge was to be a suspension bridge, whose roadway would hang in the air from cables strung between two huge towers, and would immediately sink into three hundred feet of water if it were destroyed.

The best order is
A.   II, III, I, IV, V
B.   I, II, III, V, IV
C.   IV, II, I, III, V
D.   IV, I, III, V, II

2.

   I.   Plastic surgeons have already begun to use virtual reality to map out the complex nerve and tissue structures of a particular patient's face, in order to prepare for delicate surgery.

   II.   A virtual reality program responds to these movements by adjusting the Images that a person sees on a screen or through goggles, thereby creating an "interactive" world in which a person can see and touch three-dimensional graphic objects.

   III.   No more than a computer program that is designed to build and display graphic images, the virtual reality program takes graphic programs a step further by sensing a person's head and body movements.

   IV.   The computer technology known as virtual reality, now in its very first stages of development, is already revolutionizing some aspects of contemporary life.

   V.   Virtual reality computers are also being used by the space program, most recently to simulate conditions for the astronauts who were launched on a repair mission to the Hubble telescope.

The best order is
A. IV, II, I, V, III
B. III, I, V, II, IV
C. IV, III, II, I, V
D. III, I, II, IV, V

3.

   I.   Before you plant anything, the soil in your plant bed should be carefully raked level, a small section at a time, and any clods or rocks that can't be broken up should be removed.

   II.   Your plant should be placed in a hole that will position it at the same level it was at the nursery, and a small indentation should be pressed into the soil around the plant in order to hold water near it roots.

   III.   Before placing the plant in the soil, lightly separate any roots that may have been matted together in the container, cutting away any thick masses that can't be separated, so that the remaining roots will be able to grow outward.

   IV.   After the bed is ready, remove your plant from its container by turning it upside down and tapping or pushing on the bottom — never remove it by pulling on the plant.

   V.   When you bring home a small plant in an individual container from the nursery, there are several things to remember while preparing to plant it in your own garden.

The best order is
A. V, IV, III, II, I
B. V, I, IV, III, II
C. I, IV, II, III, V
D. I, IV, V, II, III

4.   4._____

    I.   The motte and its tower were usually built first, so that sentries could use it as a lookout to warn the castle workers of any danger that might approach the castle.

    II.   Though the moat and palisade offered the bailey a good deal of protection, it was linked to the motte by a set of stairs that led to a retractable drawbridge at the motte's gate, to enable people to evacuate and retreat onto the motte in case of an attack.

    III. The *motte* of these early castles was a fortified hill, sometimes as high as one hundred feet, on which stood a palisade and tower.

    IV. The *bailey* was a clear, level spot below the motte, also enclosed by a palisade, which in turn was surrounded by a large trench or moat.

    V.   The earliest castles built in Europe were not the magnificent stone giants that still tower over much of the European landscape, but simpler wooden constructions called motte-and-bailey castles.

The best order is
A. V, III, I, IV, II
B. V, IV, I, II, III
C. I, IV, IIII, II, V
D. I, III, II, IV, V

5.   5._____

    I.   If an infant is left alone or abandoned for a short while, its immediate response is to cry loudly, accompanying its screams with aggressive flailing of its legs and limbs.

    II.   If a child has been abandoned for a longer period of time, it becomes completely still and quiet, as if realizing that now its only chance for survival is to shut its mouth and remain motionless.

    III. Along with their intense fear of the dark, the crying behavior of human infants offers insights into how prehistoric newborn children might have evolved instincts that would prevent them from becoming victims of predators.

    IV. This behavior often surprises people who enter a hospital's maternity ward for the first time and encounter total silence from a roomful of infants.

    V.   This violent screaming response is quite different from an infant's cries of discomfort or hunger, and seems to serve as either the child's first line of defense against an unwanted intruder, or a desperate attempt to communicate its position to the mother.

The best order is
A. III, II, IV, I, V
B. III, I, V, II, IV
C. I, V, IV, II, III
D. II, IV, I, V, III

6.

I.   When two cats meet who are strangers, their first actions and gestures determine who the "dominant" cat will be, at least for the time being.

II.   Unlike dogs, cats are typically a solitary animal species who avoid social interaction, but they do display specific social responses to each other upon meeting.

III.   This is unlikely, however; before such a point of open hostility is reached, one of the cats will usually take the "submissive" position of crouching down while looking away from the other cat.

IV.   If a cat desires dominance or sees the other cat as a threat to its territory, it will stare directly at the intruder with a lowered tail.

V.   If the other cat responds with a similar gesture, or with the strong defensive posture of an arched back, laid-back ears and raised tail, a fight or chase is likely if neither cat gives in.

The best order is
A. IV, II, I, V, III
B. I, II, IV, V, III
C. I, IV, V, III, II
D. II, I, IV, V, III

7.

I.   A star or planet's gravitational force can best be explained in this way: anything passing through this "dent" in space will veer toward the star or planet as if it were rolling into a hole.

II.   Objects that are massive or heavy, such as stars or planets, "sink" into this surface, creating a sort of dent or concavity in the surrounding space.

III.   Black holes, the most massive objects known to exist in space, create dents so large and deep that the space surrounding them actually folds in on itself, preventing anything that falls in — even light — from ever escaping again.

IV.   The sort of dent a star or planet makes depends on how massive it is; planets generally have weak gravitational pulls, but stars, which are larger and heavier, make a bigger "dent" that will attract more matter.

V.   In outer space, the force of gravity works as if the surrounding space is a soft, flat surface.

The best order is
A. III, V, II, I, IV
B. III, IV, I, V, II
C. V, II, I, IV, III
D. I, V, II, IV, III

8.   8._____

    I.   Eventually, the society of Kyoto gave the world one of its first and greatest novels when Japan's most prominent writer, Lady Murasaki Shikibu, wrote her chronicle of Kyoto's society, *The Tale of Genji*, which preceded the first European novels by more than 500 years.

    II.   The society of Kyoto was dedicated to the pleasures of art; the courtiers experimented with new and colorful methods of sculpture, painting, writing, decorative gardening, and even making clothes.

    III.   Japanese culture began under the powerful authority of Chinese Buddhism, which influenced every aspect of Japanese life from religion to politics and art.

    IV.   This new, vibrant culture was so sophisticated that all the people in Kyoto's imperial court considered themselves poets, and the line between life and art hardly existed — lovers corresponded entirely through written verses, and even government officials communicated by writing poems to each other.

    V.   In the eighth century, when the emperor established the town of Kyoto as the capital of the Japanese empire, Japanese society began to develop its own distinctive style.

The best order is
A.   V, II, IV, I, III
B.   II, I, V, IV, III
C.   V, III, IV, I, II
D.   III, V, II, IV, I

9.   9._____

    I.   Instead of wheels, the HSST uses two sets of magnets, one which sits on the track, and another that is carried by the train; these magnets generate an identical magnetic field which forces the two sets apart.

    II.   In the last few decades, railway travel has become less popular throughout the world, because it is much slower than travel by airplane, and not much less expensive.

    III.   The HSST's designers say that the train can take passengers from one town to another as quickly as a jet plane — while consuming less than half the energy.

    IV.   This repellent effect is strong enough to lift the entire train above the trackway, and the train, literally traveling on air, rockets along at speeds of up to 300 miles per hour.

    V.   The revolutionary technology of magnetic levitation, currently being tested by Japan's experimental HSST (High Speed Surface Transport), may yet bring passenger trains back from the dead.

The best order is
A.   II, V, I, IV, III
B.   II, I, IV, III, V
C.   V, II, III, I, IV
D.   V, I, III, IV, II

10.   10._____

    I.   When European countries first began to colonize the African continent, their impression of the African people was of a vast group of loosely organized tribal societies, without any great centralized source of power or wealth.

    II. The legend of Timbuktu persisted until the nineteenth century, when a French adventurer visited Timbuktu and found that raids by neighboring tribesmen had made the city a shadow of its former self.

    III. In the fifteenth century, when the stories of travelers who had traveled Africa's Sudan region began circulating around Europe, this impression began to change.

    IV. In 1470, an Italian merchant named Benedetto Dei traveled to Timbuktu and confirmed these rumors, describing a thriving metropolis where rich and poor people worshipped together in the city's many ornate mosques — there was even a university in Timbuktu, much like its European counterparts, where African scholars pursued their studies in the arts and sciences.

    V. The travelers' legends told of an enormous city in the western Sudan, Timbuktu, where the streets were crowded with goods brought by faraway caravans, and where there was a stone palace as large as any in Europe.

The best order is
A. III, V, I, IV, II
B. I, II, IV, III, V
C. I, III, V, IV, II
D. II, I, III, IV, V

11.   11._____

    I.   Also, our reference points in sighting the moon may make us believe that its size is changing; when the moon is rising through the trees, it seems huge, because our brains unconsciously compare the size of the moon with the size of the trees in the foreground.

    II. To most people, the sky itself appears more distant at the horizon than directly overhead, and if the moon's size — which remains constant — is projected from the horizon, the apparent distance of the horizon makes the moon look bigger.

    III. Up higher in the sky, the moon is set against tiny stars in the background, which will make the moon seem smaller.

    IV. People often wonder why the moon becomes bigger when it approaches the horizon, but most scientists agree that this is a complicated optical illusion, produced by at least three factors.

    V. The moon illusion may also be partially explained by a phenomenon that has nothing to do with errors in our perception — light that enters the earth's atmosphere is sometimes refracted, and so the atmosphere may act as a kind of magnifying glass for the moon's image.

The best order is
A. IV, III, V, II, I
B. IV, II, I, III, V
C. V, II, I, III, IV
D. II, I, III, IV, V

12.

12._____

I.   When the Native Americans were introduced to the horses used by white explorers, they were amazed at their new alternative — here was an animal that was strong and swift, would patiently carry a person or other loads on its back, and, they later discovered, was right at home on the plains.

II.   Before the arrival of European explorers to North America, the natives of the American plains used large dogs to carry their travois-long lodgepoles loaded with clothing, gear, and food.

III.   These horses, it is now known, were not really strangers to North America; the very first horses originated here, on this continent, tens of thousands of years ago, and migrated into Asia across the Bering Land Bridge, a strip of land that used to link our continent with the Eastern world.

IV.   At first, the natives knew so little about horses that at least one tribe tried to feed their new animals pieces of dried meat and animal fat, and were surprised when the horses turned their heads away and began to eat the grass of the prairie.

V.   The American horse eventually became extinct, but its Asian cousins were reintroduced to the New World when the European explorers brought them to live among the Native Americans.

The best order is
A. II, I, IV, III, V
B. II, IV, I, III, V
C. I, II, IV, III, V
D. I, III, V, II, IV

13.

13._____

I.   The dress worn by the dancer is believed to have been adorned in the past by shells which would strike each other as the dancer performed, creating a lovely sound.

II.   Today's jingle-dress is decorated with the tin lids of snuff cans, which are rolled into cones and sewn onto the dress.

III.   During the jingle-dress dance, the dancer must blend complicated footwork with a series of gentle hops that cause the cones to jingle in rhythm to a drumbeat.

IV.   When contemporary Native American tribes meet for a pow-wow, one of the most popular ceremonies to take place is the women's jingle-dress dance.

V.   Besides being more readily available than shells, the lids are thought by many dancers to create a softer, more subtle sound.

The best order is
A. II, IV, V, I, III
B. IV, II, I, III, V
C. II, I, III, V, IV
D. IV, I, II, V, III

14.   14._____

   I.   If a homeowner lives where seasonal climates are extreme, deciduous shade trees — which will drop their leaves in the winter and allow sunlight to pass through the windows — should be planted near the southern exposure in order to keep the house cool during the summer.

   II.   This trajectory is shorter and lower in the sky than at any other time of year during the winter, when a house most requires heating; the northern-facing parts of a house do not receive any direct sunlight at all.

   III. In designing an energy-efficient house, especially in colder climates, it is important to remember that most of the house's windows should face south.

   IV. Though the sun always rises in the east and sets in the west, the sun of the northern hemisphere is permanently situated in the southern portion of the sky.

   V.   The explanation for why so many architects and builders want this "southern exposure"
is related to the path of the sun in the sky.

The best order is
A. III, I, V, IV, II
B. III, V, IV, II, I
C. I, III, IV, II, V
D. I, II, V, IV, III

15.   15._____

   I.   His journeying lasted twenty-four years and took him over an estimated 75,000 miles, a distance that would not be surpassed by anyone other than Magellan — who sailed around the world — for another six hundred years.

   II.   Perhaps the most far-flung of these lesser-known travelers was Ibn Batuta, an African Moslem who left his birthplace of Tangier in the summer of 1325.

   III. Ibn Batuta traveled all over Africa and Asia, from Niger to Peking, and to the islands of Maldive and Indonesia.

   IV. However, a few explorers of the Eastern world logged enough miles and adventures to make Marco Polo's voyage look like an evening stroll.

   V.   In America, the most well-known of the Old World's explorers are usually Europeans such as Marco Polo, the Italian who brought many elements of Chinese culture to the Western world.

The best order is
A. V, IV, II, III, I
B. V, IV, III, II, I
C. III, II, I, IV, V
D. II, III, I, IV, V

16.

16._____

I. In the rain forests of South America, a rare species of frog practices a reproductive method that is entirely different from this standard process.

II. She will eventually carry each of the tadpoles up into the canopy and drop each into its own little pool, where it will be easy to locate and safe from most predators.

III. After fertilization, the female of the species, who lives almost entirely on the forest floor, lays between 2 and 16 eggs among the leaf litter at the base of a tree, and stands watch over these eggs until they hatch.

IV. Most frogs are pond-dwellers who are able to deposit hundreds of eggs in the water and then leave them alone, knowing that enough eggs have been laid to insure the survival of some of their offspring.

V. Once the tadpoles emerge, the female backs in among them, and a tadpole will wriggle onto her back to be carried high into the forest canopy, where the female will deposit it in a little pool of water cupped in the leaf of a plant.

The best order is
A. I, IV, III, II, V
B. I, III, V, II, IV
C. IV, III, II, V, I
D. IV, I, III, V, II

17.

17._____

I. Eratosthenes had heard from travelers that at exactly noon on June 21, in the ancient city of Aswan, Egypt, the sun cast no shadow in a well, which meant that the sun must be directly overhead.

II. He knew the sun always cast a shadow in Alexandria, and so he figured that if he could measure the length of an Alexandria shadow at the time when there was no shadow in Aswan, he could calculate the angle of the sun, and therefore the circumference of the earth.

III. The evidence for a round earth was not new in 1492; in fact, Eratosthenes, an Alexandrian geographer who lived nearly sixteen centuries before Columbus's voyage (275-195 B.C.), actually developed a method for calculating the circumference of the earth that is still in use today.

IV. Eratosthenes's method was correct, but his result — 28,700 miles — was about 15 percent too high, probably because of the inaccurate ancient methods of keeping time, and because Aswan was not due south of Alexandria, as Eratosthenes had believed.

V. When Christopher Columbus sailed across the Atlantic Ocean for the first time in 1492, there were still some people in the world who ignored scientific evidence and believed that the earth was flat, rather than round.

The best order is
A. I, II, V, III, IV
B. V, III, IV, I, II
C. V, III, I, II, IV
D. III, V, I, II, IV

18.

I.   The first name for the child is considered a trial naming, often impersonal and neutral, such as the Ngoni name *Chabwera*, meaning "it has arrived."

II.   This sort of name is not due to any parental indifference to the child, but is a kind of silent recognition of Africa's sometimes high infant death rate; most parents ease the pain of losing a child with the belief that it is not really a person until it has been given a final name.

III.   In many tribal African societies, families often give two different names to their children, at different periods in time.

IV.   After the trial naming period has subsided and it is clear that the child will survive, the parents choose a final name for the child, an act that symbolically completes the act of birth.

V.   In fact, some African first-given names are explicitly uncomplimentary, translating as "I am dead" or "I am ugly," in order to avoid the jealousy of ancestral spirits who might wish to take a child that is especially healthy or attractive.

The best order is
A. III, I, II, V, IV
B. III, IV, II, I, V
C. IV, III, I, II, V
D. IV, V, III, I, II

19.

I.   Though uncertain of the definite reasons for this behavior, scientists believe the birds digest the clay in order to counteract toxins contained in the seeds of certain fruits that are eaten by macaws.

II.   For example, all macaws flock to riverbanks at certain times of the year to eat the clay that is found in river mud.

III.   The macaws of South America are not only among the largest and most beautifully colored of the world's flying birds, but they are also one of the smartest.

IV.   It is believed that macaws are forced to resort to these toxic fruits during the dry season, when foods are more scarce.

V.   The macaw's intelligence has led to intense study by scientists, who have discovered some macaw behaviors that have not yet been explained.

The best order is
A. III, IV, I, II, V
B. III, V, II, I, IV
C. V, II, I, IV, III
D. IV, I, II, III, V

20.

20._____

I.   Although Maggie Kuhn has since passed away, the Gray Panthers are still waging a campaign to reinstate the historical view of the elderly as people whose experience allows them to make their greatest contribution in their later years.

II.   In 1972, an elderly woman named Maggie Kuhn responded to this sort of treatment by forming a group called the Gray Panthers, an organization of both old and young adults with the common goal of creating change.

III.   This attitude is reflected strongly in the way elderly people are treated by our society; many are forced into early retirement, or are placed in rest homes in which they are isolated from their communities.

IV.   Unlike most other cultures around the world, Americans tend to look upon old age with a sense of dread and sadness.

V.   Kuhn believed that when the elderly are forced to withdraw into lives that lack purpose, society loses one of its greatest resources: people who have a lifetime of experience and wisdom to offer their communities.

The best order is
A. IV, III, II, V, I
B. IV, II, I, III, V
C. II, IV, III, V, I
D. II, I, IV, III, V

21.

21._____

I.   The current theory among most anthropologists is that humans evolved from apes who lived in trees near the grasslands of Africa.

II.   Still, some anthropologists insist that such an invention was necessary for the survival of early humans, and point to the Kung Bushmen of central Africa as a society in which the sling is still used in this way.

III.   Two of these inventions — fire, and weapons such as spears and clubs — were obvious defenses against predators, and there is archaeological evidence to support the theory of their use.

IV.   Once people had evolved enough to leave the safety of trees and walk upright, they needed the protection of several inventions in order to survive.

V.   But another invention, a leather or fiber sling that allowed mothers to carry children while leaving their hands free to gather roots or berries, would certainly have decomposed and left behind no trace of itself.

The best order is
A. I, II, III, V, IV
B. IV, I, II, III, V
C. I, IV, III, V, II
D. IV, III, V, II, I

22.

I. The person holding the bird should keep it in hot water up to its neck, and the person cleaning should work a mild solution of dishwashing liquid into the bird's plumage, paying close attention to the head and neck.

II. When rinsing the bird, after all the oil has been removed, the running water should be directed against the lay of its feathers, until water begins to bead off the surface of the feathers — a sign that all the detergent has been rinsed out.

III. If you have rescued a sea bird from an oil spill and want to restore it to clean and normal living, you need a large sink, a constant supply of running hot water (a little over 100° F), and regular dishwashing liquid.

IV. This cleaning with detergent solution should be repeated as many times as it takes to remove all traces of oil from the bird's feathers, sometimes over a period of several days.

V. But before you begin to clean the bird, you must first find a partner, because cleaning an oiled bird is a two-person job.

The best order is
A. III, I, II, IV, V
B. III, V, I, IV, II
C. III, I, IV, V, II
D. III, IV, V, I, II

23.

I. The most difficult time of year for the Tsaatang is the spring calving, when the reindeer leave their wintering ground and rush to their accustomed calving place, without stopping by night or by day.

II. Reindeer travel in herds, and though some animals are tamed by the Tsaatang for riding or milking, the herds are allowed to roam free.

III. This journey is hard for the Tsaatang, who carry all their possessions with them, but once it's over it proves worthwhile; the Tsaatang can immediately begin to gather milk from reindeer cows who have given birth.

IV. The Tsaatang, a small tribe who live in the far northwest corner of Mongolia, practice a lifestyle that is completely dependent on the reindeer, their main resource for food, clothing, and transport.

V. The people must follow their yearly migrations, living in portable shelters that resemble Native American tepees.

The best order is
A. I, III, II, V, IV
B. I, IV, II, V, III
C. IV, I, III, V, II
D. IV, II, V, I, III

24.   24._____

    I.   The Romans later improved this system by installing these heated pipe net-
          works throughout walls and ceilings, supplying heat to even the uppermost
          floors of a building — a system that, to this day, hasn't been much improved.

    II.   Air-conditioning, the method by which humans control indoor temperatures,
          was practiced much earlier than most people think.

    III.   The earliest heating devices other than open fires were used in 350 B.C. by
          the ancient Greeks, who directed air that had been heated by underground
          fires into baked clay pipes that ran under the floor.

    IV.   Ironically, the first successful cooling system, patented in England in 1831,
          used fire as its main energy source — fires were lit in the attic of a building,
          creating an updraft of air that drew cool air into the building through ducts
          that had underground openings near the river Thames.

    V.   Cooling buildings was more of a challenge, and wasn't attempted until 1500:
          a water-based system, designed by Leonardo da Vinci, does not appear to
          have been successful, since it was never used again.

The best order is
A. III, V, IV, I, II
B. III, I, II, V, IV
C. II, III, I, V, IV
D. IV, II, III, I, V

25.   25._____

    I.   Cold, dry air from Canada passes over the Rocky Mountains and sweeps
          down onto the plains, where it collides with warm, moist air from the waters
          of the Gulf of Mexico, and when the two air masses meet, the resulting
          disturbance sometimes forms a violent funnel cloud that strikes the earth
          and destroys virtually everything in its path.

    II.   Hurricanes, storms which are generally not this violent and last much longer,
          are usually given names by meteorologists, but this tradition cannot be applied
          to tornados, which have a life span measured in minutes and disappear in the
          same way as they are born — unnamed.

    III.   A tornado funnel forms rotating columns of air whose speed reaches three
          hundred miles an hour — a speed that can only be estimated, because no
          wind-measuring devices in the direct path of a storm have ever survived.

    IV.   The natural phenomena known as tornados occur primarily over the mid-
          western grasslands of the United States.

    V.   It is here, meteorologists tell us, that conditions for the formation of tornados
          are sometimes perfect during the spring months.

The best order is
A. II, IV, V, I, III
B. II, III, I, V, IV
C. IV, V, I, III, II
D. IV, III, I, V, II

KEY (CORRECT ANSWERS)

1.	C	11.	B
2.	C	12.	A
3.	B	13.	D
4.	A	14.	B
5.	B	15.	A
6.	D	16.	D
7.	C	17.	C
8.	D	18.	A
9.	A	19.	B
10.	C	20.	A

21.	C
22.	B
23.	D
24.	C
25.	C

PREPARING WRITTEN MATERIALS

EXAMINATION SECTION
TEST 1

DIRECTIONS: Each of the two sentences in the following questions may contain errors in punctuation, capitalization, or grammar.
If there is an error in only Sentence I, mark your answer A. If there is an error in only Sentence II, mark your answer B.
If there is an error in both Sentence I and Sentence II, mark your answer C. If both Sentence I and Sentence II are correct, mark your answer D.

1. I.   The task of typing these reports is to be divided equally between you and me.   1.____
    II. If I was he, I would use a different method for filing these records.

2. I.   The new clerk is just as capable as some of the older employees, if not more capa-   2.____
         ble.
    II. Using his knowledge of arithmetic to check the calculations, the supervisor found
         no errors in the report.

3. I.   A typist who does consistently superior work probably merits promotion.   3.____
    II. In its report on the stenographic unit, the committee pointed out that neither the
         stenographers nor the typists were adequately trained.

4. I.   Entering the office, the desk was noticed immediately by the visitor.   4.____
    II. Arrangements have been made to give this training to whoever applies for it.

5. I.   The office manager estimates that this assignment, which is to be handled by you   5.____
         and I, will require about two weeks for completion.
    II. One of the recommendations of the report is that these kind of forms be dis-
         carded because they are of no value.

6. I.   The supervisor knew that the typist was a quiet, cooperative, efficient, employee.   6.____
    II. The duties of a stenographer are to take dictation notes at conferences and tran-
         scribing them.

7. I.   The stenographer has learned that she, as well as two typists, is being assigned to   7.____
         the new unit.
    II. We do not know who you have designated to take charge of the new program.

8. I.   He asked, "When do you expect to return?"   8.____
    II. I doubt whether this system will be successful here; it is not suitable for the work
         of our agency.

9. I.   It is a policy of this agency to encourage punctuality as a good habit for we employ-   9.____
         ees to adopt.
    II. The successful completion of the task was due largely to them cooperating
         effectively with the supervisor.

10. I.   Mr. Smith, who is a very competent executive has offered his services to our   10.____
         department.
    II. Every one of the stenographers who work in this office is considered trustworthy.

11.   I.   It is very annoying to have a pencil sharpener, which is not in proper working order.   11.____
      II. The building watchman checked the door of Charlie's office and found that the lock has been jammed.

12.   I.   Since he went on the New York City council a year ago, one of his primary concerns has been safety in the streets.   12.____
      II. After waiting in the doorway for about 15 minutes, a black sedan appeared.

13.   I.   When you are studying a good textbook is important.   13.____
      II. He said he would divide the money equally between you and me.

14.   I.   The question is, "How can a large number of envelopes be sealed rapidly without the use of a sealing machine?"   14.____
      II. The administrator assigned two stenographers, Mary and I, to the new bureau.

15.   I.   A dictionary, in addition to the office management textbooks, were placed on his desk.   15.____
      II. The concensus of opinion is that none of the employees should be required to work overtime.

16.   I.   Mr. Granger has demonstrated that he is as courageous, if not more courageous, than Mr. Brown.   16.____
      II. The successful completion of the project depends on the manager's accepting our advisory opinion.

17.   I.   Mr. Ames was in favor of issuing a set of rules and regulations for all of us employees to follow.   17.____
      II. It is inconceivable that the new clerk knows how to deal with that kind of correspondence.

18.   I.   The revised referrence manual is to be used by all of the employees.   18.____
      II. Mr. Johnson told Miss Kent and me to accumulate all the letters that we receive.

19.   I.   The supervisor said, that before any changes would be made in the attendance report, there must be ample justification for them.   19.____
      II. Each of them was asked to amend their preliminary report.

20.   I.   Mrs. Peters conferred with Mr. Roberts before she laid the papers on his desk.   20.____
      II. As far as this report is concerned, Mr. Williams always has and will be responsible for its preparation.

KEY (CORRECT ANSWERS)

1.	B		11.	C
2.	D		12.	C
3.	D		13.	A
4.	A		14.	B
5.	C		15.	C
6.	C		16.	A
7.	B		17.	B
8.	D		18.	A
9.	C		19.	C
10.	A		20.	B

TEST 2

DIRECTIONS: Each question or incomplete statement is followed by several suggested answers or completions. Select the one that BEST answers the question or completes the statement. *PRINT THE LETTER OF THE CORRECT ANSWER IN THE SPACE AT THE RIGHT.*

Questions 1-9.

DIRECTIONS: Questions 1 through 9 consist of pairs of sentences which may or may not contain errors in grammar, capitalization, or punctuation.
If both sentences are correct, mark your answer A.
If the first sentence only is correct, mark your answer B.
If the second sentence only is correct, mark your answer C.
If both sentences are incorrect, mark your answer D.
NOTE: Consider a sentence correct if it contains no errors, although there may be other correct ways of writing the sentence.

1. I. An unusual conference will be held today at George Washington high school.   1.____
    II. The principal of the school, Dr. Pace, described the meeting as "a unique opportunity for educators to exchange ideas."

2. I. Studio D, which they would ordinarily use, will be occupied at that time.   2.____
    II. Any other studio, which is properly equipped, may be used instead.

3. I. D.H. Lawrence's Sons and Lovers were discussed on today's program.   3.____
    II. Either Eliot's or Yeats's work is to be covered next week.

4. I. This program is on the air for three years now, and has a well-established audience.   4.____
    II. We have received many complimentary letters from listeners, and scarcely no critical ones.

5. I. Both Mr. Owen and Mr. Mitchell have addressed the group.   5.____
    II. As has Mr. Stone, whose talks have been especially well received.

6. I. The original program was different in several respects from the version that eventually went on the air.   6.____
    II. Each of the three announcers who Mr. Scott thought had had suitable experience was asked whether he would be willing to take on the special assignment.

7. I. A municipal broadcasting system provides extensive coverage of local events, but also reports national and international news.   7.____
    II. A detailed account of happenings in the South may be carried by a local station hundreds of miles away.

8. I. Jack Doe the announcer and I will be working on the program.   8.____
    II. The choice of musical selections has been left up to he and I.

9. I. Mr. Taylor assured us that "he did not anticipate any difficulty in making arrange-   9.____
        ments for the broadcast ."
    II. Although there had seemed at first to be certain problems; these had been
        solved.

Questions 10-14.

DIRECTIONS: Questions 10 through 14 consist of pairs of sentences which may contain
             errors in grammar, sentence structure, punctuation, or spelling, or both sen-
             tences may be correct. Consider a sentence correct if it contains no errors,
             although there may be other correct ways of writing the sentence.
             If only Sentence I contains an error, mark your answer A.
             If only Sentence II contains an error, mark your answer B.
             If both sentences contain errors, mark your answer C.
             If both sentences are correct, mark your answer D.

10. I. No employee considered to be indispensable will be assigned to the new office.   10.____
     II. The arrangement of the desks and chairs give the office a neat appearance.

11. I. The recommendation, accompanied by a report, was delivered this morning.   11.____
     II. Mr. Green thought the procedure would facilitate his work; he knows better now.

12. I. Limiting the term "property" to tangible property, in the criminal mischief setting, 12.____
         accords with prior case law holding that only tangible property came within the pur-
         view of the offense of malicious mischief.
     II. Thus, a person who intentionally destroys the property of another, but under an
         honest belief that he has title to such property, cannot be convicted of criminal
         mischief under the Revised Penal Law.

13. I. Very early in its history, New York enacted statutes from time to time punishing,   13.____
         either as a felony or as a misdemeanor, malicious injuries to various kinds of prop-
         erty: piers, booms, dams, bridges, etc.
     II. The application of the statute is necessarily restricted to trespassory takings with
         larcenous intent: namely with intent permanently or virtually permanently to
         "appropriate" property or "deprive" the owner of its use.

14. I. Since the former Penal Law did not define the instruments of forgery in a general   14.____
         fashion, its crime of forgery was held to be narrower than the common law offense
         in this respect and to embrace only those instruments explicitly specified in the
         substantive provisions.
     II. After entering the barn through an open door for the purpose of stealing, it was
         closed by the defendants.

Questions 15-20.

DIRECTIONS: Questions 15 through 20 consist of pairs of sentences which may or may not
             contain errors in grammar, capitalization, or punctuation.
             If both sentences are correct, mark your answer A.
             If the first sentence only is correct, mark your answer B.
             If the second sentence only is correct, mark your answer C.
             If both sentences are incorrect, mark your answer D.

NOTE: Consider a sentence correct if it contains no errors, although there may be other correct ways of writing the sentence.

15. I. The program, which is currently most popular, is a news broadcast. 15.____
     II. The engineer assured his supervisor that there was no question of his being late again.

16. I. The announcer recommended that the program originally scheduled for that time be cancelled. 16.____
     II. Copies of the script may be given to whoever is interested.

17. I. A few months ago it looked like we would be able to broadcast the concert live. 17.____
     II. The program manager, as well as the announcers, were enthusiastic about the plan.

18. I. No speaker on the subject of education is more interesting than he. 18.____
     II. If he would have had the time, we would have scheduled him for a regular weekly broadcast.

19. I. This quartet, in its increasingly complex variations on a simple theme, admirably illustrates Professor Baker's point. 19.____
     II. Listeners interested in these kind of ideas will find his recently published study of Haydn rewarding.

20. I. The Commissioner's resignation at the end of next month marks the end of a long public service career. 20.____
     II. Outstanding among his numerous achievements were his successful implementation of several revolutionary schemes to reorganize the agency.

KEY (CORRECT ANSWERS)

1.	C	11.	D
2.	B	12.	C
3.	C	13.	B
4.	D	14.	A
5.	B	15.	C
6.	A	16.	A
7.	A	17.	D
8.	D	18.	B
9.	D	19.	B
10.	B	20.	B

PREPARING WRITTEN MATERIALS

EXAMINATION SECTION
TEST 1

DIRECTIONS: Each question consists of a sentence which may be classified appropriately under one of the following four categories:
- A. Incorrect because of faulty grammar or sentence structure;
- B. Incorrect because of faulty punctuation;
- C. Incorrect because of faulty capitalization;
- D. Correct.

Examine each sentence carefully. Then, in the space at the right, indicate the letter preceding the category which is the BEST of the four suggested above. Each incorrect sentence contains only one type of error. Consider a sentence correct if it contains no errors, although there may be other correct ways of expressing the same thought.

1. All the employees, in this office, are over twenty-one years old. 1.____

2. Neither the clerk nor the stenographer was able to explain what had happened. 2.____

3. Mr. Johnson did not know who he would assign to type the order. 3.____

4. Mr. Marshall called her to report for work on Saturday. 4.____

5. He might of arrived on time if the train had not been delayed. 5.____

6. Some employees on the other hand, are required to fill out these forms every month. 6.____

7. The supervisor issued special instructions to his subordinates to prevent their making errors. 7.____

8. Our supervisor Mr. Williams, expects to be promoted in about two weeks. 8.____

9. We were informed that prof. Morgan would attend the conference. 9.____

10. The clerks were assigned to the old building; the stenographers, to the new building. 10.____

11. The supervisor asked Mr. Smith and I to complete the work as quickly as possible. 11.____

12. He said, that before an employee can be permitted to leave, the report must be finished. 12.____

13. An adding machine, in addition to the three typewriters, are needed in the new office. 13.____

14. Having made many errors in her work, the supervisor asked the typist to be more careful. 14.____

15. "If you are given an assignment," he said, "you should begin work on it as quickly as possible." 15.____

16. All the clerks, including those who have been appointed recently are required to work on the new assignment. 16.____

17. The office manager asked each employee to work one Saturday a month.   17._____

18. Neither Mr. Smith nor Mr. Jones was able to finish his assignment on time.   18._____

19. The task of filing these cards is to be divided equally between you and he.   19._____

20. He is an employee whom we consider to be efficient.   20._____

21. I believe that the new employees are not as punctual as us.   21._____

22. The employees, working in this office, are to be congratulated for their work.   22._____

23. The delay in preparing the report was caused, in his opinion, by the lack of proper supervision and coordination.   23._____

24. John Jones accidentally pushed the wrong button and then all the lights went out.   24._____

25. The investigator ought to of had the witness sign the statement.   25._____

―――――――

KEY (CORRECT ANSWERS)

1.	B		11.	A
2.	D		12.	B
3.	A		13.	A
4.	C		14.	A
5.	A		15.	D
6.	B		16.	B
7.	D		17.	C
8.	B		18.	D
9.	C		19.	A
10.	D		20.	D

21.	A
22.	B
23.	D
24.	D
25.	A

―――――――

TEST 2

Questions 1-10.

DIRECTIONS: Each of the following sentences may be classified under one of the following
four options:
A. Faulty; contains an error in grammar only
B. Faulty; contains an error in spelling only
C. Faulty; contains an error in grammar and an error in spelling
D. Correct; contains no error in grammar or in spelling

Examine each sentence carefully to determine under which of the above four
options it is BEST classified. Then, in the space at the right, write the letter preceding the option which is the best of the four listed above.

1. A recognized principle of good management is that an assignment should be given to   1._____
    whomever is best qualified to carry it out.

2. He considered it a privilege to be allowed to review and summarize the technical reports   2._____
    issued annually by your agency.

3. Because the warehouse was in an inaccessable location, deliveries of electric fixtures   3._____
    from the warehouse were made only in large lots.

4. Having requisitioned the office supplies, Miss Brown returned to her desk and resumed   4._____
    the computation of petty cash disbursements.

5. One of the advantages of this chemical solution is that records treated with it are not   5._____
    inflamable.

6. The complaint of this employee, in addition to the complaints of the other employees,   6._____
    were submitted to the grievance committee.

7. A study of the duties and responsibilities of each of the various categories of employees   7._____
    was conducted by an unprejudiced classification analyst.

8. Ties of friendship with this subordinate compels him to withold the censure that the sub-   8._____
    ordinate deserves.

9. Neither of the agencies are affected by the decision to institute a program for rehabilitat- 9._____
    ing physically handi-caped men and women.

10. The chairman stated that the argument between you and he was creating an intolerable   10._____
    situation.

Questions 11-25.

DIRECTIONS: Each of the following sentences may be classified under one of the following
four options:

A. Correct
B. Sentence contains an error in spelling
C. Sentence contains an error in grammar
D. Sentence contains errors in both grammar and spelling.

11. He reported that he had had a really good time during his vacation although the farm was located in a very inaccessible portion of the country.　　11._____

12. It looks to me like he has been fasinated by that beautiful painting.　　12._____

13. We have permitted these kind of pencils to accumulate on our shelves, knowing we can sell them at a profit of five cents apiece any time we choose.　　13._____

14. Believing that you will want an unexagerated estimate of the amount of business we can expect, I have made every effort to secure accurate figures.　　14._____

15. Each and every man, woman and child in that untrameled wilderness carry guns for protection against the wild animals.　　15._____

16. Although this process is different than the one to which he is accustomed, a good chemist will have no trouble.　　16._____

17. Insensible to the fuming and fretting going on about him, the engineer continued to drive the mammoth dynamo to its utmost capacity.　　17._____

18. Everyone had studied his lesson carefully and was consequently well prepared when the instructor began to discuss the fourth dimention.　　18._____

19. I learned Johnny six new arithmetic problems this afternoon.　　19._____

20. Athletics is urged by our most prominent citizens as the pursuit which will enable the younger generation to achieve that ideal of education, a sound mind in a sound body.　　20._____

21. He did not see whoever was at the door very clearly but thinks it was the city tax appraiser.　　21._____

22. He could not scarsely believe that his theories had been substantiated in this convincing fashion.　　22._____

23. Although you have displayed great ingenuity in carrying out your assignments, the choice for the position still lies among Brown and Smith.　　23._____

24. If they had have pleaded at the time that Smith was an accessory to the crime, it would have lessened the punishment.　　24._____

25. It has proven indispensible in his compilation of the facts in the matter.　　25._____

KEY (CORRECT ANSWERS)

1.	A		11.	A
2.	D		12.	D
3.	B		13.	C
4.	D		14.	B
5.	B		15.	D
6.	A		16.	C
7.	D		17.	A
8.	C		18.	B
9.	C		19.	C
10.	A		20.	A

21.	B
22.	D
23.	C
24.	D
25.	B

TEST 3

Questions 1-5.

DIRECTIONS: Questions 1 through 5 consist of sentences which may or may not contain errors in grammar or spelling or both. Sentences which do not contain errors in grammar or spelling or both are to be considered correct, even though there may be other correct ways of expressing the same thought. Examine each sentence carefully. Then, in the space at the right, write the letter of the answer which is the BEST of those suggested below:
- A. If the sentence is correct;
- B. If the sentence contains an error in spelling;
- C. If the sentence contains an error in grammar;
- D. If the sentence contains errors in both grammar and spelling.

1. Brown is doing fine although the work is irrevelant to his training.   1.____

2. The conference of sales managers voted to set its adjournment at one o'clock in order to give those present an opportunity to get rid of all merchandise.   2.____

3. He decided that in view of what had taken place at the hotel that he ought to stay and thank the benificent stranger who had rescued him from an embarassing situation.   3.____

4. Since you object to me criticizing your letter, I have no alternative but to consider you a mercenary scoundrel.   4.____

5. I rushed home ahead of schedule so that you will leave me go to the picnic with Mary.   5.____

Questions 6-15.

DIRECTIONS: Some of the following sentences contain an error in spelling, word usage, or sentence structure, or punctuation. Some sentences are correct as they stand although there may be other correct ways of expressing the same thought. All incorrect sentences contain only one error. Mark your answer to each question in the space at the right as follows:
- A. If the sentence has an error in spelling;
- B. If the sentence has an error in punctuation or capitalization;
- C. If the sentence has an error in word usage or sentence structure;
- D. If the sentence is correct.

6. Because the chairman failed to keep the participants from wandering off into irrelevant discussions, it was impossible to reach a consensus before the meeting was adjourned.   6.____

7. Certain employers have an unwritten rule that any applicant, who is over 55 years of age, is automatically excluded from consideration for any position whatsoever.   7.____

8. If the proposal to build schools in some new apartment buildings were to be accepted by the builders, one of the advantages that could be expected to result would be better communication between teachers and parents of schoolchildren.   8.____

9. In this instance, the manufacturer's violation of the law against deseptive packaging was discernible only to an experienced inspector.   9.____

10. The tenants' anger stemmed from the president's going to Washington to testify without consulting them first.　　10.＿＿＿

11. Did the president of this eminent banking company say; "We intend to hire and train a number of these disadvan-taged youths?"　　11.＿＿＿

12. In addition, today's confidential secretary must be knowledgable in many different areas: for example, she must know modern techniques for making travel arrangements for the executive.　　12.＿＿＿

13. To avoid further disruption of work in the offices, the protesters were forbidden from entering the building unless they had special passes.　　13.＿＿＿

14. A valuable secondary result of our training conferences is the opportunities afforded for management to observe the reactions of the participants.　　14.＿＿＿

15. Of the two proposals submitted by the committee, the first one is the best.　　15.＿＿＿

Questions 16-25.

DIRECTIONS:　Each of the following sentences may be classified MOST appropriately under one of the following three categories:
　　　　A.　Faulty because of incorrect grammar
　　　　B.　Faulty because of incorrect punctuation
　　　　C.　Correct

Examine each sentence. Then, print the capital letter preceding the BEST choice of the three suggested above. All incorrect sentences contain only one type of error. Consider a sentence correct if it contains none of the types of errors mentioned, even though there may be other ways of expressing the same thought.

16. He sent the notice to the clerk who you hired yesterday.　　16.＿＿＿

17. It must be admitted, however that you were not informed of this change.　　17.＿＿＿

18. Only the employees who have served in this grade for at least two years are eligible for promotion.　　18.＿＿＿

19. The work was divided equally between she and Mary.　　19.＿＿＿

20. He thought that you were not available at that time.　　20.＿＿＿

21. When the messenger returns; please give him this package.　　21.＿＿＿

22. The new secretary prepared, typed, addressed, and delivered, the notices.　　22.＿＿＿

23. Walking into the room, his desk can be seen at the rear.　　23.＿＿＿

24. Although John has worked here longer than she, he produces a smaller amount of work.　　24.＿＿＿

25. She said she could of typed this report yesterday.　　25.＿＿＿

KEY (CORRECT ANSWERS)

1.	D		11.	B
2.	A		12.	A
3.	D		13.	C
4.	C		14.	D
5.	C		15.	C
6.	A		16.	A
7.	B		17.	B
8.	D		18.	C
9.	A		19.	A
10.	D		20.	C

21.	B
22.	B
23.	A
24.	C
25.	A

TEST 4

Questions 1-5.

DIRECTIONS: Each of the following sentences may be classified MOST appropriately under one of the following three categories:
- A. Faulty because of incorrect grammar
- B. Faulty because of incorrect punctuation
- C. Correct

Examine each sentence. Then, print the capital letter preceding the BEST choice of the three suggested above. All incorrect sentences contain only one type of error. Consider a sentence correct if it contains none of the types of errors mentioned, even though there may be other correct ways of expressing the same thought.

1. Neither one of these procedures are adequate for the efficient performance of this task.   1.____

2. The typewriter is the tool of the typist; the cash register, the tool of the cashier.   2.____

3. "The assignment must be completed as soon as possible" said the supervisor.   3.____

4. As you know, office handbooks are issued to all new employees.   4.____

5. Writing a speech is sometimes easier than to deliver it before an audience.   5.____

Questions 6-15.

DIRECTIONS: Each statement given in Questions 6 through 15 contains one of the faults of English usage listed below. For each, choose from the options listed the MAJOR fault contained.
- A. The statement is not a complete sentence.
- B. The statement contains a word or phrase that is redundant.
- C. The statement contains a long, less commonly used word when a shorter, more direct word would be acceptable.
- D. The statement contains a colloquial expression that normally is avoided in business writing.

6. The fact that this activity will afford an opportunity to meet your group.   6.____

7. Do you think that the two groups can join together for next month's meeting?   7.____

8. This is one of the most exciting new innovations to be introduced into our college.   8.____

9. We expect to consummate the agenda before the meeting ends tomorrow at noon.   9.____

10. While this seminar room is small in size, we think we can use it.   10.____

11. Do you think you can make a modification in the date of the Budget Committee meeting?   11.____

12. We are cognizant of the problem but we think we can ameliorate the situation.   12.____

13. Shall I call you around three on the day I arrive in the City?   13.____

14. Until such time that we know precisely that the students will be present.   14._____

15. The consensus of opinion of all the members present is reported in the minutes.   15._____

Questions 16-25.

DIRECTIONS: For each of Questions 16 through 25, select from the options given below the
MOST applicable choice.
   A.   The sentence is correct.
   B.   The sentence contains a spelling error only.
   C.   The sentence contains an English grammar error only.
   D.   The sentence contains both a spelling error and an English grammar
        error.

16. Every person in the group is going to do his share.   16._____

17. The man who we selected is new to this University.   17._____

18. She is the older of the four secretaries on the two staffs that are to be combined.   18._____

19. The decision has to be made between him and I.   19._____

20. One of the volunteers are too young for this complecated task, don't you think?   20._____

21. I think your idea is splindid and it will improve this report considerably.   21._____

22. Do you think this is an exagerated account of the behavior you and me observed this
morning?   22._____

23. Our supervisor has a clear idea of excelence.   23._____

24. How many occurences were verified by the observers?   24._____

25. We must complete the typing of the draft of the questionaire by noon tomorrow.   25._____

———————

KEY (CORRECT ANSWERS)

1.	A		11.	C
2.	C		12.	C
3.	B		13.	D
4.	C		14.	A
5.	A		15.	B
6.	A		16.	A
7.	B		17.	C
8.	B		18.	C
9.	C		19.	C
10.	B		20.	D

21.	B
22.	D
23.	B
24.	B
25.	B

PREPARING WRITTEN MATERIAL

EXAMINATION SECTION
TEST 1

DIRECTIONS: Each question consists of a sentence which may or may not be an example of good English usage. Examine each sentence, considering grammar, punctuation, spelling, capitalization, and awkwardness. Then choose the correct statement about it from the four choices below it. If the English usage in the sentence given is better than any of the changes suggested in choices B, C, or D, pick choice A. (Do not pick a choice that will change the meaning of the sentence.)

1. We attended a staff conference on Wednesday the new safety and fire rules were discussed.

    A. This is an example of acceptable writing.
    B. The words "safety," "fire" and "rules" should begin with capital letters.
    C. There should be a comma after the word "Wednesday."
    D. There should be a period after the word "Wednesday" and the word "the" should begin with a capital letter

1.____

2. Neither the dictionary or the telephone directory could be found in the office library.

    A. This is an example of acceptable writing.
    B. The word "or" should be changed to "nor."
    C. The word "library" should be spelled "libery."
    D. The word "neither" should be changed to "either."

2.____

3. The report would have been typed correctly if the typist could read the draft.

    A. This is an example of acceptable writing.
    B. The word "would" should be removed.
    C. The word "have" should be inserted after the word "could."
    D. The word "correctly" should be changed to "correct."

3.____

4. The supervisor brought the reports and forms to an employees desk.

    A. This is an example of acceptable writing.
    B. The word "brought" should be changed to "took."
    C. There should be a comma after the word "reports" and a comma after the word "forms."
    D. The word "employees" should be spelled "employee's."

4.____

5. It's important for all the office personnel to submit their vacation schedules on time.

    A. This is an example of acceptable writing.
    B. The word "It's" should be spelled "Its."
    C. The word "their" should be spelled "they're."
    D. The word "personnel" should be spelled "personal."

5.____

6. The report, along with the accompanying documents, were submitted for review. 6.____

    A. This is an example of acceptable writing.
    B. The words "were submitted" should be changed to "was submitted."
    C. The word "accompanying" should be spelled "accompaning."
    D. The comma after the word "report" should be taken out.

7. If others must use your files, be certain that they understand how the system works, but 7.____
insist that you do all the filing and refiling.

    A. This is an example of acceptable writing.
    B. There should be a period after the word "works," and the word "but" should start a
new sentence
    C. The words "filing" and "refiling" should be spelled "fileing" and "refileing."
    D. There should be a comma after the word "but."

8. The appeal was not considered because of its late arrival. 8.____

    A. This is an example of acceptable writing.
    B. The word "its" should be changed to "it's."
    C. The word "its" should be changed to "the."
    D. The words "late arrival" should be changed to "arrival late."

9. The letter must be read carefuly to determine under which subject it should be filed. 9.____

    A. This is an example of acceptable writing.
    B. The word "under" should be changed to "at."
    C. The word "determine" should be spelled "determin."
    D. The word "carefuly" should be spelled "carefully."

10. He showed potential as an office manager, but he lacked skill in delegating work. 10.____

    A. This is an example of acceptable writing.
    B. The word "delegating" should be spelled "delagating."
    C. The word "potential" should be spelled "potencial."
    D. The words "he lacked" should be changed to "was lacking."

KEY (CORRECT ANSWERS)

1.	D	6.	B
2.	B	7.	A
3.	C	8.	A
4.	D	9.	D
5.	A	10.	A

TEST 2

DIRECTIONS: Each question consists of a sentence which may or may not be an example of good English usage. Examine each sentence, considering grammar, punctuation, spelling, capitalization, and awkwardness. Then choose the correct statement about it from the four choices below it. If the English usage in the sentence given is better than any of the changes suggested in choices B, C, or D, pick choice A. (Do not pick a choice that will change the meaning of the sentence.)

1. The supervisor wants that all staff members report to the office at 9:00 A.M.

    A. This is an example of acceptable writing.
    B. The word "that" should be removed and the word "to" should be inserted after the word "members."
    C. There should be a comma after the word "wants" and a comma after the word "office."
    D. The word "wants" should be changed to "want" and the word "shall" should be inserted after the word "members."

    1._____

2. Every morning the clerk opens the office mail and distributes it.

    A. This is an example of acceptable writing.
    B. The word "opens" should be changed to "open."
    C. The word "mail" should be changed to "letters."
    D. The word "it" should be changed to "them."

    2._____

3. The secretary typed more fast on a desktop computer than on a laptop computer.

    A. This is an example of acceptable writing.
    B. The words "more fast" should be changed to "faster."
    C. There should be a comma after the words "desktop computer."
    D. The word "than" should be changed to "then."

    3._____

4. The new stenographer needed a desk a computer, a chair and a blotter.

    A. This is an example of acceptable writing.
    B. The word "blotter" should be spelled "blodder."
    C. The word "stenographer" should begin with a capital letter.
    D. There should be a comma after the word "desk."

    4._____

5. The recruiting officer said, "There are many different goverment jobs available."

    A. This is an example of acceptable writing.
    B. The word "There" should not be capitalized.
    C. The word "goverment" should be spelled "government".
    D. The comma after the word "said" should be removed.

    5._____

6. He can recommend a mechanic whose work is reliable.

    A. This is an example of acceptable writing.
    B. The word "reliable" should be spelled "relyable."
    C. The word "whose" should be spelled "who's."
    D. The word "mechanic" should be spelled "mecanic."

    6._____

7. She typed quickly; like someone who had not a moment to lose.   7.____

    A. This is an example of acceptable writing.
    B. The word "not" should be removed.
    C. The semicolon should be changed to a comma.
    D. The word "quickly" should be placed before instead of after the word "typed."

8. She insisted that she had to much work to do.   8.____

    A. This is an example of acceptable writing.
    B. The word "insisted" should be spelled "incisted."
    C. The word "to" used in front of "much" should be spelled "too."
    D. The word "do" should be changed to "be done."

9. He excepted praise from his supervisor for a job well done.   9.____

    A. This is an example of acceptable writing.
    B. The word "excepted" should be spelled "accepted."
    C. The order of the words "well done" should be changed to "done well."
    D. There should be a comma after the word "supervisor."

10. What appears to be intentional errors in grammar occur several times in the passage.   10.____

    A. This is an example of acceptable writing.
    B. The word "occur" should be spelled "occurr."
    C. The word "appears" should be changed to "appear."
    D. The phrase "several times" should be changed to "from time to time."

KEY (CORRECT ANSWERS)

1.	B		6.	A
2.	A		7.	C
3.	B		8.	C
4.	D		9.	B
5.	C		10.	C

TEST 3

Questions 1-5.

DIRECTIONS: Same as for Tests 1 and 2.

1. The clerk could have completed the assignment on time if he knows where these materi-   1.____
    als were located.

    A.   This is an example of acceptable writing.
    B.   The word "knows" should be replaced by "had known."
    C.   The word "were" should be replaced by "had been."
    D.   The words "where these materials were located" should be replaced by "the loca-
         tion of these materials."

2. All employees should be given safety training. Not just those who have accidents.   2.____

    A.   This is an example of acceptable writing.
    B.   The period after the word "training" should be changed to a colon.
    C.   The period after the word "training" should be changed to a semicolon, and the first
         letter of the word "Not" should be changed to a small "n."
    D.   The period after the word "training" should be changed to a comma, and the first
         letter of the word "Not" should be changed to a small "n."

3. This proposal is designed to promote employee awareness of the suggestion program, to   3.____
    encourage employee participation in the program, and to increase the number of
    suggestions submitted.

    A.   This is an example of acceptable writing.
    B.   The word "proposal" should be spelled "preposal."
    C.   The words "to increase the number of suggestions submitted" should be changed
         to "an increase in the number of suggestions is expected."
    D.   The word "promote" should be changed to "enhance" and the word "increase"
         should be changed to "add to."

4. The introduction of inovative managerial techniques should be preceded by careful anal-   4.____
    ysis of the specific circumstances and conditions in each department.

    A.   This is an example of acceptable writing.
    B.   The word "techniques" should be spelled "techneques."
    C.   The word "inovative" should be spelled "innovative."
    D.   A comma should be placed after the word "circumstances" and after the word "con-
         ditions."

5. This occurrence indicates that such criticism embarrasses him.   5.____

    A.   This is an example of acceptable writing.
    B.   The word "occurrence" should be spelled "occurence."
    C.   The word "criticism" should be spelled "critisism."
    D.   The word "embarrasses" should be spelled "embarasses."

KEY (CORRECT ANSWERS)

1. B
2. D
3. A
4. C
5. A

WRITTEN ENGLISH EXPRESSION
EXAMINATION SECTION
TEST 1

DIRECTIONS: The questions that follow the paragraph below are designed to test your appreciation of correctness and effectiveness of expression in English. The paragraph is presented first in full so that you may read it through for sense. Disregard the errors you find, as you will be asked to correct them in the questions that follow. The paragraph is then presented sentence by sentence with portions underlined and numbered. At the end of this material, you will find numbers corresponding to those below the underlined portions, each followed by five alternatives lettered A to E. In every case, the usage in the alternative lettered A is the same as that in the original paragraph and is followed by four possible usages. Choose the usage you consider best in each case.

When this war is over, no nation will either be isolated in war or peace. Each will be within trading distance of all the others and will be able to strike them. Every nation will be most as dependent on the rest for the maintainance of peace as is any of our own American states on all the others. The world that we have known was a world made up of individual nations, each of which had the priviledge of doing about as they pleased without being embarassed by outside interference. The world has dissolved before the impact of an invention, the airplane has done to our world what gun powder did to the feudal world. Whether the coming century will be a period of further tragedy or one of peace and progress depend very largely on the wisdom and skill with which the present generation adjusts their thinking to the problems immediately at hand. Examining the principal movements sweeping through the world, it can be seen that they are being accelerated by the war. There is undoubtedly many of these whose courses will be affected for good or ill by the settlements that will follow the war. The United States will share the responsibility of these settlements with Russia, England and China. The influence of the United States, however, will be great. This country is likely to emerge from the war stronger than any other nation. Having benefitted by the absence of actual hostilities on our own soil, we shall probably be less exhausted than our allies and better able than them to help restore the devastated areas. However many mistakes have been made in our past, the tradition of America, not only the champion of freedom but also fair play, still lives among millions who can see light and hope scarcely nowhere else.

When this war is over, no nation will $\underline{\text{either be isolated in war or peace.}}$
$$1$$

1.   A.   either be isolated in war or peace.   1.____
     B.   be either isolated in war or peace.
     C.   be isolated in neither war nor peace.
     D.   be isolated either in war or in peace.
     E.   be isolated neither in war or peace

$\dfrac{\text{Each}}{2}$ will be

2.   A.   Each   B.   It   C.   Some   D.   They   E.   A nation   2.____

within trading distance of all the others and will be able to strike them.

3

3. A. within trading distance of all the others and will be able to strike them.   3.___
   B. near enough to trade with and strike all the others.
   C. trading and striking the others.
   D. within trading and striking distance of all the others.
   E. able to strike and trade with all the others.

Every nation will be <u>most</u> as dependent on

4

4. A. most   B. wholly   C. much   D. mostly   E. almost   4.___

the rest for the <u>maintainance</u> of peace as is

5

5. A. maintainance   B. maintainence   C. maintenence   5.___
   D. maintenance   E. maintanence

any of our own American states on all the others. The world that we have known was a
world made up of individual <u>nations, each</u>

6

6. A. nations, each   B. nations. Each   C. nations: each   6.___
   D. nations; each   E. nations each

of which had the <u>priviledge</u> of doing about as

7

7. A. priviledge   B. priveledge   C. privelege   7.___
   D. privalege   E. privilege

<u>they</u> pleased without being

8

8. A. they   B. it   8.___
   C. they individually   D. he
   E. the nations

<u>embarassed</u> by outside interference. That

9

9. A. embarassed   B. embarrassed   C. embaressed   9.___
   D. embarrased   E. embarressed

world has dissolved before the impact of an <u>invention, the</u> airplane has done to our world
                                                    10
what gunpowder did to the feudal world. Whether the coming century will be a period of
further tragedy or one of peace and

10.   A. invention, the   B. invention but the   10.____
       C. invention: the   D. invention. The
       E. invention and the

progress <u>depend</u> very largely on the wisdom and skill with which the present generation
          11

11.   A. depend   B. will have depended   11.____
       C. depends   D. depended
       E. shall depend

<u>adjusts their</u> thinking to the problems immediately at hand.
       12

12.   A. adjusts their   B. adjusts there   C. adjusts its   12.____
       D. adjust our   E. adjust it's

<u>Examining the principal movements sweeping through the world, it can be seen</u>
                                    13

13.   A. Examining the principal movements sweeping through the world, it can be seen   13.____
       B. Having examined the principal movements sweeping through the world, it can be
           seen
       C. Examining the principal movements sweeping through the world can be seen
       D. Examining the principal movements sweeping through the world, we can see
       E. It can be seen examining the principal movements sweeping through the world

that they are being <u>accelerated</u> by the war.
                        14

14.   A. accelerated   B. acelerated   C. accelarated   14.____
       D. acellerated   E. acelerrated

There <u>is</u> undoubtedly many of these whose courses will be affected for good or ill by the
       15
settlements that will follow the war. The United States will share the responsibility of these
settlements with Russia, England and China. The influence of the United

15.   A. is   B. were   C. was   D. are   E. might be   15.____

States, <u>however</u>, will be great. This country is likely to emerge from the war stronger
          16
than any other nation.

16. A. , however,   B. however,   C. , however   16.___
     D. however   E. ; however,

Having _benefitted_ by the absence of actual hostilities on our own soil, we shall probably

17

be less exhausted

17. A. benefitted   B. benifitted   C. benefited   17.___
     D. benifited   E. benafitted

than our allies and better able than _them_ to help restore the devasted areas. However

18

many mistakes have been made in our past, the tradition of American,

18. A. them   B. themselves   C. they   18.___
     D. the world   E. the nations

not only the champion of freedom but also fair play, still lives among millions who can

19

19. A. not only the champion of freedom but also fair play,   19.___
     B. the champion of not only freedom but also of fair play,
     C. the champion not only of freedom but also of fair play,
     D. not only the champion but also freedom and fair play,
     E. not the champion of freedom only, but also fair play,

see light and hope _scarcely nowhere else._

20

20. A. scarcely nowhere else   B. elsewhere   20.___
     C. nowheres   D. scarcely anywhere else
     E. anywhere

———

KEY (CORRECT ANSWERS)

1.	D	11.	C
2.	A	12.	C
3.	D	13.	D
4.	E	14.	A
5.	D	15.	D
6.	A	16.	A
7.	E	17.	C
8.	B	18.	C
9.	B	19.	C
10.	D	20.	D

———

TEST 2

DIRECTIONS: The questions that follow the selection below are designed to test your appreciation of correctness and effectiveness of expression in English. The selection is presented first in full so that you may read it through for sense. Disregard the errors you find, as you will be asked to correct them in the questions that follow. The selection is then presented sentence by sentence, with portions underlined and numbered. At the end of this material, you will find numbers corresponding to those below the underlined portions, each followed by five alternatives lettered A to E. In some cases the usage in the underlined portion is correct. In other cases it requires correction. In every case, the usage in the alternative lettered A is the same as that in the original selection and is followed by four other possible usages. Choose the usage you consider best in each case and indicate your answer.

The use of the machine produced up to the present time outstanding changes in our modern world. One of the most significant of these changes have been the marked decreases in the length of the working day and the working week. The fourteen-hour day not only has been reduced to one of ten hours but also, in some lines of work, to one of eight or even six. The trend toward a decrease is further evidenced in the longer weekend already given to employees in many business establishments. There seems also to be a trend toward shorter working weeks and longer summer vacations. An important feature of this development is that leisure is no longer the privilege of the wealthy few, - it has become the common right of most people. Using it wisely, leisure promotes health, efficiency, and happiness, for there is time for each individual to live their own "more abundant life" and having opportunities for needed recreation.

Recreation, like the name implies, is a process of revitalization. In giving expression to the play instincts of the human race, new vigor and effectiveness are afforded by recreation to the body and to the mind. Of course not all forms of amusement, by no means, constitute recreation. Furthermore, an activity that provides recreation for one person may prove exhausting for another. Today, however, play among adults, as well as children, is regarded as a vital necessity of modern life. Play being recognized as an important factor in improving mental and physical health and thereby reducing human misery and poverty.

Among the most important forms of amusement available at the present time are the automobile, the moving picture, the radio, television, and organized sports. The automobile, especially, has been a boon to the American people, since it has been the chief means of them getting out into the open. The motion picture, the radio and television have tremendous opportunities to supply wholesome recreation and to promote cultural advancement. A criticism often leveled against organized sports as a means of recreation is because they make passive spectators of too many people. It has been said "that the American public is afflicted with "spectatoritis," but there is some recreational advantages to be gained even from being a spectator at organized games. Such sports afford a release from the monotony of daily toil, get people outdoors and also provide an exhilaration that is tonic in its effect.

The chief concern, of course, should be to eliminate those forms of amusement that are socially undesirable. There are, however, far too many people who, we know, do not use their leisure to the best advantage. Sometimes leisure leads to idleness, and idleness may lead to demoralization. The value of leisure both to the individual and to society will depend on the uses made of it.

The use of the machine <u>produced</u> up to the

                               1

1.   A. produced   B. produces   1.____
       C. has produced   D. had produced
       E. will have produced

present time many outstanding changes in our modern world. One of the most significant

of these changes <u>have been</u> the marked

                      2

2.   A. have been   B. was   C. were   2.____
       D. has been   E. will be

decreases in the length of the working day and the working week.

  <u>The fourteen - hour day not only has been reduced</u> to one of ten hour but also , in some

                            3

lineof work , to one of eight or even six.

3.   A. The fourteen-hour day not only has been reduced   3.____
       B. Not only the fourteen-hour day has been reduced
       C. Not the fourteen-hour day only has been reduced
       D. The fourteen-hour day has not only been reduced
       E. The fourteen-hour day has been reduced not only

The trend toward a decrease is further evidenced in the longer week end <u>already</u> given

                                                              4

4.   A. already   B. all ready   C. allready   4.____
       D. ready   E. all in all

to employees in many business establishments. There seems also to be a trend toward
shorter working weeks and longer summer vacations. An important feature of this development is that leisure is no longer the privilege of the wealthy few <u>, - it</u> has become the

                                                                     5

common right of people.

5.   A. , - it   B. :it   C. ; it   5.____
       D. ... it   E. omit punctuation

  <u>Using it wisely,</u> leisure promotes health, efficiency, and happiness, for there is time for

               6

each individual to live <u>their</u> own "more abundant life" and <u>having</u> opportunities for

                           7   8

needed recreation.

6.   A. Using it wisely   B. If used wisely   6.___
       C. Having used it widely   D. Because of its wise use
       E. Because of usefulness

7.   A. their   B. his   C. its   D. our   E. your   7.___

8.   A. having   B. having had   C. to have   8.____
        D. to have had   E. had

Recreation, _like_ the name implies, is a
          9

9.   A. like   B. since   C. through   D. for   E. as   9.____

process of revitalization. In giving expression to the play instincts of the human race,
new vigor and effectiveness are afforded by recreation to the body and to the mind.
                                      10

10.   A. new vigor and effectiveness are afforded by recreation to the body and to the mind.   10.____
      B. recreation affords new vigor and effectiveness to the body and to the mind.
      C. there are afforded new vigor and effectiveness to the body and to the mind.
      D. by recreation the body and mind are afforded new vigor and effectiveness.
      E. the body and the mind afford new vigor and effectiveness to themselves by rec-
          reation.

Of course not all forms of amusement, _by no means_ constistute recreation. Further-
                                  11
more, an activity that provides recreation for one person may prove exhausting for
another. Today, however, play among adults, as well as children, is regarded as a vital
necessity of modern life.

11.   A. by no means   B. by those means   11.____
      C. by some means   D. by every means
      E. by any means

Play being recognized as an important factor in improving mental and physical health
              12
and thereby reducing human misery and poverty.

12.   A. . Play being recognized as   12.____
      B. . by their recognizing play as
      C. . They recognizing play as
      D. . Recognition of it being
      E. , for play is recognized as

Among the most important forms of amusement available at the present time are the
automobile, the moving picture, the radio, television, and organized sports. The automobile, especially, has been a boon to the American people, since it has been the chief

means of _them_ getting out into the open. The motion picture, the radio, and television
           13
have tremendous opportunities to supply wholesome recreation and to promote cultural
advancement. A criticism often leveled against organized

13.   A. them   B. their   C. his   13.____
      D. our   E. the people

sports as a means of recreation is __because__ they make passive spectators of too many
                                        14
people.

14.   A. because   B. since   C. as   D. that   E. why   14.___

It has been said " __that__ the American public is afflicted with "spectatoritis," but there
                      15

__is__ some recreational advantages to be gained even from being a spectator at organized
16
games.

15.   A. "that   B. "that"   C. that"   D. 'that   E. that   15.___

16.   A. is   B. was   C. are   D. were   E. will be   16.___

Such sports afford a release from the monotony of daily toil, get people outdoors and also
provide an exhilaration that is tonic in its effect. The chief concern, of course, should be to
eliminate those forms of amusement that are socially undesirable. There are, however, far

too many people __who,__ we know, do not use their leisure to the best advantage. Some-
                        17
times leisure leads to idleness, and idleness may lead to demoralization. The value of leisure both to the individual and to society will depend on the uses made of it.

17.   A. who   B. whom   C. which   17.___
       D. such as   E. that which

KEY (CORRECT ANSWERS)

1.	C		11.	E
2.	D		12.	E
3.	E		13.	B
4.	A		14.	D
5.	C		15.	E
6.	B		16.	C
7.	B		17.	A
8.	C			
9.	E			
10.	B			

TEST 3

DIRECTIONS: The questions that follow the selection below are designed to test your appreciation of correctness and effectiveness of expression in English. The selection is presented first in full so that you may read it through for sense. Disregard the errors you find, as you will be asked to correct them in the questions that follow. The selection is then presented sentence by sentence, with portions underlined and numbered. At the end of this material, you will find numbers corresponding to those below the underlined portions, each followed by five alternatives lettered A to E. In some cases the usage in the underlined portion is correct. In other cases it requires correction. In every case, the usage in the alternative lettered A is the same as that in the original selection and is followed by four other possible usages. Choose the usage you consider best in each case.

The process by which the community influence the actions of its members is known as social control. Imitation which takes place when the action of one individual awakens the impulse in each other to attempt the same thing, is one of the means by which society gains this control. When the child acts as other members of his group acts, he receives their approval. There is also adults who seem almost equally imitative. Advertisers of luxuries are careful to convey the idea that important persons use and indorse the merchandise concerned, for most folk will do their utmost to follow the example of those whom they think are the best people.

Akin to imitation as a means of social control is suggestion. The child is taught to think and feel as do the adults of his community. He is neither encouraged to be critical or to examine all the evidence for his opinions. To be sure, there would be scarcely no time left for other things if school children would have been expected to have considered all sides of every matter on which they hold opinions. It is possible, however and probably very desirable, for pupils of high school age to learn that the point of view accepted in their community is not the only one, and that many widely held opinions may be mistaken. The way in which suggestion operates is illustrated by advertising methods. Depending on skillful suggestion, argument is seldom used in advertising. The words accompanying the picture do not seek to convince the reason but only to intensify the suggestion.

Some persons are more susceptible to suggestion than others. The ignorant person is more easily moved to action by suggestion than he who is well educated, education developing the habit of criticizing what is read and heard. Whoever would think clearly, freeing himself from emotion and prejudice, must beware of the influence of the crowd or mob. A crowd is a group of people in a highly suggestible condition, each stimulating the feelings of the others until an intense uniform emotion has control of the group. Such a crowd may become irresponsible and anonymous, and whose activity may lead in any direction. The educated person ought to be beyond reach of this kind of appeal, no one may be said to have a real individuality who, at the mercy of the suggestions of others, allow themselves to succumb to "crowd-mindedness."

The process by which the community <u>infiuence the action of its members</u> is known as

                                                                   1

social control.

1. A. influence the actions of its members
    B. influences the actions of its members
    C. had influenced the actions of its members
    D. influences the actions of their members
    E. will influence the actions of its members

    1.____

Imitation <u>which</u> takes place when the action
            2

2. A. which   B. , which   C. --- which   2.____
    D. that   E. what

of one individual awakens the impulse <u>in each other</u> to attempt the same thing, is one of
                                          3
the means by which society gains this control.

3. A. each other   B. some other   C. one other   3.____
    D. another   E. one another

When the child acts as other members of his group <u>acts,</u> he receives their approval.
                                                      4

4. A. acts   B. act   C. has acted   4.____
    D. will act   E. will have acted

There <u>is</u> also adults who seem almost equally imitative.
       5

5. A. is   B. are   C. was   D. were   E. will be   5.____

Advertisers of luxuries are careful to convey the idea that important persons use and
indorse the merchandise concerned, for most folk will do their utmost to follow the exam-

ple of those <u>whom</u> they think are the best people.
                6

6. A. whom   B. what   C. which   6.____
    D. who   E. that which

Akin to imitation as a means of social control is suggestion. The child is taught to think
and feel as <u>do</u> the adults of his community.
              7

7. A. do   B. does   C. had   D. may   E. might   7.____

He <u>is neither encouraged to be critical or to examine all</u> the evidence for his opinions.
                                    8

8. A. neither encouraged to be critical or to examine   8.____
    B. neither encouraged to be critical nor to examine
    C. either encouraged to be critical or to examine
    D. encouraged either to be critical nor to examine
    E. not encouraged either to be critical or to examine

To be sure, there would be scarcely no time left for other things
                            _____
                                 9

9. A. scarcely no   B. hardly no   C. scarcely any   9.____
    D. enough   E. but only

if school children would have been expected
                    _____
                          10

10. A. would have been   B. should have been   10.____
    C. would have   D. were
    E. will be

to have considered all sides of every matter on which they hold opinions.
_____
        11

11. A. to have considered   B. to be considered   11.____
    C. to consider   D. to have been considered
    E. and have considered

It is possible, however and probably very desirable, for pupils of high school age to learn
                _____
                  12
that the point of view accepted in their community is not the only one, and that many
widely held opinions may be mistaken. The way in which suggestion operates is illustrated by advertising methods.

12. A. , however   B. however,   C. ; however,   12.____
    D. however   E. , however,

Depending on skillful suggestion, argument is seldom used in advertising. The words
_____
                                    13
accompanying the picture do not seek to convince the reason but only to intensify the
suggestion.

13. A. Depending on skillful suggestion, argument is seldom used in advertising.   13.____
    B. Argument is seldom used by advertisers, who depend instead on skillful suges-
        tion.
    C. Skillful suggestion is depended on by advertisers instead of argument.
    D. Suggestion, which is more skillful, is used in place of argument by advertisers.
    E. Instead of suggestion, depending on argument is used by skillful advertisers.

Some persons are more susceptible to suggestion than others. The ignorant person is more easily moved to action by suggestion than he who is well educated, education developing the habit of criticizing what is read and heard. Whoever would
_____
14

think clearly, freeing himself from emotion and prejudice, must beware of the influence of the crowd or mob.

14. A.   , education developing   B.   , education developed by   14.__
     C.   , for education develops   D.   . Education will develop
     E.   . Education developing

A crowd is a group of people in a highly suggestible condition, each stimulating the feelings of the others until an intense uniform emotion has control of the group. Such a crowd may become irresponsible and anonymous, and whose activity may lead in any direc-
                                          _____
                                             15

tion. The educated person ought to be beyond reach of this kind of appeal,

15. A.   and whose   B.   whose   C.   and its   15.__
     D.   and the   E.   and the crowd's

no one may be said to have a real individuality who,
__
16

16. A.   , no   B.   : no   C.   --no   16.__
     D.   . No   E.   omit punctuation

at the mercy of the suggestions of others, allow themselves to succumb to "crowd-
                                            _____
                                                  17

mindedness."

17. A.   allow themselves   B.   allows themselves   17.__
     C.   allow himself   D.   allows himself
     E.   allow ourselves

KEY (CORRECT ANSWERS)

1.	B	11.	C
2.	B	12.	E
3.	D	13.	B
4.	B	14.	C
5.	B	15.	C
6.	D	16.	D
7.	A	17.	D
8.	E		
9.	C		
10.	D		

TEST 4

DIRECTIONS: The questions that follow are designed to test your appreciation of correctness and effectiveness of expression in English. In each statement, you will find underlined portions. In some cases, the usage in the underlined portion is correct. In other cases, it requires correction. Five (5) alternatives lettered A to E are presented. In every case, the usage in the alternative lettered A *(No Change)* is the same as that in the original statement and is followed by four (4) other possible usages. Choose the usage you consider best in each case.

Sample Questions and Answers

Questions

1. John <u>ran</u> home.
   A. No change
   B. run
   C. runned
   D. runed
   E. None right

2. John <u>aint</u> here.
   A. No change
   B. ain't
   C. am not
   D. are'nt
   E. None right

Answers

1. A
   (The sentence is obviously correctly written. Therefore, the correct answer is A. No change.)

2. E
   (word <u>aint</u> is unacceptable in usage today. The correct answer should be <u>is not</u> or <u>isn't.</u> Since the alternatives offered in A, B, C, and D are all incorrect, the correct answer is, therefore, E. None right.)

1. It takes study <u>to become</u> a lawyer.   1.____

   A. No change   B. before you can become
   C. in becoming   D. for becoming
   E. None right

2. His novels never <u>concern old people who wished</u> to be young.   2.____

   A. No change
   B. concerned old people who wish
   C. concerned old people who had wished
   D. concern old people who wish
   E. None right

3. You people like <u>we boys as much as we.</u> boys like you.   3.____

   A. No change   B. we boys as much as us
   C. us boys as much as us   D. us boys as much as we
   E. None right

4. Jane and Mary are <u>more poised than he, but Bill is the brighter</u> of all three.   4.____

   A. No change
   B. more poised than he, but Bill is the brightest
   C. more poised than him, but Bill is the brightest
   D. more poised than him, but Bill is the brighter
   E. None right

5. It is a thing of joy, beauty, <u>and containing</u> terror.   5.___

     A. No change   B. and abounding in
     C. and of   D. and contains
     E. None right

6. If he <u>was able, he would demand that she return</u> home.   6.___

     A. No change
     B. were able, he would demand that she return
     C. was able, he would demand that she returns
     D. were able, he would demand that she returns
     E. None right

7. He <u>use to visit when he was supposed to.</u>   7.___

     A. No change
     B. use to visit when he was suppose to.
     C. used to visit when he was suppose to.
     D. used to visit when he was supposed to .
     E. None right

8. I saw the <u>seamstress and asked her for a needle, hook and eye,</u> and thimble.   8.___

     A. No change
     B. seamstress, and asked her for a needle, hook and eye
     C. seamstress and asked her for a needle, hook and eye
     D. seamstress, and asked her for a needle, hook and eye,
     E. None right

9. A tall, young<u>, man threw the heavy, soggy,</u> ball.   9.___

     A. No change
     B. , young man threw the heavy, soggy
     C. young man threw the heavy, soggy
     D. , young man threw the heavy soggy
     E. None right

10. The week <u>before my sister, thinking of other matters,</u> thrust her hand into the fire.   10.___

     A. No change
     B. before, my sister thinking of other matters
     C. before my sister thinking of other matters,
     D. before my sister, thinking of other matters
     E. None right

11. We seldom eat a roast at our house. <u>My</u> wife being a vegetarian.   11.___

     A. No change   B. my   C. , my
     D. ; my   E. None right

12. I have only one request. <u>That</u> you leave at once.   12.___

     A. No change   B. that   C. ; that
     D. : that   E. None right

13. I admire stimulating conversation and appreciative listening, <u>therefore</u> I talk to myself.   13._____

    A. No change   B. , therefore,   C. therefore
    D. therefore,   E. None right

14. The <u>battle-scarred veteran was as bald as a newlaid egg.</u>   14._____

    A. No change
    B. battlescarred veteran was as bald as a new-laid egg.
    C. battle-scarred veteran was as bald as a new-laid egg.
    D. battle scarred veteran was as bald as a new laid egg.
    E. None right

15. The President's proclamation opened with the following statement: <u>"The intention of the</u>   15._____
<u>government is,</u> to make the people aware of one of the greatest dangers to the safety of
the country."

    A. No change
    B. , "The intention of the government is
    C. : "The intention of the government is:
    D. : "The intention of the government is
    E. None right

16. I get only a <u>week vacation after two years work.</u>   16._____

    A. No change
    B. week's vacation after two years work.
    C. week's vacation after two years' work.
    D. weeks vacation after two years work.
    E. None right

17. <u>You first</u> wash your brush in turpentine. Then hang it up to dry.   17._____

    A. No change   B. First you
    C. First you should   D. First
    E. None right

18. The teacher insisted that you and <u>he were responsible for the mistakes of Joe and me.</u>   18._____

    A. No change
    B. him were responsible for the mistakes of Joe and me.
    C. he were responsible for the mistakes of Joe and I.
    D. him were responsible for the mistakes of Joe and I.
    E. None right

19. <u>He sometimes in a generous mood gave the flowers to others</u> that he had grown in his   19._____
garden.

    A. No change
    B. He in a generous mood sometimes gave to others the flowers
    C. In a generous mood he sometimes gave the flowers to others
    D. Sometimes in a generous mood he gave to others the flowers
    E. None right

20. He <u>is attending</u> college since September.   20.____

    A. No change   B. has attended
    C. was attending   D. attended
    E. None right

21. He enjoys <u>me hearing him singing.</u>   21.____

    A. No change   B. my hearing him sing
    C. me hearing him sing   D. me hearing his singing
    E. None right

22. Even patients of anxious <u>temperament occasionally feel an element of primitive</u> plea-   22.____
sure.

    A. No change
    B. temperament occassionally feel an element of primitive
    C. temperment occasionally feel an element of primitive
    D. temperament occasionally feel an element of primitive
    E. None right

23. <u>Undoubtedly even the loneliest patient feels tranquill.</u>   23.____

    A. No change
    B. Undoubtably even the loneliest patient feels tranquill.
    C. Undoubtedly even the loneliest patient feels tranquil.
    D. Undoubtably even the loneliest patient feels tranquil.
    E. None right

24. <u>Sophmores taking behavioral psychology must pay a labratory</u> fee.   24.____

    A. No change
    B. Sophmores taking behavioral psychology must pay a laboratory
    C. Sophmores taking behavioral psychology must pay a laboratory
    D. Sophomores taking behavioral psychology must pay a labratory
    E. None right

25. <u>Atheletic heroes often find their studies an unnecessary hinderance.</u>   25.____

    A. No change
    B. Athletic heroes often find their studies an unnecessary hinderance.
    C. Athletic heros often find their studies an unnecessary hindrance.
    D. Athletic heroes often find their studies an unnecessary hindrance.
    E. None right

KEY (CORRECT ANSWERS)

1.	A		11.	C
2.	D		12.	D
3.	D		13.	E
4.	B		14.	C
5.	E		15.	D
6.	B		16.	C
7.	D		17.	D
8.	D		18.	A
9.	C		19.	D
10.	E		20.	B

21. B
22. A
23. E
24. C
25. D

TEST 5

DIRECTIONS: The questions that follow are designed to test your appreciation of correctness and effectiveness of expression in English. In each statement, you will find underlined portions. In some cases, the usage in the underlined portion is correct. In other cases, it requires correction. Five (5) alternatives lettered A to E are presented. In every case, the usage in the alternative lettered A *(No Change)* is the same as that in the original statement and is followed by four (4) other possible usages. Choose the usage you consider best in each case.

1. Many of the <u>childrens' games were supervised by students who' s</u> interests lay in teaching.   1.____

   A.   No change
   B.   children's games were supervised by students who's
   C.   childrens' games were supervised by students whose
   D.   children's games were supervised by students whose
   E.   None right

2. I told <u>father that a college president</u> was invited to speak.   2.____

   A.   No change
   B.   Father that a college president
   C.   father that a College President
   D.   Father that a College president
   E.   None right

3. One should <u>either be able to read</u> German or French.   3.____

   A.   No change
   B.   be able either to read
   C.   be able to either read
   D.   be able to read either
   E.   None right

4. <u>Twirling around on my piano stool, my head begins to swim.</u>   4.____

   A.   No change
   B.   My head begins to swim, twirling around on my piano stool.
   C.   Twirling around on my piano stool, a dizzy spell ensues.
   D.   Twirling around on my piano stool, I begin to feel dizzy.
   E.   None right

5. As the reverberations of my deep bass voice <u>increase, one of my dogs starts</u> to howl.   5.____

   A.   No change
   B.   increase, one of my dogs start
   C.   increases, one of my dogs start
   D.   increases, one of my dogs starts
   E.   None right

6. Roy bellows at Eve that it is <u>her, not he,</u> who shouts.   6.____

    A. No change   B. her, not him
    C. she, not him   D. she, not he
    E. None right

7. The only man <u>who I think will knock out whoever</u> he fights is Roy.   7.____

    A. No change
    B. who I think will knock out whomever
    C. whom I think will knock out whomever
    D. whom I think will knock out whoever
    E. None right

8. The <u>more prettier</u> of my eyes is the glass one.   8.____

    A. No change   B. most pretty
    C. prettier   D. prettiest
    E. None right

9. When a good actress cries, she <u>feels real sad.</u>   9.____

    A. No change   B. feels real sadly
    C. feels really sadly   D. really feels sad
    E. None right

10. I asked the instructor what I should do with this examina-paper. <u>Can you imagine what</u>   10.____
<u>he</u> said?

    A. No change
    B. ? Can you imagine what he said.
    C. ? Can you imagine what he said?
    D. . Can you imagine what he said.
    E. None right

11. Not wishing to hurt my friend's feelings, <u>I tell him that I am leaving,</u> because I have a pre-   11.____
vious engagement.

    A. No change
    B. I tell him that I am leaving
    C. , I tell him that I am leaving
    D. I tell him that I am leaving,
    E. None right

12. I remember Utopia <u>College where I studied, while I lived abroad,</u> when the world was at   12.____
peace.

    A. No change
    B. College where I studied, while I lived abroad
    C. College, where I studied while I lived abroad,
    D. College, where I studied, while I lived abroad
    E. None right

13. Would Robinson Crusoe have survived if he <u>was</u> less unimaginative? 13.___

    A. No change   B. were
    C. had been   D. would have been
    E. None right

14. Neither time nor tide <u>delay either the traveler or the stay-at-home from his</u> pastime. 14.___

    A. No change
    B. delays either the traveler or the stay-at-home from his
    C. delay either the traveler or the stay-at-home from their
    D. delays either the traveler or the stay-at-home from their
    E. None right

15. When the committee reports <u>its findings somebody will lose their</u> composure. 15.___

    A. No change
    B. their findings somebody will lose their
    C. their findings somebody will lose his
    D. its findings somebody will lose his
    E. None right

16. The worst one of the problems which <u>is confronting me concern</u> money. 16.___

    A. No change
    B. are confronting me concern
    C. is confronting me concerns
    D. are confronting me concerns
    E. None right

17. Far in the distance <u>rumble the motors of the convoy, but there's</u> no signs of it yet. 17.___

    A. No change
    B. rumbles the motors of the convoy, but there is
    C. rumbles the motors of the convoy, but there are
    D. rumble the motors of the convoy, but there are
    E. None right

18. Neither of the parents <u>believe that Hansel or Gretel are</u> alive. 18.___

    A. No change
    B. believes that Hansel or Gretel are
    C. believe that Hansel or Gretel is
    D. believes that Hansel or Gretel is
    E. None right

19. <u>Its in untried emergencies that a man's native metal receives its</u> ultimate test. 19.___

    A. No change
    B. It's in untried emergencies that a man's native metal receives its
    C. It's in untried emergencies that a mans' native metal receives its
    D. It's in untried emergencies that a man's native metal receives its'
    E. None right

20. Expecting my friends to be on time, <u>their tardiness seemed almost an insult.</u>   20._____

    A. No change
    B. it seemed that their tardiness was almost an insult.
    C. resentment at their tardiness grew in my mind.
    D. only an accident on the way could account for their tardiness.
    E. None right

21. <u>On first reading "The Wasteland" seems obscure.</u>   21._____

    A. No change
    B. On first reading it, "The Wasteland" seems obscure.
    C. "The Wasteland" seems an obscure poem on first reading it.
    D. On first reading "The Wasteland," it seems an obscure poem.
    E. None right

22. <u>A special light will be required to inspect the engine.</u>   22._____

    A. No change
    B. To inspect the engine, a special light will be required.
    C. To inspect the engine, you will require a special light.
    D. To inspect the engine, your light must be special.
    E. None right

23. When <u>mixing it,</u> the cake batter must be thoroughly beaten.   23._____

    A. No change   B. mixing
    C. being mixed   D. being mix
    E. None right

24. What you say may be different <u>from me.</u>   24._____

    A. No change   B. from what I say
    C. than me   D. than mine
    E. None right

25. Trumping is <u>playing</u> a trump when another suit has been led.   25._____

    A. No change   B. to play
    C. if you play   D. where one plays
    E. None right

KEY (CORRECT ANSWERS)

1.	D	11.	C
2.	A	12.	C
3.	D	13.	C
4.	D	14.	B
5.	A	15.	D
6.	D	16.	D
7.	B	17.	D
8.	C	18.	D
9.	D	19.	B
10.	A	20.	E

21.	B
22.	B
23.	C
24.	B
25.	A

EXAMINATION SECTION
TEST 1

DIRECTIONS: Each question or incomplete statement is followed by several suggested answers or completions. Select the one that BEST answers the question or completes the statement. *PRINT THE LETTER OF THE CORRECT ANSWER IN THE SPACE AT THE RIGHT.*

1. Which of the following sentences is punctuated INCORRECTLY?　　　　1.＿＿＿

    A. Johnson said, "One tiny virus, Blanche, can multiply so fast that it will become 200 viruses in 25 minutes."
    B. With economic pressures hitting them from all sides, American farmers have become the weak link in the food chain.
    C. The degree to which this is true, of course, depends on the personalities of the people involved, the subject matter, and the atmosphere in general.
    D. "What loneliness, asked George Eliot, is more lonely than distrust?"

2. Which of the following sentences is punctuated INCORRECTLY?　　　　2.＿＿＿

    A. Based on past experiences, do you expect the plumber to show up late, not have the right parts, and overcharge you.
    B. When polled, however, the participants were most concerned that it be convenient.
    C. No one mentioned the flavor of the coffee, and no one seemed to care that china was used instead of plastic.
    D. As we said before, sometimes people view others as things; they don't see them as living, breathing beings like themselves.

3. Convention members travelled here from Kingston New York Pittsfield Massachusetts Bennington Vermont and Hartford Connecticut.　　　　3.＿＿＿
How many commas should there be in the above sentence?

    A. 3　　　　B. 4　　　　C. 5　　　　D. 6

4. Of the two speakers the one who spoke about human rights is more famous and more humble.　　　　4.＿＿＿
How many commas should there be in the above sentence?

    A. 1　　　　B. 2　　　　C. 3　　　　D. 4

5. Which sentence is punctuated INCORRECTLY?　　　　5.＿＿＿

    A. Five people voted no; two voted yes; one person abstained.
    B. Well, consider what has been said here today, but we won't make any promises.
    C. Anthropologists divide history into three major periods: the Stone Age, the Bronze Age, and the Iron Age.
    D. Therefore, we may create a stereotype about people who are unsuccessful; we may see them as lazy, unintelligent, or afraid of success.

6. Which sentence is punctuated INCORRECTLY?　　　　6.＿＿＿

    A. Studies have found that the unpredictability of customer behavior can lead to a great deal of stress, particularly if the behavior is unpleasant or if the employee has little control over it.

B. If this degree of emotion and variation can occur in spectator sports, imagine the role that perceptions can play when there are <u>real</u> stakes involved.

C. At other times, however hidden expectations may sabotage or severely damage an encounter without anyone knowing what happened.

D. There are usually four issues to look for in a conflict: differences in values, goals, methods, and facts.

Questions 7-10.

DIRECTIONS: Questions 7 through 10 test your ability to distinguish between words that sound alike but are spelled differently and have different meanings. In the following groups of sentences, one of the underlined words is used incorrectly.

7. A. By <u>accepting</u> responsibility for their actions, managers promote trust.   7.____
    B. Dropping hints or making <u>illusions</u> to things that you would like changed sometimes leads to resentment.
    C. The entire unit <u>loses</u> respect for the manager and resents the reprimand.
    D. Many people are <u>averse</u> to confronting problems directly; they would rather avoid them.

8. A. What does this say about the <u>effect</u> our expectations have on those we supervise?   8.____
    B. In an effort to save time between 9 A.M. and 1 P.M., the staff members devised <u>their</u> own interpretation of what was to be done on these forms.
    C. The task master's <u>principal</u> concern is for getting the work done; he or she is not concerned about the needs or interests of employees.
    D. The advisor's main objective was increasing Angela's ability to invest her <u>capitol</u> wisely.

9. A. A typical problem is that people have to cope with the internal <u>censer</u> of their feelings.   9.____
    B. Sometimes, in their attempt to sound more learned, people speak in ways that are barely <u>comprehensible</u>.
    C. The <u>council</u> will meet next Friday to decide whether Abrams should continue as representative.
    D. His <u>descent</u> from grace was assured by that final word.

10. A. The doctor said that John's leg had to remain <u>stationary</u> or it would not heal properly.   10.____
    B. There is a city <u>ordinance</u> against parking too close to fire hydrants.
    C. Meyer's problem is that he is never <u>discrete</u> when talking about office politics.
    D. Mrs. Thatcher probably worked harder <u>than</u> any other British Prime Minister had ever worked.

Questions 11-20.

DIRECTIONS: For each of the following groups of sentences in Questions 11 through 20, select the sentence which is the BEST example of English usage and grammar.

11. A. She is a woman who, at age sixty, is distinctly attractive and cares about how they look.
    B. It was a seemingly impossible search, and no one knew the problems better than she.
    C. On the surface, they are all sweetness and light, but his morbid character is under it.
    D. The minicopier, designed to appeal to those who do business on the run like architects in the field or business travelers, weigh about four pounds.

11.____

12. A. Neither the administrators nor the union representative regret the decision to settle the disagreement.
    B. The plans which are made earlier this year were no longer being considered.
    C. I would have rode with him if I had known he was leaving at five.
    D. I don't know who she said had it.

12.____

13. A. Writing at a desk, the memo was handed to her for immediate attention.
    B. Carla didn't water Carl's plants this week, which she never does.
    C. Not only are they good workers, with excellent writing and speaking skills, and they get to the crux of any problem we hand them.
    D. We've noticed that this enthusiasm for undertaking new projects sometimes interferes with his attention to detail.

13.____

14. A. It's obvious that Nick offends people by being unruly, inattentive, and having no patience.
    B. Marcia told Genie that she would have to leave soon.
    C. Here are the papers you need to complete your investigation.
    D. Julio was startled by you're comment.

14.____

15. A. The new manager has done good since receiving her promotion, but her secretary has helped her a great deal.
    B. One of the personnel managers approached John and tells him that the client arrived unexpectedly.
    C. If somebody can supply us with the correct figures, they should do so immediately.
    D. Like zealots, advocates seek power because they want to influence the policies and actions of an organization.

15.____

16. A. Between you and me, Chris probably won't finish this assignment in time.
    B. Rounding the corner, the snack bar appeared before us.
    C. Parker's radical reputation made to the Supreme Court his appointment impossible.
    D. By the time we arrived, Marion finishes briefing James and returns to Hank's office.

16.____

17. A. As we pointed out earlier, the critical determinant of the success of middle managers is their ability to communicate well with others.   17.____
    B. The lecturer stated there wasn't no reason for bad supervision.
    C. We are well aware whose at fault in this instance.
    D. When planning important changes, it's often wise to seek the participation of others because employees often have much valuable
       ideas to offer.

18. A. Joan had ought to throw out those old things that were damaged when the roof   18.____
       leaked.
    B. I spose he'll let us know what he's decided when he finally comes to
       a decision.
    C. Carmen was walking to work when she suddenly realized that she
       had left her lunch on the table as she passed the market.
    D. Are these enough plants for your new office?

19. A. First move the lever forward, and then they should lift the ribbon casing before try-   19.____
       ing to take it out.
    B. Michael finished quickest than any other person in the office.
    C. There is a special meeting for we committee members today at 4
       p.m.
    D. My husband is worried about our having to work overtime next
       week.

20. A. Another source of conflicts are individuals who possess very poor interpersonal   20.____
       skills.
    B. It is difficult for us to work with him on projects because these kinds
       of people are not interested in team building.
    C. Each of the departments was represented at the meeting.
    D. Poor boy, he never should of past that truck on the right.

Questions 21-28.

DIRECTIONS: In Questions 21 through 28, there may be a problem with English grammar or usage. If a problem does exist, select the letter that indicates the most effective change. If no problem exists, select choice A.

21. He rushed her to the hospital and stayed with her, even though this took quite a bit of his   21.____
    time, he didn't charge her anything.

    A. No changes are necessary
    B. Change even though to although
    C. Change the first comma to a period and capitalize even
    D. Change rushed to had rushed

22. Waiting that appears unfairly feels longer than waiting that seems justified.   22.____

    A. No changes are necessary
    B. Change unfairly to unfair
    C. Change appears to seems
    D. Change longer to longest

23. May be you and the person who argued with you will be able to reach an agreement.   23.____

    A.   No changes are necessary
    B.   Change will be to <u>were</u>
    C.   Change <u>argued with</u> to <u>had an argument with</u>
    D.   Change <u>May be</u> to <u>Maybe</u>

24. Any one of them could of taken the file while you were having coffee.   24.____

    A.   No changes are necessary
    B.   Change <u>any one</u> to <u>anyone</u>
    C.   Change <u>of</u> to <u>have</u>
    D.   Change <u>were having</u> to <u>were out having</u>

25. While people get jobs or move from poverty level to better paying employment, they stop   25.____
receiving benefits and start paying taxes.

    A.   No changes are necessary
    B.   Change <u>While</u> to <u>As</u>
    C.   Change <u>stop</u> to <u>will stop</u>
    D.   Change <u>get</u> to <u>obtain</u>

26. Maribeth's phone rang while talking to George about the possibility of their meeting Tom   26.____
at three this afternoon.

    A.   No changes are necessary
    B.   Change <u>their</u> to <u>her</u>
    C.   Move <u>to George</u> so that it follows <u>Tom</u>
    D.   Change <u>talking</u> to <u>she was talking</u>

27. According to their father, Lisa is smarter than Chris, but Emily is the smartest of the three   27.____
sisters.

    A.   No changes are necessary
    B.   Change <u>their</u> to <u>her</u>
    C.   Change <u>is</u> to <u>was</u>
    D.   Make two sentences, changing the second comma to a period and omitting <u>but</u>

28. Yesterday, Mark and he claim that Carl took Carol's ideas and used them inappropriately.   28.____

    A.   No changes are necessary
    B.   Change <u>claim</u> to <u>claimed</u>
    C.   Change <u>inappropriately</u> to <u>inappropriate</u>
    D.   Change <u>Carol's</u> to <u>Carols'</u>

Questions 29-34.

DIRECTIONS: For each group of sentences in Questions 29 through 34, select the choice
that represents the BEST editing of the problem sentence.

29. The managers expected employees to be at their desks at all times, but they would   29.____
always be late or leave unannounced.

A. The managers wanted employees to always be at their desks, but they would always be late or leave unannounced.
B. Although the managers expected employees to be at their desks no matter what came up, they would always be late and leave without telling anyone.
C. Although the managers expected employees to be at their desks at all times, the managers would always be late or leave without telling anyone.
D. The managers expected the employee to never leave their desks, but they would always be late or leave without telling anyone.

30. The one who is department manager he will call you to discuss the problem tomorrow morning at 10 A.M.   30.____

    A. The one who is department manager will call you tomorrow morning at ten to discuss the problem.
    B. The department manager will call you to discuss the problem tomorrow at 10 A.M.
    C. Tomorrow morning at 10 A.M., the department manager will call you to discuss the problem.
    D. Tomorrow morning the department manager will call you to discuss the problem.

31. A conference on child care in the workplace the $200 cost of which to attend may be prohibitive to childcare workers who earn less than that weekly.   31.____

    A. A conference on child care in the workplace that costs $200 may be too expensive for childcare workers who earn less than that each week.
    B. A conference on child care in the workplace, the cost of which to attend is $200, may be prohibitive to childcare workers who earn less than that weekly.
    C. A conference on child care in the workplace who costs $200 may be too expensive for childcare workers who earn less than that a week.
    D. A conference on child care in the workplace which costs $200 may be too expensive to childcare workers who earn less than that on a weekly basis.

32. In accordance with estimates recently made, there are 40,000 to 50,000 nuclear weapons in our world today.   32.____

    A. Because of estimates recently, there are 40,000 to 50,000 nuclear weapons in the world today.
    B. In accordance with estimates made recently, there are 40,000 to 50,000 nuclear weapons in the world today.
    C. According to estimates made recently, there are 40,000 to 50,000 weapons in the world today.
    D. According to recent estimates, there are 40,000 to 50,000 nuclear weapons in the world today.

33. Motivation is important in problem solving, but they say that excessive motivation can inhibit the creative process.   33.____

    A. Motivation is important in problem solving, but, as they say, too much of it can inhibit the creative process.
    B. Motivation is important in problem solving and excessive motivation will inhibit the creative process.
    C. Motivation is important in problem solving, but excessive motivation can inhibit the creative process.

D. Motivation is important in problem solving because excessive motivation can inhibit the creative process.

34. In selecting the best option calls for consulting with all the people that are involved in it.   34._____

    A. In selecting the best option consulting with all the people concerned with it.
    B. Calling for the best option, we consulted all the affected people.
    C. We called all the people involved to select the best option.
    D. To be sure of selecting the best option, one should consult all the people involved.

35. There are a number of problems with the following letter. From the options below, select the version that is MOST in accordance with standard business style, tone, and form.   35._____

Dear Sir:

We are so sorry that we have had to backorder your order for 15,000 widgets and 2,300 whatzits for such a long time. We have been having incredibly bad luck lately. When your order first came in no one could get to it because my secretary was out with the flu and her replacement didn't know what she was doing, then there was the dock strike in Cucamonga which held things up for awhile, and then it just somehow got lost. We think it may have fallen behind the radiator.

We are happy to say that all these problems have been taken care of, we are caught up on supplies, and we should have the stuff to you soon, in the near future --about two weeks. You may not believe us after everything you've been through with us, but it's true.

We'll let you know as soon as we have a secure date for delivery. Thank you so much for continuing to do business with us after all the problems this probably has caused you.

Yours very sincerely,

Rob Barker

    A. Dear Sir:

    We are so sorry that we have had to backorder your order for 15,000 widgets and 2,300 whatzits. We have been having problems with staff lately and the dock strike hasn't helped anything.

    We are happy to say that all these problems have been taken care of. I've told my secretary to get right on it, and we should have the stuff to you soon. Thank you so much for continuing to do business with us after all the problems this must have caused you.

    We'll let you know as soon as we have a secure date for delivery.

    Sincerely,

    Rob Barker

B. Dear Sir:

We regret that we haven't been able to fill your order for 15,000 widgets and 2,300 whatzits in a timely fashion.

We'll let you know as soon as we have a secure date for delivery.

Sincerely,

Rob Barker

C. Dear Sir:

We are so very sorry that we haven't been able to fill your order for 15,000 widgets and 2,300 whatzits. We have been having incredibly bad luck lately, but things are much better now.

Thank you so much for bearing with us through all of this. We'll let you know as soon as we have a secure date for delivery.

Sincerely,

Rob Barker

D. Dear Sir:

We are very sorry that we haven't been able to fill your order for 15,000 widgets and 2,300 whatzits. Due to unforeseen difficulties, we have had to back-order your request. At this time, supplies have caught up to demand, and we foresee a delivery date within the next two weeks.

We'll let you know as soon as we have a secure date for delivery. Thank you for your patience.

Sincerely,

Rob Barker

———

KEY (CORRECT ANSWERS)

1.	D		16.	A
2.	A		17.	A
3.	B		18.	D
4.	A		19.	D
5.	B		20.	C
6.	C		21.	C
7.	B		22.	B
8.	D		23.	D
9.	A		24.	C
10.	C		25.	B
11.	B		26.	D
12.	D		27.	A
13.	D		28.	B
14.	C		29.	C
15.	D		30.	B

31.	A
32.	D
33.	C
34.	D
35.	D

ARITHMETICAL REASONING
EXAMINATION SECTION
TEST 1

DIRECTIONS: Each question or incomplete statement is followed by several suggested answers or completions. Select the one that BEST answers the question or completes the statement. *PRINT THE LETTER OF THE CORRECT ANSWER IN THE SPACE AT THE RIGHT.*

1. If a secretary answered 28 phone calls and typed the addresses for 112 credit statements in one morning, what is the RATIO of phone calls answered to credit statements typed for that period of time?

    A. 1:4   B. 1:7   C. 2:3   D. 3:5

1.____

2. According to a suggested filing system, no more than 10 folders should be filed behind any one file guide and from 15 to 25 file guides should be used in each file drawer for easy finding and filing.
The MAXIMUM number of folders that a five-drawer file cabinet can hold to allow easy finding and filing is

    A. 550   B. 750   C. 1,100   D. 1,250

2.____

3. An employee had a starting salary of $19,353. He received a salary increase at the end of each year, and at the end of the seventh year his salary was $25,107.
What was his AVERAGE annual increase in salary over these seven years?

    A. $765   B. $807   C. $822   D. $858

3.____

4. The 55 typists and 28 senior clerks in a certain agency were paid a total of $1,457,400 in salaries in 2005.
If the average annual salary of a typist was $16,800, the average annual salary of a senior clerk was

    A. $19,050   B. $19,950   C. $20,100   D. $20,250

4.____

5. A typist has been given a three-page report to type. She has finished typing the first two pages. The first page has 283 words, and the second page has 366 words.
If the total report consists of 954 words, how many words will she have to type on the third page of the report?

    A. 202   B. 287   C. 305   D. 313

5.____

6. In one day, Clerk A processed 30% more forms than Clerk B, and Clerk C processed 1 1/4 as many forms as Clerk A.
If Clerk B processed 40 forms, how many more forms were processed by Clerk C than Clerk B?

    A. 12   B. 13   C. 21   D. 25

6.____

7. A clerk who earns a gross salary of $678 every 2 weeks has the following deductions taken from her paycheck: 15% for city, state, and federal taxes; 2 1/2% for Social Security; $1.95 for health insurance; and $9.00 for union dues.
The amount of her take-home pay is

    A. $429.60   B. $468.60   C. $497.40   D. $548.40

7.___

8. In 2002, an agency spent $400 to buy pencils at a cost of $1.00 a dozen.
If the agency used 3/4 of these pencils in 2002 and used the same number of pencils in 2003, how many more pencils did it have to buy to have enough pencils for all of 2003?

    A. 1,200   B. 2,400   C. 3,600   D. 4,800

8.___

9. A clerk who worked in Agency X earned the following salaries: $15,105 the first year, $15,750 the second year, and $16,440 the third year. Another clerk who worked in Agency Y for three years earned $15,825 a year for two years and $16,086 the third year.
The DIFFERENCE between the average salaries received by both clerks over a three-year period is

    A. $147   B. $153   C. $261   D. $423

9.___

10. An employee who works more than 40 hours in any week receives overtime payment for the extra hours at time and one-half (1 1/2 times) his hourly rate of pay. An employee who earns $13.60 an hour works a total of 45 hours during a certain week.
His TOTAL pay for that week would be

    A. $564.40   B. $612.00   C. $646.00   D. $824.00

10.___

11. Suppose that the amount of money spent for supplies in 2006 for a division in a city department was $156,500. This represented an increase of 12% over the amount spent for supplies for this division in 2005.
The amount of money spent for supplies for this division in 2005 was MOST NEARLY

    A. $139,730   B. $137,720   C. $143,460   D. $138,720

11.___

12. Suppose that a group of five clerks have been assigned to insert 24,000 letters into envelopes. The clerks perform this work at the following rates of speed: Clerk A, 1,100 letters an hour; Clerk B, 1,450 letters an hour; Clerk C, 1,200 letters an hour; Clerk D, 1,300 letters an hour; Clerk E, 1,250 letters an hour. At the end of two hours of work, Clerks C and D are assigned to another task.
From the time that Clerks C and D were taken off the assignment, the number of hours required for the remaining clerks to complete this assignment is

    A. less than 3 hours
    B. 3 hours
    C. more than 3 hours, but less than 4 hours
    D. more than 4 hours

12.___

13. The number 60 is 40% of

    A. 24   B. 84   C. 96   D. 150

13.___

14. If 3/8 of a number is 96, the number is

    A. 132   B. 36   C. 256   D. 156

14.___

15. A city department uses an average of 25 20-cent, 35 30-cent, and 350 40-cent postage   15.____
stamps each day.
The TOTAL cost of stamps used by the department in a five-day period is

    A. $29.50   B. $155.50   C. $290.50   D. $777.50

16. A city department issued 12,000 applications in 2000. The number of applications that   16.____
the department issued in 1998 was 25% greater than the number it issued in 2000.
If the department issued 10% fewer applications in 1996 than it did in 1998, the number it issued in 1996 was

    A. 16,500   B. 13,500   C. 9,900   D. 8,100

17. A clerk can add 40 columns of figures an hour by using an adding machine and 20 col-   17.____
umns of figures an hour without using an adding machine.
The TOTAL number of hours it would take him to add 200 columns if he does 3/5 of the
work by machine and the rest without the machine is

    A. 6   B. 7   C. 8   D. 9

18. In 1997, a city department bought 500 dozen pencils at $1.20 per dozen. In 2000, only   18.____
75 percent as many pencils were bought as were bought in 1997, but the price was 20
percent higher than the 1997 price. The TOTAL cost of the pencils bought in 2000 was

    A. $540   B. $562.50   C. $720   D. $750

19. A clerk is assigned to check the accuracy of the entries on 490 forms. He checks 40   19.____
forms an hour. After working one hour on this task, he is joined by another clerk, who
checks these forms at the rate of 35 an hour.
The TOTAL number of hours required to do the entire assignment is

    A. 5   B. 6   C. 7   D. 8

20. Assume that there are a total of 420 employees in a city agency. Thirty percent of the   20.____
employees are clerks, and 1/7 are typists.
The DIFFERENCE between the number of clerks and the number of typists is

    A. 126   B. 66   C. 186   D. 80

21. Assume that a duplicating machine produces copies of a bulletin at a cost of 2 cents per   21.____
copy. The machine produces 120 copies of the bulletin per minute.
If the cost of producing a certain number of copies was $12, how many minutes of
operation did it take the machine to produce this number of copies?

    A. 5   B. 2   C. 10   D. 6

22. An assignment is completed by 32 clerks in 22 days. Assuming that all the clerks work at   22.____
the same rate of speed, the number of clerks that would be needed to complete this
assignment in 16 days is

    A. 27   B. 38   C. 44   D. 52

23. A department head hired a total of 60 temporary employees to handle a seasonal increase in the department's workload. The following lists the number of temporary employees hired, their rates of pay, and the duration of their employment:

    One-third of the total were hired as clerks, each at the rate of $27,500 a year, for two months.

    30 percent of the total were hired as office machine operators, each at the rate of $31,500 a year, for four months.

    22 stenographers were hired, each at the rate of $30,000 a year, for three months.

The total amount paid to these temporary employees was MOST NEARLY

23.____

    A. $1,780,000
    C. $650,000
    B. $450,000
    D. $390,000

24. Assume that there are 2,300 employees in a city agency. Also, assume that five percent of these employees are accountants, that 80 percent of the accountants have college degrees, and that one-half of the accountants who have college degrees have five years of experience. Then, the number of employees in the agency who are accountants with college degrees and five years of experience is

24.____

    A. 46   B. 51   C. 460   D. 920

25. Assume that the regular 8-hour working day of a laborer is from 8 A.M. to 5 P.M., with an hour off for lunch. He earns a regular hourly rate of pay for these 8 hours and is paid at the rate of time-and-a-half for each hour worked after his regular working day.

If, on a certain day, he works from 8 A.M. to 6 P.M., with an hour off for lunch, and earns $171, his regular hourly rate of pay is

25.____

    A. $16.30   B. $17.10   C. $18.00   D. $19.00

KEY (CORRECT ANSWERS)

1. A		11. A
2. D		12. B
3. C		13. D
4. A		14. C
5. C		15. D
6. D		16. B
7. D		17. B
8. B		18. A
9. A		19. C
10. C		20. B

21. A
22. C
23. B
24. A
25. C

SOLUTIONS TO PROBLEMS

1. 28/112 is equivalent to 1:4

2. Maximum number of folders = (10)(25)(5) = 1250

3. Average annual increase = ($25,107-19,353) ÷ 7 = $822

4. $1,457,400 - (55)($16,800) = $533,400 = total amount paid to senior clerks. Average senior clerk's salary = $533,400 ÷ 28 = $19,050

5. Number of words on 3rd page = 954 - 283 - 366 = 305

6. Clerk A processed (40)(1.30) = 52 forms and clerk C processed (52)(1.25) = 65 forms. Finally, 65 - 40 = 25

7. Take-home pay = $678 - (.15)($678) - (.025)($678) - $1.95 - $9.00 = $548.40

8. (400)(12) = 4800 pencils. In 2002, (3/4)(4800) = 3600 were used, so that 1200 pencils were available at the beginning of 2003. Since 3600 pencils were also used in 2003, the agency had to buy 3600 - 1200 = 2400 pencils.

9. Average salary for clerk in Agency X = ($15,105+$15,750+$16,440)/3 = $15,765. Average salary for clerk in Agency Y = ($15,825+ $15,825+$16,086) ÷ 3 = $15,912. Difference in average salaries = $147.

10. Total pay = ($13.60)(40) + ($20.40)(5) = $646.00

11. In 2005, amount spent = $156,500 ÷ 1.12 ≈ $139,730 (Actual value = $139,732.1429)

12. At the end of 2 hours, (1100)(2) + (1450)(2) + (1200)(2) + (1300X2) + (1250X2) = 12,600 letters have been inserted into envelopes. The remaining 11,400 letters done by clerks A, B, and C will require 11,400 ÷ (1100+1450+1250) = 3 hours.

13. 60 ÷ .40 = 150

14. 96 ÷ 3/8 = (96)(8/3) = 256

15. Total cost = (5)[(25)(.20)+(35)(.30)+(350)(.40)]= $777.50

16. In 1998, (12,000) (1.25) = 15,000 applications were issued In 1996, (15,000)(.90) = 13,500 applications were issued

17. Total number of hours $=\dfrac{120}{40}+\dfrac{80}{20}=7$

18. (.75)(500 dozen) = 375 dozen purchased in 2000 at a cost of ($1.20)(1.20) = $1.44 per dozen. Total cost for 2000 = ($1.44) (375) = $540

19. Total time = 1 hour + 450/75 hrs. = 7 hours

20. (.30)(420) - (1/7)(420) = 126 - 60 = 66

21. Cost per minute = (120)(.02) = $2.40. Then, $12 ÷ $2.40 = 5 minutes

22. (32)(22) ÷ 16 = 44 clerks

23. Total amount paid = (20)($27,500)(2/12) + (18)($31,500) (4/12) + (22)($30,000)(3/12) = $445,666.$\overline{6}$ ≈ $450,000

24. Number of accountants with college degrees and five years of experience = (2300)(.05)(.80)(1/2) = 46

25. Let x = regular hourly pay. Then, (8)(x) + (1)(1.5x) = $1.71 So, 9.5x = 171. Solving, x = $18

————

TEST 2

DIRECTIONS: Each question or incomplete statement is followed by several suggested answers or completions. Select the one that BEST answers the question or completes the statement. *PRINT THE LETTER OF THE CORRECT ANSWER IN THE SPACE AT THE RIGHT.*

1. Assume that you know the capacity of a filing cabinet, the extent of which it is filled, and the daily rate at which material is being added to the file.
   In order to estimate how many more days it will take for the cabinet to be filled to capacity, you should

   A. divide the extent to which the cabinet is filled by the daily rate
   B. take the difference between the capacity of the cabinet and the material in it, and multiply the result by the daily rate of adding material
   C. divide the daily rate of adding material by the difference between the capacity of the cabinet and the material in it
   D. take the difference between the capacity of the cabinet and the material in it, and divide the result by the daily rate of adding material

   1.____

2. Suppose you have been asked to compute the average salary earned in your department during the past year. For each of the divisions of the department, you are given the number of employees and the average salary.
   In order to find the requested overall average salary for the department, you should

   A. add the average salaries of the various divisions and divide the total by the number of divisions
   B. multiply the number of employees in each division by the corresponding average salary, add the results and divide the total by the number of employees in the department
   C. add the average salaries of the various divisions and divide the total by the total number of employees in the department
   D. multiply the sum of the average salaries of the various divisions by the total number of divisions and divide the resulting product by the total number of employees in the department

   2.____

3. Suppose that a group of six clerks has been assigned to assemble the duplicated pages of a report into completed copies. After four hours of work, they have been able to complete one-third of the job.
   In order to assemble all the remaining copies in three more hours of work, the number of clerks which will have to be added to the original six, assuming that all the clerks assigned to this task work at the same rate of speed, is

   A. 10   B. 16   C. 2   D. 6

   3.____

4. A study of the grades of students in a certain college revealed that in 2005, 15% fewer students received a passing grade in mathematics than in 2004, whereas in 2006 the number of students passing mathematics increased 15% over 2005.
   On the basis of this study, it would be MOST accurate to conclude that

   A. the same percentage of students passed mathematics in 2004 as in 2006
   B. of the three years studied, the greatest percentage of students passed mathematics in 2006

   4.____

C. the percentage of students who passed mathematics in 2006 was less than the percentage passing this subject in 2004
D. the percentage of students passing mathematics in 2004 was 15% greater than the percentage of students passing this subject in 2006

5. A city department employs 1,400 people, of whom 35% are clerks and 1/8 are stenographers.
The number of employees in the department who are neither clerks nor stenographers is

   A. 640   B. 665   C. 735   D. 760

6. Assume that there are 190 papers to be filed and that Clerk A and Clerk B are assigned to file these papers. If Clerk A files 40 papers more than Clerk B, then the number of papers that Clerk A files is

   A. 75   B. 110   C. 115   D. 150

7. A stock clerk had on hand the following items:
      500 pads, each worth 16 cents
      130 pencils, each worth 12 cents
      50 dozen rubber bands, worth 8 cents a dozen
   If, from this stock, he issued 125 pads, 45 pencils, and 48 rubber bands, the value of the remaining stock would be

   A. $25.72   B. $27.80   C. $70.52   D. $73.88

8. In a particular agency, there were 160 accidents in 2002. Of these accidents, 75% were due to unsafe acts and the rest were due to unsafe conditions. In the following year, a special safety program was established. The number of accidents in 2004 due to unsafe acts was reduced to 35% of what it had been in 2002.
   How many accidents due to unsafe acts were there in 2004?

   A. 20   B. 36   C. 42   D. 56

9. At the end of every month, the petty cash fund of Agency A is reimbursed for payments made from the fund during the month. During the month of February, the amounts paid from the fund were entered on receipts as follows: 10 bus fares of $1.40 each and one taxi fare of $14.00. At the end of the month, the money left in the fund was in the following denominations: 60 one-dollar bills, 16 quarters, 40 dimes, and 80 nickels.
   If the petty cash fund is reduced by 20% for the following month, how much money will there be available in the petty cash fund for March?

   A. $44   B. $80   C. $86   D. $100

10. An employee worked on a job for 6 weeks, 5 days per week, and 8 hours per day.
    How many hours did he work on the job?

    A. 40   B. 48   C. 55   D. 240

11. Divide 35 by .7.

    A. 5   B. 42   C. 50   D. 245

12. .1% of 25 =   12.____

   A. .025   B. .25   C. 2.5   D. 25

13. In a city agency, 80 percent of the total number of employees are more than 25 years of   13.____
   age and 65 percent of the total number of employees are high school graduates.
   The SMALLEST possible percent of employees who are both high school graduates
   and more than 25 years of age is

   A. 35%   B. 45%   C. 55%   D. 65%

14. Two clerical units, X and Y, each having a different number of clerks, are assigned to file   14.____
   registration cards. It takes Unit X, which contains 8 clerks, 21 days to file the same number of cards that Unit Y can file in 28 days. It is also a fact that Unit X can file 174,528
   cards in 72 days.
   Assuming that all the clerks in both units work at the same rate of speed, the number
   of cards which can be filed by Unit Y in 144 days, if 4 more clerks are added to the staff
   of Unit Y, is MOST NEARLY

   A. 392,000   B. 436,000   C. 523,000   D. 669,000

15. Assume that two machines, each costing $14,750, were purchased for your office. Each   15.____
   machine requires the services of an operator at a salary of $2,000 per month. These
   machines are to replace six clerks, two of whom earn $1,550 per month each, and four of
   whom earn $1,700 per month each.
   The number of months it will take for the cost of the machines to be made up from the
   savings in salaries is

   A. less than four   B. four
   C. five   D. more than five

16. Suppose that the amount of stationery used by your department in August decreased by   16.____
   16% as compared with the amount used in July, and that the amount used in September
   increased by 25% as compared with the amount used in August.
   The amount of stationery used in September as compared with the amount used in
   July is

   A. greater by 5 percent   B. less by 5 percent
   C. greater by 9 percent   D. the same

17. An employee earns $48 a day and works 5 days a week.   17.____
   He will earn $2,160 in _____ weeks.

   A. 5   B. 7   C. 8   D. 9

18. In a certain bureau, the entire staff consists of 1 senior supervisor, 2 supervisors, 6   18.____
   assistant supervisors, and 54 associate workers.
   The percent of the staff who are not associate workers is MOST NEARLY

   A. 14   B. 21   C. 27   D. 32

19. In a certain bureau, five employees each earn $1,000 a month, another 3 employees   19.____
   each earn $2,200 a month, and another two employees each earn $1,400 a month.
   The monthly payroll for these employees is

   A. $3,600   B. $8,800   C. $11,400   D. $14,400

20. An employee contributes 5% of his salary to the pension fund.   20.____
    If his salary is $1,200 a month, the amount of his contribution to the pension fund in a
    year is

    A. $480   B. $720   C. $960   D. $1,200

21. The number of square feet in an area that is 50 feet long and 30 feet wide is   21.____

    A. 80   B. 150   C. 800   D. 1,500

22. A farm hand was paid a weekly wage of $332.16 for a 48-hour work week. As a result of   22.____
    a new labor contract, he is paid $344.96 a week for a 44-hour work week with time and
    one-half pay for time worked in excess of 44 hours in any work week.
    If he continues to work 48 hours weekly under the new contract, the amount by which
    his average hourly rate for a 48-hour work week under the new contract exceeds the
    hourly rate previously paid him lies between _____ and _____ cents, inclusive.

    A. 91;100   B. 101;110   C. 111;120   D. 121;130

23. Each side of a square room, which is being used as an office, measures 66 feet. The   23.____
    floor of the room is divided by six traffic aisles, each aisle being six feet wide. Three of
    the aisles run parallel to the east and west sides of the room, and the other three run par-
    allel to the north and south sides of the room, so that the remaining floor space is divided
    into 16 equal sections. If all of the floor space which is not being used for traffic aisles is
    occupied by desk and chair sets, and each set takes up 24 square feet of floor space, the
    number of desk and chair sets in the room is

    A. 80   B. 64   C. 36   D. 96

24. In 2005, a city agency bought 12,000 envelopes at $4.00 per hundred. In 2006, the price 24.____
    of envelopes purchased was 40 percent higher than the 2005 price, but only 60 percent
    as many envelopes were bought.
    The total cost of the envelopes purchased in 2006 was MOST NEARLY

    A. $250   B. $320   C. $400   D. $480

25. In a city agency, 25 percent of the women employees and 50 percent of the men employ-   25.____
    ees attended a general staff meeting.
    If 48 percent of all the employees in the agency are women, the percentage of all the
    employees who attended the meeting is

    A. 36%   B. 37%   C. 38%   D. 75%

KEY (CORRECT ANSWERS)

1.	D		11.	C
2.	B		12.	A
3.	A		13.	B
4.	C		14.	A
5.	C		15.	C
6.	C		16.	A
7.	D		17.	D
8.	C		18.	A
9.	B		19.	D
10.	D		20.	B

21.	D
22.	D
23.	D
24.	C
25.	C

SOLUTIONS TO PROBLEMS

1. To determine number of days required to fill cabinet to capacity, subtract material in it from capacity amount, then divide by daily rate of adding material. Example: A cabinet already has 10 folders in it, and the capacity is 100 folders. Suppose 5 folders per day are added. Number of days to fill to capacity = $(100-10) \div 5 = 18$

2. To determine overall average salary, multiply number of employees in each division by that division's average salary, add results, then divide by total number of employees. Example: Division A has 4 employees with average salary of $40,000; division B has 6 employees with average salary of $36,000; division C has 2 employees with average salary of $46,000. Average salary = $[(4)(\$40,000)+(6)(\$36,000)+(2)(\$46,000)] / 12 = \$39,000$

3. $(6)(4) = 24$ clerk-hours. Since only one-third of work has been done, $(24) (3) - 24 = 48$ clerk-hours remain. Then, 48 3 = 16 clerks. Thus, $16 - 6 = 10$ additional clerks.

4. The percentage of students passing math in 2006 was less than the percentage of those passing math in 2004. Example: Suppose 400 students passed math in 2004. Then, $(400)(.85) = 340$ passed in 2005. Finally, $(340)(1.15) = 391$ passed in 2006.

5. $1400 - (.35)(1400) - (1/8)(1400) = 735$

6. Let x = number of papers filed by clerk A, x-40 = number of papers filed by clerk B. Then, $x + (x-40) = 190$ Solving, $x = 115$

7. $(500-125)(.16) + (130-45)(.12) + (50 - 48/12)(.08) = \$60.00 + \$10.20 + \$3.68 = \$73.88$

8. $(160)(.75) = 120$ accidents due to unsafe acts in 2002. In 2004, $(120)(.35) = 42$ accidents due to unsafe acts

9. Original amount at beginning of February in the fund = $(10)(\$1.40) + (1)(\$14.00) + (60)(\$1) + (16)(.25) + (40)(.10) + (80)(.05) = \$100$. Finally, for March, $(\$100)(.80) = \$80$ will be available

10. Total hours = $(6)(5)(8) = 240$

11. $35 \div .7 = 50$

12. .1% of 25 = $(.001)(25) = .025$

13. Let A = percent of employees who are at least 25 years old and B = percent of employees who are high school graduates. Also, let N = percent of employees who fit neither category and J = percent of employees who are in both categories.
Then, $100 = A + B + N - J$. Substituting, $100 = 80 + 65 + N - J$ To minimize J, let N = 0. So, $100 = 80 + 65 + 0 - J$. Solving, $J = 45$

14. Let Y = number of clerks in Unit Y. Then, $(8)(21) = (4)(28)$, so Y = 6. Unit X has 8 clerks who can file 174,528 cards in 72 flays; thus, each clerk in Unit X can file $174,528 \div 72 \div 8 = 303$ cards per day. Adding 4 clerks to Unit Y will yield 10 clerks in that unit. Since their rate is equal to that of Unit X, the clerks in Unit Y will file, in 144 days, is $(303)(10)(144) = 436,320 \approx 436,000$ cards.

15. Let x = required number of months. The cost of the machines in x months = (2)(14,750) + (2)(2000)(x) = 29,500 + 4000x. The savings in salaries for the displaced clerks = x[(2)(1550) +(4)(1700)] = 9900x. Thus, 29,500 + 4000x = 9900x. Solving, x = 5. So, five months will elapse in order to achieve a savings in cost.

16. Let x = amount used in July, so that .84x = amount used in August. For September, the amount used = (.84x)(1.25) = 1.05x. This means the amount used in September is 5% more than the amount used in July.

17. Each week he earns ($48)(5) = $240. Then, $2160 ÷ $240 = 9 weeks

18. (1+2+6) ÷ 63 = 1/7 ≈ 14%

19. Monthly payroll = (5)($1000) + (3)($2200) + (2)($1400) = $14,400

20. Yearly contribution to pension fund = (12)($1200)(.05) = $720

21. (50')(30') = 1500 sq.ft.

22. Old rate = 332.16 ÷ 48 = 6.92 (48 hours)
New rate = 344.96 (44 hours)
Overtime rate = 344.96 ÷ 44 = 7.75/hr. x 1.5 x 4 = 46.48
344.96 + 46.48 = 391.44
391.44 ÷ 48 = 8.15
815 - 692 = 123 cents an hour more

23. Each of the 16 sections is a square with side [66'-(3)(6')] ÷ 4 = 12'. So each section contains (12')(12') = 144 sq.ft.
The number of desk and chair sets = (144 ÷ 24) (16) = 96

24. In 2006, (.60)(12,000) = 7200 envelopes were bought and the price per hundred was ($4.00)(1.40) = $5.60. The total cost = (5.60)(72) = $403.20 ≈ $400

25. (.25)(.48) + (.50)(.52) = .38 = 38%

_____

TEST 3

DIRECTIONS: Each question or incomplete statement is followed by several suggested answers or completions. Select the one that BEST answers the question or completes the statement. *PRINT THE LETTER OF THE CORRECT ANSWER IN THE SPACE AT THE RIGHT.*

1. According to one suggested filing system, no more than 12 folders should be filed behind any one file guide and from 10 to 20 file guides should be used in each file drawer. Based on this filing system, the MAXIMUM number of folders that a four-drawer file cabinet can hold is

   A. 240   B. 480   C. 960   D. 1,200

   1.____

2. A certain office uses three different forms. Last year, it used 3,500 copies of Form L, 6,700 copies of Form M, and 10,500 copies of Form P. This year, the office expects to decrease the use of each of these forms by 5%. The TOTAL number of these three forms which the office expects to use this year is

   A. 10,350   B. 16,560   C. 19,665   D. 21,735

   2.____

3. The hourly rate of pay for a certain part-time employee is computed by dividing his yearly salary rate by the number of hours in the work year. The employee's yearly salary rate is $18,928, and there are 1,820 hours in the work year.
   If this employee works 18 hours during one week, his TOTAL earnings for these 18 hours are

   A. $180.00   B. $183.60   C. $187.20   D. $190.80

   3.____

4. Assume that the regular work week of an employee is 35 hours and that the employee is paid for any extra hours worked according to the following schedule. For hours worked in excess of 35 hours, up to and including 40 hours, the employee receives his regular hourly rate of pay. For hours worked in excess of 40 hours, the employee receives 1 1/2 times his hourly rate of pay.
   If the employee's hourly rate of pay is $11.20 and he works 43 hours during a certain week, his TOTAL pay for the week would be

   A. $481.60   B. $498.40   C. $556.00   D. $722.40

   4.____

5. A clerk divided his 35 hour work week as follows:
   1/5 of his time in sorting mail;
   1/2 of his time in filing letters; and
   1/7 of his time in reception work.
   The rest of his time was devoted to messenger work. The percentage of time spent on messenger work by the clerk during the week was MOST NEARLY

   A. 6%   B. 10%   C. 14%   D. 16%

   5.____

6. A city department has set up a computing unit and has rented 5 computing machines at a yearly rental of $700 per machine. In addition, the cost to the department for the maintenance and repair of each of these machines is $50 per year. Five computing machine operators, each receiving an annual salary of $15,000, and a supervisor, who receives $19,000 a year, have been assigned to this unit. This unit will perform the work previously performed by 10 employees whose combined salary was $162,000 a year.
   On the basis of these facts, the savings that will result from the operation of this computing unit for 5 years will be MOST NEARLY

   A. $250,000   B. $320,000   C. $330,000   D. $475,000

   6.____

240

7. Twelve clerks are assigned to enter certain data on index cards. This number of clerks could perform the task in 18 days. After these clerks have worked on this assignment for 6 days, 4 more clerks are added to the staff to do this work.
Assuming that all the clerks work at the same rate of speed, the entire task, instead of taking 18 days, will be performed in _____ days.

7._____

    A. 9   B. 12   C. 15   D. 16

8. Suppose that a file cabinet, which has a capacity of 3,000 cards, now contains approximately 2,200 cards. Cards are added to the file at the average rate of 30 cards a day.
To find the number of days it will take to fill the cabinet to capacity,

8._____

    A.   divide 3,000 by 30
    B.   divide 2,200 by 3,000
    C.   divide 800 by 30
    D.   multiply 30 by the fraction 2,200 divided by 3,000

9. Six gross of special drawing pencils were purchased for use in a city department.
If the pencils were used at the rate of 24 a week, the MAXIMUM number of weeks that the six gross of pencils would last is _____ weeks.

9._____

    A. 6   B. 12   C. 24   D. 36

10. A stock clerk had 600 pads on hand. He then issued 3/8 of his supply of pads to Division X, 1/4 to Division Y, and 1/6 to Division Z.
The number of pads remaining in stock is

10._____

    A. 48   B. 125   C. 240   D. 475

11. If a certain job can be performed by 18 clerks in 26 days, the number of clerks needed to perform the job in 12 days is _____ clerks.

11._____

    A. 24   B. 30   C. 39   D. 52

12. In anticipation of a seasonal increase in the amount of work to be performed by his division, a division chief prepared the following list of additional temporary employees needed by his division and the amount of time they would be employed:
    26 cashiers, each at $24,000 a year, for 2 months
    15 laborers, each at $85.00 a day, for 50 days
    6 clerks, each at $21,000 a year, for 3 months
The total approximate cost for this additional personnel would be MOST NEARLY

12._____

    A. $200,000   B. $250,000   C. $500,000   D. $600,000

13. A copy machine company offered to sell a city agency 4 copy machines at a discount of 15% from the list price, and to allow the agency $850 for each of its two old machines.
The list price of the new machines is $6,250 per machine.
If the city agency accepts this offer, the amount of money it will have to provide for the purchase of these 4 machines is

13._____

    A. $17,350   B. $22,950   C. $19,550   D. $18,360

14. A stationery buyer was offered bond paper at the following price scale: 14.__
    $1.43 per ream for the first 1,000 reams
    $1.30 per ream for the next 4,000 reams
    $1.20 per ream for each additional ream beyond 5,000 reams
    If the buyer ordered 10,000 reams of paper, the average cost per ream, computed to
    the nearest cent, was

    A. $1.24   B. $1.26   C. $1.31   D. $1.36

15. A clerk has 5.70 percent of his salary deducted for his retirement pension. 15.__
    If this clerk's annual salary is $20,400, the monthly deduction for his retirement pen-
    sion is

    A. $298.20   B. $357.90   C. $1,162.80   D. $96.90

16. In a certain bureau, two-thirds of the employees are clerks and the remainder are typists. 16.__
    If there are 90 clerks, then the number of typists in this bureau is

    A. 135   B. 45   C. 120   D. 30

17. The number of investigations conducted by an agency in 1999 was 3,600. In 2000, the 17.__
    number of investigations conducted was one-third more than in 1999. The number of
    investigations conducted in 2001 was three-fourths of the number conducted in 2000. It
    is anticipated that the number of investigations conducted in 2002 will be equal to the
    average of the three preceding years. On the basis of this information, the MOST accu-
    rate of the following statements is that the number of investigations conducted in

    A. 1999 is larger than the number anticipated for 2002
    B. 2000 is smaller than the number anticipated for 2002
    C. 2001 is equal to the number conducted in 1999
    D. 2001 is larger than the number anticipated in 2002

18. A city agency engaged in repair work uses a small part which the city purchases for 14 18.__
    each. Assume that, in a certain year, the total expenditure of the city for this part was
    $700.
    How many of these parts were purchased that year?

    A. 50   B. 200   C. 2,000   D. 5,000

19. The work unit which you supervise is responsible for processing 15 reports per month. 19.__
    If your unit has 4 clerks and the best worker completes 40% of the reports himself, how
    many reports would each of the other clerks have to complete if they all do an equal
    number?

    A. 1   B. 2   C. 3   D. 4

20. Assume that the work unit in which you work has 24 clerks and 18 stenographers.   20._____
    In order to change the ratio of stenographers to clerks so that there is 1 stenographer
    for every 4 clerks, it would be necessary to REDUCE the number of stenographers by

    A. 3   B. 6   C. 9   D. 12

21. The arithmetic mean salary for five employees earning $18,500, $18,300, $18,600,   21._____
    $18,400, and $18,500, respectively, is

    A. $18,450   B. $18,460   C. $18,475   D. $18,500

22. Last year, a city department which is responsible for purchasing supplies ordered bond 22._____
    paper in equal quantities from 22 different companies. The price was exactly the same
    for each company, and the total cost for the 22 orders was $693,113.
    Assuming prices did not change during the year, the cost of each order was MOST
    NEARLY

    A. $31,490   B. $31,495   C. $31,500   D. $31,505

23. Suppose that a large bureau has 187 employees. On a particular day, approximately   23._____
    14% of these employees are not available for work because of absences due to vacation,
    illness, or other reasons. Of the remaining employees, 1/7 are assigned to a special
    project while the balance are assigned to the normal work of the bureau. The number of
    employees assigned to the normal work of the bureau on that day is

    A. 112   B. 124   C. 138   D. 142

24. Suppose that you are in charge of a typing pool of 8 typists. Two typists type at the rate of 24._____
    38 words per minute; three type at the rate of 40 words per minute; three type at the rate
    of 42 words per minute. The average typewritten page consists of 50 lines, 12 words per
    line. Each employee works from 9 to 5 with one hour off for lunch.
    The total number of pages typed by this pool in one day is, on the average, CLOSEST
    to _____ pages.

    A. 205   B. 225   C. 250   D. 275

25. Suppose that part-time workers are paid $7.20 an hour, prorated to the nearest half hour, 25._____
    with pay guaranteed for a minimum of four hours if services are required for less than
    four hours. In one operation, part-time workers signed the time sheet as follows:

Worker	In	Out
A	8:00 A.M.	11:35 A.M.
B	8:30 A.M.	3:20 P.M.
C	7:55 A.M.	11:00 A.M.
D	8:30 A.M.	2:25 P.M.

    How much would TOTAL payment to these part-time workers amount to for this opera-
    tion, assuming that those who stayed after 12 Noon were not paid for one hour which
    they took off for lunch?

    A. $134.40   B. $136.80   C. $142.20   D. $148.80

KEY (CORRECT ANSWERS)

1.	C	11.	C
2.	C	12.	A
3.	C	13.	C
4.	B	14.	B
5.	D	15.	D
6.	B	16.	B
7.	C	17.	C
8.	C	18.	D
9.	D	19.	C
10.	B	20.	D

21.	B
22.	D
23.	C
24.	B
25.	B

SOLUTIONS TO PROBLEMS

1. Maximum number of folders = (4)(12)(20) = 960

2. (3500+6700+10,500)(.95) = 19,665

3. Hourly rate = $18,928 ÷ 1820 = $10.40. Then, the pay for 18 hours = ($10.40)(18) = $187.20

4. Total pay = ($11.20)(40) + ($11.20)(1.5)(3) = $498.40

5. (1 - 1/5 - 1/2 - 1/7)(100)% ≈ 16%

6. Previous cost for five years = ($324,000)(5) = $1,620,000
   Present cost for five years = (5)(5)($1,400) + (5)(5)($100) + (5)(5)($30,000) + (1)(5)($38,000) = $977,500   The net savings = $642,500 ≈ $640,000

7. (12)(18) = 216 clerk-days. Then, 216 - (12)(6) = 144 clerk-days of work left when 4 more clerks are added. Now, 16 clerks will finish the task in 144 ÷ 16 = 9 more days. Finally, the task will require a total of 6 + 9 = 15 days.

8. Number of days needed = (3000-2200) ÷ 30 = 26.7, which is equivalent to dividing 800 by 30.

9. (6)(144) = 864 pencils purchased. Then, 864 ÷ 24 = 36 maximum number of weeks

10. Number of remaining pads = 600 - (1)(600) - (1/4)(600) - (1/6)(600) = 125

11. (18)(26) ÷ 12 = 39 clerks

12. Total cost = (26)($24,000)(2/12) + (15)($85)(50) + (6)($21,000)(3/12) = $199,250
    $200,000

13. (4)($6250)(.85) - (2)($850) = $19,550

14. Total cost = ($1.43)(1000) + ($1.30)(4000) + ($1.20X5000) = $12,630. Average cost per ream = $12,630 10,000 ≈ $1.26

15. Monthly salary = $20,400 ÷ 12 = $1700. Thus, the monthly deduction for his pension = ($1700)(.057) + $96.90

16. Number of employees = 90 ÷ 2/3 = 135. Then, the number of typists = (1/3)(135) = 45

17. The number of investigations for each year is as follows:
    1999: 3600
    2000: (3600)(1 1/3) = 4800
    2001: (4800)(3/4) = 3600
    2002: (3600+4800+3600)/3 = 4000
    So, the number of investigations were equal for 1999 and 2001.

18. $700 ÷ .14 = 5000 parts

19. The best worker does (.40)(15) = 6 reports. The other 9 reports are divided equally among the other 3 clerks, so each clerk does 9 ÷ 3 = 3 reports.

20. 1:4 = 6:24 . Thus, the number of stenographers must be reduced by 18 - 6 = 12

21. Mean = ($18,500+$18,300+$18,400+$18,500) ÷ 5 = $18,460

22. The cost per order = $693,113 ÷ 22 ≈ $31,505

23. 187 - (.14) = 26. 187 - 26 = 161 - 1/7 (161) = 23
    161 - 23 = 138

24. Number of words typed in 1 min. = (2)(38) + (3)(40) + (3)(42) = 322. For 7 hours, the total number of words typed = (7)(60)(322) = 135,240. Each page contains (on the average) (50)(12) = 600 words. Finally, 135,240 ÷ 600 ≈ 225 pages

25. Worker A = ($7.20)(4) = $28.80
    Worker B = ($7.20)(3 1/2) + ($7.20)(2 1/2) = $43.20
    Worker C = ($7.20)(4) = $28.80
    Worker D = ($7.20)(3 1/2) + ($7.20)(1 1/2) = $36.00
    Total for all 4 workers = $136.80
    Note: Workers A and C received the guaranteed minimum 4 hours pay each.

PHILOSOPHY, PRINCIPLES, PRACTICES AND TECHNICS
OF
SUPERVISION, ADMINISTRATION, MANAGEMENT AND ORGANIZATION

TABLE OF CONTENTS

		Page
I.	MEANING OF SUPERVISION	1
II.	THE OLD AND THE NEW SUPERVISION	1
III.	THE EIGHT (8) BASIC PRINCIPLES OF THE NEW SUPERVISION	1
	1. Principle of Responsibility	1
	2. Principle of Authority	2
	3. Principle of Self-Growth	2
	4. Principle of Individual Worth	2
	5. Principle of Creative Leadership	2
	6. Principle of Success and Failure	2
	7. Principle of Science	3
	8. Principle of Cooperation	3
IV.	WHAT IS ADMINISTRATION?	3
	1. Practices commonly classed as "Supervisory"	3
	2. Practices commonly classed as "Administrative"	3
	3. Practices classified as both "Supervisory" and "Administrative"	4
V.	RESPONSIBILITIES OF THE SUPERVISOR	4
VI.	COMPETENCIES OF THE SUPERVISOR	4
VII.	THE PROFESSIONAL SUPERVISOR—EMPLOYEE RELATIONSHIP	4
VIII.	MINI-TEXT IN SUPERVISION, ADMINISTRATION, MANAGEMENT AND ORGANIZATION	5
	A. Brief Highlights	5
	1. Levels of Management	5
	2. What the Supervisor Must Learn	6
	3. A Definition of Supervision	6
	4. Elements of the Team Concept	6
	5. Principles of Organization	6
	6. The Four Important Parts of Every Job	6
	7. Principles of Delegation	6
	8. Principles of Effective Communications	7
	9. Principles of Work Improvement	7

10. Areas of Job Improvement 7
11. Seven Key Points in Making Improvements 7
12. Corrective Techniques for Job Improvement 7
13. A Planning Checklist 8
14. Five Characteristics of Good Directions 8
15. Types of Directions 8
16. Controls 8
17. Orienting the New Employee 8
18. Checklist for Orienting New Employees 8
19. Principles of Learning 9
20. Causes of Poor Performance 9
21. Four Major Steps in On-The-Job Instructions 9
22. Employees Want Five Things 9
23. Some Don'ts in Regard to Praise 9
24. How to Gain Your Workers' Confidence 9
25. Sources of Employee Problems 9
26. The Supervisor's Key to Discipline 10
27. Five Important Processes of Management 10
28. When the Supervisor Fails to Plan 10
29. Fourteen General Principles of Management 10
30. Change 10

B. Brief Topical Summaries 11
    I.   Who/What is the Supervisor? 11
    II.   The Sociology of Work 11
    III.   Principles and Practices of Supervision 12
    IV.   Dynamic Leadership 12
    V.   Processes for Solving Problems 12
    VI.   Training for Results 13
    VII.   Health, Safety and Accident Prevention 13
    VIII.   Equal Employment Opportunity 13
    IX.   Improving Communications 14
    X.   Self-Development 14
    XI.   Teaching and Training 14
            A. The Teaching Process 14
                1. Preparation 14
                2. Presentation 15
                3. Summary 15
                4. Application 15
                5. Evaluation 15
            B. Teaching Methods 15
                1. Lecture 15
                2. Discussion 15
                3. Demonstration 16
                4. Performance 16
                5. Which Method to Use 16

PHILOSOPHY, PRINCIPLES, PRACTICES, AND TECHNICS
OF
SUPERVISION, ADMINISTRATION, MANAGEMENT AND ORGANIZATION

I. MEANING OF SUPERVISION

The extension of the democratic philosophy has been accompanied by an extension in the scope of supervision. Modern leaders and supervisors no longer think of supervision in the narrow sense of being confined chiefly to visiting employees, supplying materials, or rating the staff. They regard supervision as being intimately related to all the concerned agencies of society, they speak of the supervisor's function in terms of "growth", rather than the "improvement," of employees.

This modern concept of supervision may be defined as follows:

Supervision is leadership and the development of leadership within groups which are cooperatively engaged in inspection, research, training, guidance and evaluation.

II. THE OLD AND THE NEW SUPERVISION

TRADITIONAL
1. Inspection
2. Focused on the employee
3. Visitation
4. Random and haphazard
5. Imposed and authoritarian
6. One person usually

MODERN
1. Study and analysis
2. Focused on aims, materials, methods, supervisors, employees, environment
3. Demonstrations, intervisitation, workshops, directed reading, bulletins, etc.
4. Definitely organized and planned (scientific)
5. Cooperative and democratic
6. Many persons involved (creative)

III THE EIGHT (8) BASIC PRINCIPLES OF THE NEW SUPERVISION

1. *PRINCIPLE OF RESPONSIBILITY*
Authority to act and responsibility for acting must be joined.
- a. If you give responsibility, give authority.
- b. Define employee duties clearly.
- c. Protect employees from criticism by others.
- d. Recognize the rights as well as obligations of employees.
- e. Achieve the aims of a democratic society insofar as it is possible within the area of your work.
- f. Establish a situation favorable to training and learning.
- g. Accept ultimate responsibility for everything done in your section, unit, office, division, department.
- h. Good administration and good supervision are inseparable.

2. PRINCIPLE OF AUTHORITY
The success of the supervisor is measured by the extent to which the power of authority is not used.

    a. Exercise simplicity and informality in supervision.
    b. Use the simplest machinery of supervision.
    c. If it is good for the organization as a whole, it is probably justified.
    d. Seldom be arbitrary or authoritative.
    e. Do not base your work on the power of position or of personality.
    f. Permit and encourage the free expression of opinions.

3. PRINCIPLE OF SELF-GROWTH
The success of the supervisor is measured by the extent to which, and the speed with which, he is no longer needed.

    a. Base criticism on principles, not on specifics.
    b. Point out higher activities to employees.
    c. Train for self-thinking by employees, to meet new situations.
    d. Stimulate initiative, self-reliance and individual responsibility.
    e. Concentrate on stimulating the growth of employees rather than on removing defects.

4. PRINCIPLE OF INDIVIDUAL WORTH
Respect for the individual is a paramount consideration in supervision.

    a. Be human and sympathetic in dealing with employees.
    b. Don't nag about things to be done.
    c. Recognize the individual differences among employees and seek opportunities to permit best expression of each personality.

5. PRINCIPLE OF CREATIVE LEADERSHIP
The best supervision is that which is not apparent to the employee.

    a. Stimulate, don't drive employees to creative action.
    b. Emphasize doing good things.
    c. Encourage employees to do what they do best.
    d. Do not be too greatly concerned with details of subject or method.
    e. Do not be concerned exclusively with immediate problems and activities.
    f. Reveal higher activities and make them both desired and maximally possible.
    g. Determine procedures in the light of each situation but see that these are derived from a sound basic philosophy.
    h. Aid, inspire and lead so as to liberate the creative spirit latent in all good employees.

6. PRINCIPLE OF SUCCESS AND FAILURE
There are no unsuccessful employees, only unsuccessful supervisors who have failed to give proper leadership.

    a. Adapt suggestions to the capacities, attitudes, and prejudices of employees.
    b. Be gradual, be progressive, be persistent.
    c. Help the employee find the general principle; have the employee apply his own problem to the general principle.
    d. Give adequate appreciation for good work and honest effort.
    e. Anticipate employee difficulties and help to prevent them.
    f. Encourage employees to do the desirable things they will do anyway.
    g. Judge your supervision by the results it secures.

7. *PRINCIPLE OF SCIENCE*
Successful supervision is scientific, objective, and experimental. It is based on facts, not on prejudices.
  a. Be cumulative in results.
  b. Never divorce your suggestions from the goals of training.
  c. Don't be impatient of results.
  d. Keep all matters on a professional, not a personal level.
  e. Do not be concerned exclusively with immediate problems and activities.
  f. Use objective means of determining achievement and rating where possible.

8. *PRINCIPLE OF COOPERATION*
Supervision is a cooperative enterprise between supervisor and employee.
  a. Begin with conditions as they are.
  b. Ask opinions of all involved when formulating policies.
  c. Organization is as good as its weakest link.
  d. Let employees help to determine policies and department programs.
  e. Be approachable and accessible - physically and mentally.
  f. Develop pleasant social relationships.

IV. WHAT IS ADMINISTRATION?

Administration is concerned with providing the environment, the material facilities, and the operational procedures that will promote the maximum growth and development of supervisors and employees. (Organization is an aspect, and a concomitant, of administration.)

There is no sharp line of demarcation between supervision and administration; these functions are intimately interrelated and, often, overlapping. They are complementary activities.

1. *PRACTICES COMMONLY CLASSED AS "SUPERVISORY"*
  a. Conducting employees conferences
  b. Visiting sections, units, offices, divisions, departments
  c. Arranging for demonstrations
  d. Examining plans
  e. Suggesting professional reading
  f. Interpreting bulletins
  g. Recommending in-service training courses
  h. Encouraging experimentation
  i. Appraising employee morale
  j. Providing for intervisitation

2. *PRACTICES COMMONLY CLASSIFIED AS "ADMINISTRATIVE"*
  a. Management of the office
  b. Arrangement of schedules for extra duties
  c. Assignment of rooms or areas
  d. Distribution of supplies
  e. Keeping records and reports
  f. Care of audio-visual materials
  g. Keeping inventory records
  h. Checking record cards and books
  i. Programming special activities
  j. Checking on the attendance and punctuality of employees

3. *PRACTICES COMMONLY CLASSIFIED AS BOTH "SUPERVISORY" AND "ADMINISTRATIVE"*
    a. Program construction
    b. Testing or evaluating outcomes
    c. Personnel accounting
    d. Ordering instructional materials

V. RESPONSIBILITIES OF THE SUPERVISOR

A person employed in a supervisory capacity must constantly be able to improve his own efficiency and ability. He represents the employer to the employees and only continuous self-examination can make him a capable supervisor.

Leadership and training are the supervisor's responsibility. An efficient working unit is one in which the employees work with the supervisor. It is his job to bring out the best in his employees. He must always be relaxed, courteous and calm in his association with his employees. Their feelings are important, and a harsh attitude does not develop the most efficient employees.

VI. COMPETENCIES OF THE SUPERVISOR

1. Complete knowledge of the duties and responsibilities of his position.
2. To be able to organize a job, plan ahead and carry through.
3. To have self-confidence and initiative.
4. To be able to handle the unexpected situation and make quick decisions.
5. To be able to properly train subordinates in the positions they are best suited for.
6. To be able to keep good human relations among his subordinates.
7. To be able to keep good human relations between his subordinates and himself and to earn their respect and trust.

VII. THE PROFESSIONAL SUPERVISOR-EMPLOYEE RELATIONSHIP

There are two kinds of efficiency: one kind is only apparent and is produced in organizations through the exercise of mere discipline; this is but a simulation of the second, or true, efficiency which springs from spontaneous cooperation. If you are a manager, no matter how great or small your responsibility, it is your job, in the final analysis, to create and develop this involuntary cooperation among the people whom you supervise. For, no matter how powerful a combination of money, machines, and materials a company may have, this is a dead and sterile thing without a team of willing, thinking and articulate people to guide it.

The following 21 points are presented as indicative of the exemplary basic relationship that should exist between supervisor and employee:

1. Each person wants to be liked and respected by his fellow employee and wants to be treated with consideration and respect by his superior.
2. The most competent employee will make an error. However, in a unit where good relations exist between the supervisor and his employees, tenseness and fear do not exist. Thus, errors are not hidden or covered up and the efficiency of a unit is not impaired.
3. Subordinates resent rules, regulations, or orders that are unreasonable or unexplained.
4. Subordinates are quick to resent unfairness, harshness, injustices and favoritism.
5. An employee will accept responsibility if he knows that he will be complimented for a job well done, and not too harshly chastised for failure; that his supervisor will check the cause of the failure, and, if it was the supervisor's fault, he will assume the blame therefore. If it was the employee's fault, his supervisor will explain the correct method or means of handling the responsibility.

6. An employee wants to receive credit for a suggestion he has made, that is used. If a suggestion cannot be used, the employee is entitled to an explanation. The supervisor should not say "no" and close the subject.
7. Fear and worry slow up a worker's ability. Poor working environment can impair his physical and mental health. A good supervisor avoids forceful methods, threats and arguments to get a job done.
8. A forceful supervisor is able to train his employees individually and as a team, and is able to motivate them in the proper channels.
9. A mature supervisor is able to properly evaluate his subordinates and to keep them happy and satisfied.
10. A sensitive supervisor will never patronize his subordinates.
11. A worthy supervisor will respect his employees' confidences.
12. Definite and clear-cut responsibilities should be assigned to each executive.
13. Responsibility should always be coupled with corresponding authority.
14. No change should be made in the scope or responsibilities of a position without a definite understanding to that effect on the part of all persons concerned.
15. No executive or employee, occupying a single position in the organization, should be subject to definite orders from more than one source.
16. Orders should never be given to subordinates over the head of a responsible executive. Rather than do this, the officer in question should be supplanted.
17. Criticisms of subordinates should, whoever possible, be made privately, and in no case should a subordinate be criticized in the presence of executives or employees of equal or lower rank.
18. No dispute or difference between executives or employees as to authority or responsibilities should be considered too trivial for prompt and careful adjudication.
19. Promotions, wage changes, and disciplinary action should always be approved by the executive immediately superior to the one directly responsible.
20. No executive or employee should ever be required, or expected, to be at the same time an assistant to, and critic of, another.
21. Any executive whose work is subject to regular inspection should, whever practicable, be given the assistance and facilities necessary to enable him to maintain an independent check of the quality of his work.

VIII. MINI-TEXT IN SUPERVISION, ADMINISTRATION, MANAGEMENT, AND ORGANIZATION

A. BRIEF HIGHLIGHTS

Listed concisely and sequentially are major headings and important data in the field for quick recall and review.

1. *LEVELS OF MANAGEMENT*

Any organization of some size has several levels of management. In terms of a ladder the levels are:

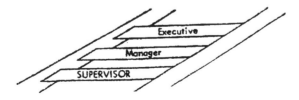

The first level is very important because it is the beginning point of management leadership.

2. *WHAT THE SUPERVISOR MUST LEARN*
A supervisor must learn to:
    (1) Deal with people and their differences
    (2) Get the job done through people
    (3) Recognize the problems when they exist
    (4) Overcome obstacles to good performance
    (5) Evaluate the performance of people
    (6) Check his own performance in terms of accomplishment

3. *A DEFINITION OF SUPERVISOR*
The term supervisor means any individual having authority, in the interests of the employer, to hire, transfer, suspend, lay-off, recall, promote, discharge, assign, reward, or discipline other employees or responsibility to direct them, or to adjust their grievances, or effectively to recommend such action, if, in connection with the foregoing, exercise of such authority is not of a merely routine or clerical nature but requires the use of independent judgment.

4. *ELEMENTS OF THE TEAM CONCEPT*
What is involved in teamwork? The component parts are:
| (1) Members | (3) Goals | (5) Cooperation |
| (2) A leader | (4) Plans | (6) Spirit |

5. *PRINCIPLES OF ORGANIZATION*
    (1) A team member must know what his job is.
    (2) Be sure that the nature and scope of a job are understood.
    (3) Authority and responsibility should be carefully spelled out.
    (4) A supervisor should be permitted to make the maximum number of decisions affecting his employees.
    (5) Employees should report to only one supervisor.
    (6) A supervisor should direct only as many employees as he can handle effectively.
    (7) An organization plan should be flexible.
    (8) Inspection and performance of work should be separate.
    (9) Organizational problems should receive immediate attention.
    (10) Assign work in line with ability and experience.

6. *THE FOUR IMPORTANT PARTS OF EVERY JOB*
    (1) Inherent in every job is the *accountability* for results.
    (2) A second set of factors in every job is *responsibilities.*
    (3) Along with duties and responsibilities one must have the *authority* to act within certain limits without obtaining permission to proceed.
    (4) No job exists in a vacuum. The supervisor is surrounded by key *relationships.*

7. *PRINCIPLES OF DELEGATION*
Where work is delegated for the first time, the supervisor should think in terms of these questions:
    (1) Who is best qualified to do this?
    (2) Can an employee improve his abilities by doing this?
    (3) How long should an employee spend on this?
    (4) Are there any special problems for which he will need guidance?
    (5) How broad a delegation can I make?

8. PRINCIPLES OF EFFECTIVE COMMUNICATIONS
     (1) Determine the media
     (2) To whom directed?
     (3) Identification and source authority
     (4) Is communication understood?

9. PRINCIPLES OF WORK IMPROVEMENT
     (1) Most people usually do only the work which is assigned to them
     (2) Workers are likely to fit assigned work into the time available to perform it
     (3) A good workload usually stimulates output
     (4) People usually do their best work when they know that results will be reviewed or inspected
     (5) Employees usually feel that someone else is responsible for conditions of work, workplace layout, job methods, type of tools/equipment, and other such factors
     (6) Employees are usually defensive about their job security
     (7) Employees have natural resistance to change
     (8) Employees can support or destroy a supervisor
     (9) A supervisor usually earns the respect of his people through his personal example of diligence and efficiency

10. AREAS OF JOB IMPROVEMENT
The areas of job improvement are quite numerous, but the most common ones which a supervisor can identify and utilize are:

(1) Departmental layout	(5) Work methods
(2) Flow of work	(6) Materials handling
(3) Workplace layout	(7) Utilization
(4) Utilization of manpower	(8) Motion economy

11. SEVEN KEY POINTS IN MAKING IMPROVEMENTS
     (1) Select the job to be improved
     (2) Study how it is being done now
     (3) Question the present method
     (4) Determine actions to be taken
     (5) Chart proposed method
     (6) Get approval and apply
     (7) Solicit worker participation

12. CORRECTIVE TECHNIQUES OF JOB IMPROVEMENT

Specific Problems	General Improvement	Corrective Techniques
(1) Size of workload	(1) Departmental layout	(1) Study with scale model
(2) Inability to meet schedules	(2) Flow of work	(2) Flow chart study
(3) Strain and fatigue	(3) Work plan layout	(3) Motion analysis
(4) Improper use of men and skills	(4) Utilization of manpower	(4) Comparison of units produced to standard allowance
(5) Waste, poor quality, unsafe conditions	(5) Work methods	(5) Methods analysis
(6) Bottleneck conditions that hinder output	(6) Materials handling	(6) Flow chart & equipment study
(7) Poor utilization of equipment and machine	(7) Utilization of equipment	(7) Down time vs. running time
(8) Efficiency and productivity of labor	(8) Motion economy	(8) Motion analysis

13. A *PLANNING CHECKLIST*

(1) Objectives	(6) Resources	(11) Safety
(2) Controls	(7) Manpower	(12) Money
(3) Delegations	(8) Equipment	(13) Work
(4) Communications	(9) Supplies and materials	(14) Timing of improvements
(5) Resources	(10) Utilization of time	

14. *FIVE CHARACTERISTICS OF GOOD DIRECTIONS*

In order to get results, directions must be:

(1) Possible of accomplishment	(3) Related to mission	(5) Unmistakably clear
(2) Agreeable with worker interests	(4) Planned and complete	

15. *TYPES OF DIRECTIONS*

(1) Demands or direct orders	(3) Suggestion or implication
(2) Requests	(4) Volunteering

16. *CONTROLS*

A typical listing of the overall areas in which the supervisor should establish controls might be:

(1) Manpower	(3) Quality of work	(5) Time	(7) Money
(2) Materials	(4) Quantity of work	(6) Space	(8) Methods

17. *ORIENTING THE NEW EMPLOYEE*

(1) Prepare for him	(3) Orientation for the job
(2) Welcome the new employee	(4) Follow-up

18. *CHECKLIST FOR ORIENTING NEW EMPLOYEES* — Yes No

(1) Do your appreciate the feelings of new employees when they first report for work? ___ ___

(2) Are you aware of the fact that the new employee must make a big adjustment to his job? ___ ___

(3) Have you given him good reasons for liking the job and the organization? ___ ___

(4) Have you prepared for his first day on the job?

(5) Did you welcome him cordially and make him feel needed?

(6) Did you establish rapport with him so that he feels free to talk and discuss matters with you? ___ ___

(7) Did you explain his job to him and his relationship to you? ___ ___

(8) Does he know that his work will be evaluated periodically on a basis that is fair and objective? ___ ___

(9) Did you introduce him to his fellow workers in such a way that they are likely to accept him? ___ ___

(10) Does he know what employee benefits he will receive?

(11) Does he understand the importance of being on the job and what to do if he must leave his duty station? ___ ___

(12) Has he been impressed with the importance of accident prevention and safe practice? ___ ___

(13) Does he generally know his way around the department? ___ ___

(14) Is he under the guidance of a sponsor who will teach the right ways of doing things? ___ ___

(15) Do you plan to follow-up so that he will continue to adjust successfully to his job? ___ ___

19. *PRINCIPLES OF LEARNING*
    (1) Motivation   (2) Demonstration or explanation   (3) Practice

20. *CAUSES OF POOR PERFORMANCE*
    (1) Improper training for job
    (2) Wrong tools
    (3) Inadequate directions
    (4) Lack of supervisory follow-up
    (5) Poor communications
    (6) Lack of standards of performance
    (7) Wrong work habits
    (8) Low morale
    (9) Other

21. *FOUR MAJOR STEPS IN ON-THE-JOB INSTRUCTION*
    (1) Prepare the worker
    (2) Present the operation
    (3) Tryout performance
    (4) Follow-up

22. *EMPLOYEES WANT FIVE THINGS*
    (1) Security (2) Opportunity (3) Recognition (4) Inclusion (5) Expression

23. *SOME DON'TS IN REGARD TO PRAISE*
    (1) Don't praise a person for something he hasn't done
    (2) Don't praise a person unless you can be sincere
    (3) Don't be sparing in praise just because your superior withholds it from you
    (4) Don't let too much time elapse between good performance and recognition of it

24. *HOW TO GAIN YOUR WORKERS' CONFIDENCE*
Methods of developing confidence include such things as:
    (1) Knowing the interests, habits, hobbies of employees
    (2) Admitting your own inadequacies
    (3) Sharing and telling of confidence in others
    (4) Supporting people when they are in trouble
    (5) Delegating matters that can be well handled
    (6) Being frank and straightforward about problems and working conditions
    (7) Encouraging others to bring their problems to you
    (8) Taking action on problems which impede worker progress

25. *SOURCES OF EMPLOYEE PROBLEMS*
On-the-job causes might be such things as:
    (1) A feeling that favoritism is exercised in assignments
    (2) Assignment of overtime
    (3) An undue amount of supervision
    (4) Changing methods or systems
    (5) Stealing of ideas or trade secrets
    (6) Lack of interest in job
    (7) Threat of reduction in force
    (8) Ignorance or lack of communications
    (9) Poor equipment
    (10) Lack of knowing how supervisor feels toward employee
    (11) Shift assignments

Off-the-job problems might have to do with:
    (1) Health   (2) Finances   (3) Housing   (4) Family

26. *THE SUPERVISOR'S KEY TO DISCIPLINE*

There are several key points about discipline which the supervisor should keep in mind:

   (1) Job discipline is one of the disciplines of life and is directed by the supervisor.
   (2) It is more important to correct an employee fault than to fix blame for it.
   (3) Employee performance is affected by problems both on the job and off.
   (4) Sudden or abrupt changes in behavior can be indications of important employee problems.
   (5) Problems should be dealt with as soon as possible after they are identified.
   (6) The attitude of the supervisor may have more to do with solving problems than the techniques of problem solving.
   (7) Correction of employee behavior should be resorted to only after the supervisor is sure that training or counseling will not be helpful.
   (8) Be sure to document your disciplinary actions.
   (9) Make sure that you are disciplining on the basis of facts rather than personal feelings.
   (10) Take each disciplinary step in order, being careful not to make snap judgments, or decisions based on impatience.

27. *FIVE IMPORTANT PROCESSES OF MANAGEMENT*

   (1) Planning   (2) Organizing   (3) Scheduling
   (4) Controlling   (5) Motivating

28. *WHEN THE SUPERVISOR FAILS TO PLAN*

   (1) Supervisor creates impression of not knowing his job
   (2) May lead to excessive overtime
   (3) Job runs itself -- supervisor lacks control
   (4) Deadlines and appointments missed
   (5) Parts of the work go undone
   (6) Work interrupted by emergencies
   (7) Sets a bad example
   (8) Uneven workload creates peaks and valleys
   (9) Too much time on minor details at expense of more important tasks

29. *FOURTEEN GENERAL PRINCIPLES OF MANAGEMENT*

   (1) Division of work
   (2) Authority and responsibility
   (3) Discipline
   (4) Unity of command
   (5) Unity of direction
   (6) Subordination of individual interest to general interest
   (7) Remuneration of personnel
   (8) Centralization
   (9) Scalar chain
   (10) Order
   (11) Equity
   (12) Stability of tenure of personnel
   (13) Initiative
   (14) Esprit de corps

30. *CHANGE*

Bringing about change is perhaps attempted more often, and yet less well understood, than anything else the supervisor does. How do people generally react to change? (People tend to resist change that is imposed upon them by other individuals or circumstances.

Change is characteristic of every situation. It is a part of every real endeavor where the efforts of people are concerned.

A. Why do people resist change?
  People may resist change because of:
  (1) Fear of the unknown
  (2) Implied criticism
  (3) Unpleasant experiences in the past
  (4) Fear of loss of status
  (5) Threat to the ego
  (6) Fear of loss of economic stability

B. How can we best overcome the resistance to change?
  In initiating change, take these steps:
  (1) Get ready to sell
  (2) Identify sources of help
  (3) Anticipate objections
  (4) Sell benefits
  (5) Listen in depth
  (6) Follow up

B. BRIEF TOPICAL SUMMARIES

I. WHO/WHAT IS THE SUPERVISOR?
1. The supervisor is often called the "highest level employee and the lowest level manager."
2. A supervisor is a member of both management and the work group. He acts as a bridge between the two.
3. Most problems in supervision are in the area of human relations, or people problems.
4. Employees expect: Respect, opportunity to learn and to advance, and a sense of belonging, and so forth.
5. Supervisors are responsible for directing people and organizing work. Planning is of paramount importance.
6. A position description is a set of duties and responsibilities inherent to a given position.
7. It is important to keep the position description up-to-date and to provide each employee with his own copy.

II. THE SOCIOLOGY OF WORK
1. People are alike in many ways; however, each individual is unique.
2. The supervisor is challenged in getting to know employee differences. Acquiring skills in evaluating individuals is an asset.
3. Maintaining meaningful working relationships in the organization is of great importance.
4. The supervisor has an obligation to help individuals to develop to their fullest potential.
5. Job rotation on a planned basis helps to build versatility and to maintain interest and enthusiasm in work groups.
6. Cross training (job rotation) provides backup skills.
7. The supervisor can help reduce tension by maintaining a sense of humor, providing guidance to employees, and by making reasonable and timely decisions. Employees respond favorably to working under reasonably predictable circumstances.
8. Change is characteristic of all managerial behavior. The supervisor must adjust to changes in procedures, new methods, technological changes, and to a number of new and sometimes challenging situations.
9. To overcome the natural tendency for people to resist change, the supervisor should become more skillful in initiating change.

III. PRINCIPLES AND PRACTICES OF SUPERVISION
1. Employees should be required to answer to only one superior.
2. A supervisor can effectively direct only a limited number of employees, depending upon the complexity, variety, and proximity of the jobs involved.
3. The organizational chart presents the organization in graphic form. It reflects lines of authority and responsibility as well as interrelationships of units within the organization.
4. Distribution of work can be improved through an analysis using the "Work Distribution Chart."
5. The "Work Distribution Chart" reflects the division of work within a unit in understandable form.
6. When related tasks are given to an employee, he has a better chance of increasing his skills through training.
7. The individual who is given the responsibility for tasks must also be given the appropriate authority to insure adequate results.
8. The supervisor should delegate repetitive, routine work. Preparation of recurring reports, maintaining leave and attendance records are some examples.
9. Good discipline is essential to good task performance. Discipline is reflected in the actions of employees on the job in the absence of supervision.
10. Disciplinary action may have to be taken when the positive aspects of discipline have failed. Reprimand, warning, and suspension are examples of disciplinary action.
11. If a situation calls for a reprimand, be sure it is deserved and remember it is to be done in private.

IV. DYNAMIC LEADERSHIP
1. A style is a personal method or manner of exerting influence.
2. Authoritarian leaders often see themselves as the source of power and authority.
3. The democratic leader often perceives the group as the source of authority and power.
4. Supervisors tend to do better when using the pattern of leadership that is most natural for them.
5. Social scientists suggest that the effective supervisor use the leadership style that best fits the problem or circumstances involved.
6. All four styles -- telling, selling, consulting, joining -- have their place. Using one does not preclude using the other at another time.
7. The theory X point of view assumes that the average person dislikes work, will avoid it whenever possible, and must be coerced to achieve organizational objectives.
8. The theory Y point of view assumes that the average person considers work to be as natural as play, and, when the individual is committed, he requires little supervision or direction to accomplish desired objectives.
9. The leader's basic assumptions concerning human behavior and human nature affect his actions, decisions, and other managerial practices.
10. Dissatisfaction among employees is often present, but difficult to isolate. The supervisor should seek to weaken dissatisfaction by keeping promises, being sincere and considerate, keeping employees informed, and so forth.
11. Constructive suggestions should be encouraged during the natural progress of the work.

V. PROCESSES FOR SOLVING PROBLEMS
1. People find their daily tasks more meaningful and satisfying when they can improve them.
2. The causes of problems, or the key factors, are often hidden in the background. Ability to solve problems often involves the ability to isolate them from their backgrounds. There is some substance to the cliché that some persons "can't see the forest for the trees."
3. New procedures are often developed from old ones. Problems should be broken down into manageable parts. New ideas can be adapted from old ones.

4. People think differently in problem-solving situations. Using a logical, patterned approach is often useful. One approach found to be useful includes these steps:

    (a) Define the problem   (d) Weigh and decide

    (b) Establish objectives   (e) Take action

    (c) Get the facts   (f) Evaluate action

VI. TRAINING FOR RESULTS

1. Participants respond best when they feel training is important to them.
2. The supervisor has responsibility for the training and development of those who report to him.
3. When training is delegated to others, great care must be exercised to insure the trainer has knowledge, aptitude, and interest for his work as a trainer.
4. Training (learning) of some type goes on continually. The most successful supervisor makes certain the learning contributes in a productive manner to operational goals.
5. New employees are particularly susceptible to training. Older employees facing new job situations require specific training, as well as having need for development and growth opportunities.
6. Training needs require continuous monitoring.
7. The training officer of an agency is a professional with a responsibility to assist supervisors in solving training problems.
8. Many of the self-development steps important to the supervisor's own growth are equally important to the development of peers and subordinates. Knowledge of these is important when the supervisor consults with others on development and growth opportunities.

VII. HEALTH, SAFETY, AND ACCIDENT PREVENTION

1. Management-minded supervisors take appropriate measures to assist employees in maintaining health and in assuring safe practices in the work environment.
2. Effective safety training and practices help to avoid injury and accidents.
3. Safety should be a management goal. All infractions of safety which are observed should be corrected without exception.
4. Employees' safety attitude, training and instruction, provision of safe tools and equipment, supervision, and leadership are considered highly important factors which contribute to safety and which can be influenced directly by supervisors.
5. When accidents do occur they should be investigated promptly for very important reasons, including the fact that information which is gained can be used to prevent accidents in the future.

VIII. EQUAL EMPLOYMENT OPPORTUNITY

1. The supervisor should endeavor to treat all employees fairly, without regard to religion, race, sex, or national origin.
2. Groups tend to reflect the attitude of the leader. Prejudice can be detected even in very subtle form. Supervisors must strive to create a feeling of mutual respect and confidence in every employee.
3. Complete utilization of all human resources is a national goal. Equitable consideration should be accorded women in the work force, minority-group members, the physically and mentally handicapped, and the older employee. The important question is: "Who can do the job?"
4. Training opportunities, recognition for performance, overtime assignments, promotional opportunities, and all other personnel actions are to be handled on an equitable basis.

IX. IMPROVING COMMUNICATIONS

1. Communications is achieving understanding between the sender and the receiver of a message. It also means sharing information -- the creation of understanding.
2. Communication is basic to all human activity. Words are means of conveying meanings; however, real meanings are in people.
3. There are very practical differences in the effectiveness of one-way, impersonal, and two-way communications. Words spoken face-to-face are better understood. Telephone conversations are effective, but lack the rapport of person-to-person exchanges. The whole person communicates.
4. Cooperation and communication in an organization go hand in hand. When there is a mutual respect between people, spelling out rules and procedures for communicating is unnecessary.
5. There are several barriers to effective communications. These include failure to listen with respect and understanding, lack of skill in feedback, and misinterpreting the meanings of words used by the speaker. It is also common practice to listen to what we want to hear, and tune out things we do not want to hear.
6. Communication is management's chief problem. The supervisor should accept the challenge to communicate more effectively and to improve interagency and intra-agency communications.
7. The supervisor may often plan for and conduct meetings. The planning phase is critical and may determine the success or the failure of a meeting.
8. Speaking before groups usually requires extra effort. Stage fright may never disappear completely, but it can be controlled.

X. SELF-DEVELOPMENT

1. Every employee is responsible for his own self-development.
2. Toastmaster and toastmistress clubs offer opportunities to improve skills in oral communications.
3. Planning for one's own self-development is of vital importance. Supervisors know their own strengths and limitations better than anyone else.
4. Many opportunities are open to aid the supervisor in his developmental efforts, including job assignments; training opportunities, both governmental and non-governmental -- to include universities and professional conferences and seminars.
5. Programmed instruction offers a means of studying at one's own rate.
6. Where difficulties may arise from a supervisor's being away from his work for training, he may participate in televised home study or correspondence courses to meet his self-develop- ment needs.

XI. TEACHING AND TRAINING

A. The Teaching Process

Teaching is encouraging and guiding the learning activities of students toward established goals. In most cases this process consists in five steps: preparation, presentation, summarization, evaluation, and application.

1. Preparation

Preparation is twofold in nature; that of the supervisor and the employee.

Preparation by the supervisor is absolutely essential to success. He must know what, when, where, how, and whom he will teach. Some of the factors that should be considered are:

(1) The objectives	(5) Employee interest
(2) The materials needed	(6) Training aids
(3) The methods to be used	(7) Evaluation
(4) Employee participation	(8) Summarization

Employee preparation consists in preparing the employee to receive the material. Probably the most important single factor in the preparation of the employee is arousing and maintaining his interest. He must know the objectives of the training, why he is there, how the material can be used, and its importance to him.

2. Presentation

In presentation, have a carefully designed plan and follow it.
The plan should be accurate and complete, yet flexible enough to meet situations as they arise. The method of presentation will be determined by the particular situation and objectives.

3. Summary

A summary should be made at the end of every training unit and program. In addition, there may be internal summaries depending on the nature of the material being taught. The important thing is that the trainee must always be able to understand how each part of the new material relates to the whole.

4. Application

The supervisor must arrange work so the employee will be given a chance to apply new knowledge or skills while the material is still clear in his mind and interest is high. The trainee does not really know whether he has learned the material until he has been given a chance to apply it. If the material is not applied, it loses most of its value.

5. Evaluation

The purpose of all training is to promote learning. To determine whether the training has been a success or failure, the supervisor must evaluate this learning.
In the broadest sense evaluation includes all the devices, methods, skills, and techniques used by the supervisor to keep him self and the employees informed as to their progress toward the objectives they are pursuing. The extent to which the employee has mastered the knowledge, skills, and abilities, or changed his attitudes, as determined by the program objectives, is the extent to which instruction has succeeded or failed.
Evaluation should not be confined to the end of the lesson, day, or program but should be used continuously. We shall note later the way this relates to the rest of the teaching process.

B. Teaching Methods

A teaching method is a pattern of identifiable student and instructor activity used in presenting training material.
All supervisors are faced with the problem of deciding which method should be used at a given time.
As with all methods, there are certain advantages and disadvantages to each method.

1. Lecture

The lecture is direct oral presentation of material by the supervisor. The present trend is to place less emphasis on the trainer's activity and more on that of the trainee.

2. Discussion

Teaching by discussion or conference involves using questions and other techniques to arouse interest and focus attention upon certain areas, and by doing so creating a learning situation. This can be one of the most valuable methods because it gives the employees 'an opportunity to express their ideas and pool their knowledge.

3. Demonstration

      The demonstration is used to teach how something works or how to do something. It can be used to show a principle or what the results of a series of actions will be. A well-staged demonstration is particularly effective because it shows proper methods of performance in a realistic manner.

4. Performance

      Performance is one of the most fundamental of all learning techniques or teaching methods. The trainee may be able to tell how a specific operation should be performed but he cannot be sure he knows how to perform the operation until he has done so.

5. Which Method to Use

      Moreover, there are other methods and techniques of teaching. It is difficult to use any method without other methods entering into it. In any learning situation a combination of methods is usually more effective than anyone method alone.

Finally, evaluation must be integrated into the other aspects of the teaching-learning process.

It must be used in the motivation of the trainees; it must be used to assist in developing understanding during the training; and it must be related to employee application of the results of training.

This is distinctly the role of the supervisor.

———